BARNS OF NEW YORK

Barns of New York

*Rural Architecture of
the Empire State*

Cynthia G. Falk

Cornell University Press
Ithaca and London

Publication of this book was made possible, in part, by a generous grant
from Furthermore: a program of the J. M. Kaplan Fund.

First published 2012 by Cornell University Press
First printing, Cornell Paperbacks, 2012

Printed in the United States of America

Library of Congress Cataloging-in-Publication Data

Falk, Cynthia G.
   Barns of New York: rural architecture of the Empire State /
Cynthia G. Falk.
      p. cm.
   Includes bibliographical references and index.
   ISBN 978-0-8014-7780-5 (pbk.: alk. paper)
   1. Barns—New York (State)   2. Farm buildings—New York
(State)   I. Title.
   NA8230.F35 2012
   725'.37209747—dc23   2011034817

Cornell University Press strives to use environmentally responsible
suppliers and materials to the fullest extent possible in the publishing of
its books. Such materials include vegetable-based, low-VOC inks and
acid-free papers that are recycled, totally chlorine-free, or partly composed
of nonwood fibers. For further information, visit our website at
www.cornellpress.cornell.edu.

Paperback printing   10 9 8 7 6 5 4 3 2 1

To my parents, Jim and Betty Layton, who introduced me to history, rural landscapes, and the great state of New York

Contents

PREFACE

The picture of the farm can be made so pleasing, and the idea of going
back to Nature as the source of all sustenance so ingratiating, that it
would be possible to build up an effective philosophy on the principle
that the architecture of the home should be made to resemble the
architecture of the farm, rather than the other way about.

ALFRED HOPKINS, *Modern Farm Buildings,* 1913

Imagine the iconic buildings of New York State. Likely what comes to mind are
New York City's skyscrapers, towering on Manhattan Island. Perhaps colonial Dutch
houses or larger nineteenth-century mansions located along the Hudson River surface from a memory bank of celebrated structures. Most people do not think of dairy
barns or their accompanying silos when they picture the Empire State's majestic
buildings. Architect-designed masterpieces trump the utilitarian structures used by
farmers to store crops and machinery, house animals, and process various products.
Yet agricultural buildings can tell us more about New York State's history and culture than the one-of-a-kind landmarks that are so often pictured in architectural
histories and tourist guidebooks. Agricultural buildings convey a sense of beauty in
their own right and, despite their apparent commonality, exemplify ingenious design
and craftsmanship that pairs form and function.

In this book I challenge our inclination to admire only the exceptional, the ar-
tistic, and the urban by celebrating barns and the farmers whose labor shaped these
buildings. Barns are indeed tangible reminders of past people, places, processes, and
practices. They also continue to be used in the present; old buildings still serve traditional functions or are adapted to help farmers perform new ones even as modern

buildings provide the means to complete new tasks or carry out old ones more efficiently. Barns and other farm structures acquaint us with the individual people who
designed and used them. They also provide evidence of broad patterns in the production, distribution, and consumption of agricultural goods. Through their form,
materials, construction, and style, they exemplify building trends that affected both
broad geographic areas and particular locales.

Farming and farm building are central to the history of New York State. Even
before European settlement, New York was an important site of agricultural production. As early as the seventeenth century, rich farmland in the river valleys allowed settlers to create surplus crops that Euro-Americans marketed internationally.
In the early nineteenth century, the opening of the Erie Canal provided farmers
with increased access to markets and led to the creation of new types of structures
such as grain elevators, which were designed to facilitate the transportation of large
quantities of field crops. Production boomed, and specialized products such as hops,
grapes, apples, cabbage, and even tobacco came to bolster the rural economy in various parts of the state. Agricultural periodicals such as the *American Agriculturalist*
and *Moore's Rural New-Yorker,* published in New York City and Rochester, respectively, documented model farm practices and the increased acceptance of progressive, scientific farming.[1]

In the early twentieth century, Ulysses Prentiss Hedrick's celebratory book *A
History of Agriculture in the State of New York* glowingly reported on the products
of the Empire State: "Farm crops in New York have ever shown a diversity hardly
equalled [*sic*] elsewhere. Almost every agricultural product of economic importance
in temperate climates is produced in the State." At that time, dairy goods, potatoes,
and forage in the form of hay, clover, and alfalfa were the state's most valuable crops,
followed by orchard products, corn, oats, wheat, and grapes.[2]

Today in New York, despite increased suburbanization and other changes in land
use, active farms still account for 7.1 million acres of land, just less than a quarter of
the state's total area. In comparison to neighboring states, the percentage of farmland
(23.8 percent) is only slightly lower than in Pennsylvania (27.3 percent) and significantly higher than in smaller states such as Massachusetts (10.4 percent), Connecticut
(13.1 percent), and New Jersey (15.6 percent). In terms of farm products, New York
State ranks second in the nation in the acreage planted in corn for silage and third in
the value of sales of milk and other dairy products. New York farmers continue to
raise a wide assortment of other agricultural goods including fruit, vegetables, field
crops, livestock, and poultry.[3]

In this book I chronicle New York's rich agricultural heritage by looking at the
buildings found on farms, both past and present. The building types addressed include those used to house animals, store or process crops, keep or maintain agricultural equipment, or provide an essential or useful purpose related to agricultural
activities.[4] As a result, I examine not only the main barn but also outbuildings and

ancillary structures, from chicken coops to smokehouses to windmills. I limit myself, however, to land-based agriculture and do not address buildings related to farming the state's rivers, lakes, and coastal waterways for fish, shellfish, and aquatic plants.

In many ways, the agricultural diversity of the Empire State makes it the ideal subject for a book about farm buildings. The vernacular architecture created to meet the needs of New York's farmers embodies the main trends in American farm life from the seventeenth century to the present day. Because of the state's varied geography and its long history of agricultural production, there are few types of agricultural structures that have been used in the United States that cannot be found in New York in some form. At the same time, the state boasts several specialized building types that are not commonly found in other places. As a case in point, New World Dutch barns from the colonial and early national periods are largely limited in their geographic distribution to areas that are now part of New York and New Jersey (Figure P.1). The hop house provides another example, this one from the nineteenth century, as during that period its construction and use in the United States was most prevalent in central New York (Figure P.2).

Studying the variations in farm buildings across New York shows just how diverse the state is in terms of climate, soil types, and topography, and therefore agricultural production. The Empire State stretches from Lake Erie in the west to Long Island in the east (Figure P.3). It includes rich valleys along the Hudson, Mohawk, and Genesee rivers; coastal regions that border the Atlantic Ocean; inland lakes in the center of the state; and mountainous areas in the Adirondacks, Catskills, and northern Alleghenies. The geography and climate of the various regions has created a historical connection between specific crops and specific places: grapes grow just east of Lake Erie, orchard crops to the south of Lake Ontario, vegetables, especially potatoes, on Long Island, and grains in the river valleys. Dairying, though common throughout the state, has been especially concentrated in central New York. While there is much overlap between the various agricultural regions within the state, there is enough variation to warrant special attention. Throughout the text and in the figure captions, trends and building types are often described by region, county, or even town to provide a clear understanding of local characteristics and agricultural practices.

While in this book I focus on common farm buildings, barns in New York are anything but ordinary. Individual farmers and builders crafted buildings that served their own unique situations and experiences. One inventive New York horticulturalist named Peter Henderson wrote to an agricultural magazine about a dual-purpose storage cellar–greenhouse built over a seven-foot-deep foundation intended for another building but left abandoned (Figure P.4). He explained, "Although I have never seen such a combination since, I am satisfied that in favorable circumstances such a structure might be made of great advantage and at trifling cost." The cellar temperature stayed cool but above freezing and therefore was ideal for cold storage; it also provided a more suitable base for the greenhouse than the frozen ground.[5] While not

Figure P.1. Detail, *Van Bergen Overmantel,* ca. 1733, attributed to John Heaten (active ca. 1730–1745), oil on cherry wood, 15 1/4" x 74 3/4". A New World Dutch barn and two hay barracks form a focal point in this painting of an early New York farmstead. Both Dutch barns and hay barracks are associated with colonial Dutch settlers and would have distinguished New York's rural landscape from that in other regions. (Fenimore Art Museum, Cooperstown, N0366.1954. Photograph by Richard Walker.)

found on the average New York farm, such a building typifies the search for practical, yet in some cases very imaginative, building solutions.

While we often think about farming as a traditional pursuit, its practice has been much more dynamic than static, even in the distant past. In 1852, for example, the agricultural journal *Moore's Rural New-Yorker* was advocating for major changes in the way farmers dealt with animals and animal waste. A columnist in *Moore's* remarked, "A new idea has dawned upon the owner of the farm and a new history opens upon those starved and plundered lands." The new idea, the construction of a cellar to store manure, was evidenced by a new type of building. *Moore's* editors, recognizing the link between architectural expression and changing practice, reported that in this case, as in many others, "the old barn stands hard by, a decayed relic of the past, a monument to the old style of farming."[6]

The 1852 article recognizes what may have been the most abrupt in a series of changes in farming and farm building. In the seventeenth and eighteenth centuries, immigrants and new Americans generally built upon agricultural practices developed in other places to make their way in what is now New York. They often found that they had to adapt to their new environment, and sometimes they borrowed from their neighbors. As a result, both the way they farmed and the buildings they built to facilitate farming balanced continuity with slow change. By the mid-nineteenth century, transformations occurred at a more rapid pace. New ideas, often published in print sources like *Moore's,* circulated among more people more quickly, and new technology both allowed and demanded new solutions to old problems.

The story of agriculture in New York after the 1840s is one of constant alteration and adjustment. While farming is often viewed nostalgically as an age-old practice, new means of transportation, new ideas about sanitation, new equipment for

Figure P.2. Hop house, ca. 1873, Town of Hartwick, Otsego County. This hop house, repaired with the assistance of a New York State barn grant, features a draft kiln with a pyramidal roof. Hops would have been dried on the second-floor level before being moved to the attached side barn for pressing. Otsego County was part of the central New York region where hops, used in flavoring beers and ales, were grown and processed. (Photograph by Cynthia Falk, July 2010.)

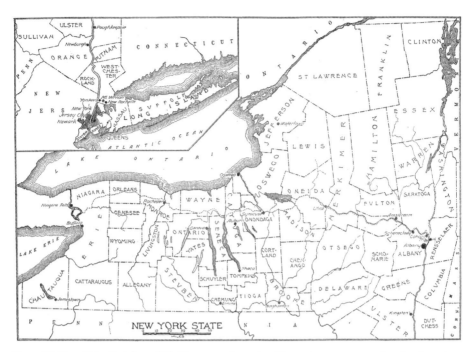

Figure P.3. Map of New York State, 1921. The names of counties, cities, and waterways are referred to throughout this book to provide a clear sense of the regional nature of New York State agriculture. (Map reproduced from Elmer O. Fippin, *Rural New York,* Rural State and Province Series [New York: Macmillan, 1921], fig. 33.)

performing routine tasks, and new construction materials have changed the way New Yorkers farmed and how they constructed the farm landscape. One of the chief developments of the mid- to late nineteenth century was the increased segregation of farm tasks. On the farm itself, an increasing array of structures replaced or supplemented multiuse buildings; even within the large main barn, tasks became compartmentalized as distinct spaces were defined for different kinds of animals and crops. At the same time, some work formerly done on the farm, such as making butter or cheese, moved away from the farmstead to rural factories. As these trends continued in the early decades of the twentieth century, new building materials also influenced the construction and appearance of farm buildings, as concrete, laminated beams and trusses, and mass-distributed building plans brought increasing standardization.

Farm building in New York generally slowed during the Great Depression and Second World War. When it resumed in the postwar period, new developments again transformed the farm landscape. Economies of scale and increasing automation became important in an era that valued modernization and increased production and consumption. Traditional buildings and approaches never disappeared, but for many farmers, new, modern methods brought about a period of rapid change much like that one hundred years earlier. When Douglas Harper spoke with farmers in New York's north country in the late 1980s, he found a divide between what he termed "craft" and "factory" farms, the latter larger in size and scale with more

A COMBINED CELLAR AND GREENHOUSE.

Figure P.4. Peter Henderson, "Combined Cellar and Greenhouse," *American Agriculturalist* 33, no. 4 (April 1874): 141.

advanced production technologies and greater division of labor.[7] His conclusions are supported by statistics. Between 1959 and 2007, the total number of farms in New York had dropped from over 82,000 to about 36,000, while average farm size had grown slightly, and the disparity in sales values between the most and least prosperous New York farms had increased exponentially.[8] As in the past, these trends are made manifest in the landscape.

People appreciate barns, particularly older barns, for a variety of reasons. Not the least of these is their endangered status. As New York's economy has become less agriculturally based, and as individual family farms have become more mechanized and, in some cases, even bought up by large agribusinesses, buildings that were once of fundamental importance have become more rare. Many barns and other agricultural buildings have been lost because they were no longer integral to the day-to-day operations of a working farm (Figure P.5). Indeed, while old barns are often seen as picturesque elements of bucolic landscapes, their maintenance and adaptation to new uses are an expensive proposition for barn owners. Barns can be attractive aesthetic resources, and important reminders of New York State's rich agricultural legacy, but the best avenue for preservation is continued serviceability.

Figure P.5. Barns of C.E. Colburn, 1901, Portlandville area, Otsego County. When built, the barn at Hillside Stock Farm cost about $6,000 and was touted as handy, comfortable, and up-to-date. Today, high maintenance costs and lack of use have jeopardized the integrity of the structure. (Photograph by Cynthia Falk, January 2010.)

For this reason, several organizations have promoted the preservation and adaptive reuse of agricultural buildings. In 1987 the National Trust for Historic Preservation and *Successful Farming* magazine began working in partnership on BARN AGAIN!, a program that provided workshops, referrals, and publications for the owners of historic barns. BARN AGAIN! also presented awards for successful barn rehabilitation projects.[9] In New York, nonprofit groups like the New York State Barn Coalition and the Dutch Barn Preservation Society continue to work to ensure that historic agricultural buildings are appreciated, preserved, and documented. Museums and historic sites such as The Farmers' Museum in Cooperstown provide the general public with the opportunity to experience old barns firsthand. The goal of all these organizations is to ensure the economic and cultural relevance of the agricultural buildings that are part of New York State's cultural heritage.

For farmers who are the stewards of historic barns, the most useful programs are those that provide grants or tax credits to keep older farm buildings well maintained and in use. Beginning in 2001, state-funded New York State Barn Restoration and Preservation Grants provided money for barn rehabilitation projects. During the first grant cycle alone, over 4,800 barn owners applied, and awards totaling

$2 million were made for 113 projects in forty-eight New York counties.[10] At this writing the state offers financial assistance to historic barn owners through tax credits rather than competitive grants. A state income tax credit calculated as a percentage of the total cost for a rehabilitation project is available for barns built before 1936, provided the project does not alter the historic appearance of the building, and it is not converted to residential use.[11] The owners of barns listed on or eligible for the National Register of Historic Places may additionally benefit from a federal income tax credit. Local municipalities and school districts can opt to phase in assessment increases on restored barns and other buildings.

My goal in writing this book is to encourage the appreciation and therefore preservation of New York's rich agricultural and architectural legacy through an increased awareness of the buildings on farms throughout the state. By writing about barns, I hope to promote further study and action. Visiting and experiencing barns in person is the best way to understand how they were built and how they function. Some organizations provide tours of working farms, often offered seasonally and geared toward particular products or industries such as maple syrup or dairying. Readers are encouraged to take advantage of these opportunities to learn how farms and farm buildings work today.

An appendix at the conclusion of this book provides a list of museums and historic sites throughout New York State that include agricultural buildings in their interpretation. These sites offer a different experience than do working farms. Their task is to use the built environment to provide a tangible connection to the past, to the experience of a specific person, location, or era. They help inform visitors about how things used to be, why barns were originally built, and what they can tell us about the people who made and used them. While many museums create a sense of nostalgia for a simpler era, often before the mechanization and automation we know today, in the best cases they connect farming in earlier eras with what we experience in the present. In an age when most people buy their food and clothes at the store, without a thought as to how they got there, an understanding of agricultural processes makes for better-informed consumers and citizens.

New York's rural landscape deserves attention just like its other architectural landmarks. I urge my readers to visit, and better yet support, a historical society, living history museum, or historic site that preserves and interprets New York State's agricultural heritage. Advocate for the preservation and adaptive reuse of old barns and farm buildings through programs that help fund maintenance, repair, and conversion to new farm uses.

Perhaps most important, we should all support local farmers. Historic barns are important cultural and aesthetic resources, but they are also important agricultural resources. As this book explains, farmers created barns to serve vital, often specialized functions on the farm. Currently more than seventeen thousand New York farms include at least one barn constructed prior to 1960.[12] These farm buildings and the rural landscapes of which they are part will endure as a legacy to the state's rich agricultural heritage by remaining part of thriving working farms where they are put to good use.

This book combines text and illustrations to help the reader connect the history of agriculture in New York with the rural landscape. It begins with an introduction about the physical characteristics of barns—the materials that are used to build them and the embellishments that make them distinctive. The remaining chapters are organized according to building type, defined primarily according to function. Chapter 1 opens with what is traditionally termed "the barn," typically a large multifunction building that is geared toward storing grain and hay, as well as housing animals, especially dairy cows. Later chapters cover more specialized buildings. Chapter 2 focuses on barns for sheltering animals, such as horse stables, pigpens, and chicken coops. Buildings associated with the storage and processing of field crops, including cereals such as wheat and corn as well as grasses such as hay, are the subject of chapter 3. Farmers who raise specialty crops—from apples to potatoes to honey—often require specialized buildings and structures, and these are detailed in chapter 4. Chapter 5 focuses on elements of the built environment, such as engine houses, which help ensure that farmers have ready access to power and water. Each chapter addresses the issue of change over time but also looks at regional variations and differences based on scale of production. Special emphasis is placed on distinct farm products associated with New York State such as hops, apples, cheese, and maple syrup (Figure P.6).

Although this book is organized to highlight individual buildings, it is important to remember that all of the structures found on a farm are part of a larger farm complex (Figure P.7). The constellation of buildings on a farmstead usually includes a residence for the family and sometimes other housing for tenants or seasonal laborers, in addition to buildings more clearly associated with agricultural work. While I do not discuss farmhouses and other domestically oriented buildings in detail, these structures were and are important components of the farm environment, as they sheltered and served the people who provided farm labor on a daily basis.

The location of buildings within the farm complex provides important information about work routines and patterns of living on the farm. Privies and woodsheds were located near the farmhouse for obvious reasons, but the reason for erecting chicken coops near the residence may be less clear until it is understood that it was farmwives and children who historically oversaw the poultry flock. Milk houses, often added to a farm complex after its initial development, were built separately from but often connected to the dairy barn to enable the separation of animals and milk products while at the same time maintaining proximity so milk did not have to be hauled a long distance. In the age of bulk tanks and off-site processing, milk houses, like garages and farm stands, also had to be oriented toward the road.

To the greatest extent possible, my interpretation is based on observation of actual farmsteads throughout New York State. Given the geographic scope of the state, however, there are biases. The Historic American Buildings Survey, New

Figure P.6. *Cider Mill,* by William Carlton (1816–1888), oil on canvas, 29" x 36" x 1 3/4". Many distinctive New York agricultural products, such as apples, require specialized spaces and equipment to be stored or processed. Here apples are made into cider at a cider mill. (Fenimore Art Museum, Cooperstown, N0427.1955. Photograph by Richard Walker.)

York State Register of Historic Places, Farm Security Administration photographs, and New York State Barn Restoration and Preservation Grant applications provided me with avenues to access the rural landscape without having to make repeated car trips. Nonetheless, central New York, particularly Otsego County, is best represented, as it was most readily studied and also best documented in the Archive of New York State Folklife and F. P. Ward files at the New York State Historical Association Research Library in Cooperstown, which served as my home base while I was writing this volume. Fortunately, Otsego County and the surrounding countryside have been exemplary of a wide variety of agricultural enterprises through the years and remain rural today, making this an ideal place to study New York's farm buildings.

When barns were not easily accessible through fieldwork, agricultural periodicals proved an important source of information. Though geared to an audience that appreciated progressive agricultural practices and full of models for ideal buildings that were beyond the reach of most farmers, the agricultural press was also a forum for practitioners who wanted to share their ideas. *Moore's Rural New-Yorker* and the

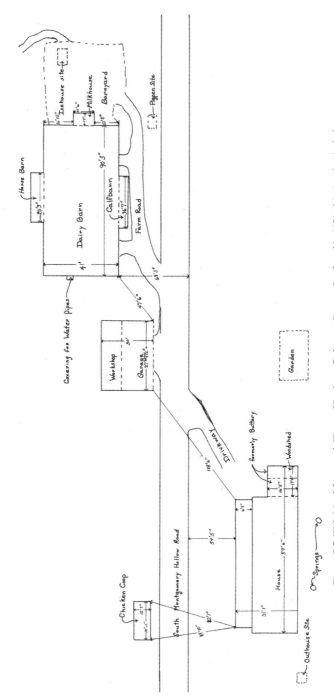

Figure P.7. Walt Mead farmstead, Town of Roxbury, Delaware County. Produced in 1974, this site plan includes the locations of the farmhouse, woodshed, garden, chicken coop, garage-workshop, dairy barn, horse barn, calf barn, milk house, and maple sugarbush, as well as the former sites of the outhouse, icehouse, and pigpen. The relationship of the buildings and landscape features to one another and to the road suggests the movement of people, animals, and equipment from one location to another over time. (Drawing by Donna Rae Gordon, Archive of New York State Folklife, New York Historical Association Research Library, Cooperstown, 74–0200.)

American Agriculturalist included articles by farmers in New York and elsewhere who were proud of their innovations and wanted to make sure others knew about a new building form, floor plan, or material they had put to use. Though less participatory in nature, books published by professionals devoted to creating the ideal farm, including those employed by the Cooperative Extension Service or other government agencies, also provided good prescriptive information about what the ideal barn should look like and how it should function. These sources are perhaps most useful when the plans they contain can be contrasted with actual buildings designed and built at the same time on working farms.

This book results from a collaboration between The Farmers' Museum, founded by Stephen C. Clark on the site of Fenimore Farm in the 1940s, and the Cooperstown Graduate Program, a two-year master's program in history museum studies cosponsored by the State University of New York College at Oneonta and the New York State Historical Association. The idea for the volume came from the museum, which recognized the need for a field guide to help readers identify and document agricultural structures from the late seventeenth century through the twentieth century. Joan K. Davidson, through her program Furthermore grants in publishing, provided generous funding and patience in seeing the project through.

This book is the work of numerous students at the Cooperstown Graduate Program, which since the 1960s has been documenting farm buildings in New York State, especially in the region immediately surrounding Cooperstown. Special thanks go to Katherine Chaison, Anne Clothier, Kira A. DeLanoy, Ryan Anthony Donaldson, Amy E. Drake, John M. Emery, Danelle N. Feddes, Amy C. Frey, Andrew Gaerte, Amy Gundrum Greene, Mehna Harders Reach, John T. Hart Jr., Erica L. Harvey, Robert Henning, Emily A. Holmes, Ashley Hopkins-Benton, Carolyn Lane, Joshua Muse, Anneke Nordmark, Leslie Poling, Dawn Reid, Brian J. Richards, Alan Rowe, Mary C. Ryan, Elizabeth Schultz, Mark A. Turdo, Greg Vadney, Lori B. White, and Cameron Wood, who did the vast majority of the research and drafted essays that served as the basis for much of the book. Sara Busch, Jennie Davy, and Amy E. Drake did the tedious work of checking and formatting the notes, and Sarah Budlong, Jennie Davy, Erica L. Harvey, and Cassandra Mundt worked to put the illustrations in order.

In addition to students and colleagues at the Cooperstown Graduate Program, this book would not have been possible without the help of numerous others. Most important are the farmers and farm owners who granted access to their property and offered their expertise. The staff at agricultural museums have also been generous with their time and knowledge, providing contacts and sources in the form of both buildings and documents. Special thanks go to librarians Wayne Wright and JoAnn VanVranken at the New York State Historical Association Research Library for their support; all of the images in this book from published sources are reprinted courtesy of the New York State Historical Association Research Library unless otherwise noted. Sally McMurry at Penn State University, who has invited me to join her in fieldwork to support her own study of farm buildings in Pennsylvania, has been an invaluable source of information. Her input, combined with that of anonymous reviewers and of Michael McGandy at Cornell University Press, has strengthened my presentation, organization, and argument.

This book is dedicated to my parents, Jim and Betty Layton, with whom I spent my early childhood in the small rural community of Wolcott in Wayne County. They, perhaps inadvertently, helped me and my brother Tim develop an early appreciation for the history and landscape of upstate New York, which we have both been able to explore more fully in our professional careers. My husband, Glenn, and children Elizabeth and Isaac have also been integral parts of this project, tolerating numerous car trips to photograph one more farm and keeping a constant eye out for unusual buildings that warranted further exploration. As book writing is often a selfish pursuit, I am most thankful for the active role they have taken in helping me see it through.

BARNS OF NEW YORK

Introduction

[July] 9th Took a pull on the river this morning with Robert and after
spending the morning very pleasantly we started for home w[h]ere we
arrived in time to help all hands lower the timbers of the barn.

Geⓞrge S. Buckmaster, New Windsor, Orange County, 1855

For eighteen-year-old George S. Buckmaster, whose family commenced building a barn in the spring of 1855, the construction of the new structure provided
lessons in geometry, woodworking, stonemasonry, accounting, and of course time
management. The Buckmasters had recently relocated from Brooklyn to New
Windsor in Orange County, and work on the barn had to be balanced with other
tasks. The Buckmasters grew a host of fruits and vegetables—strawberries, plums,
cherries, raspberries, cranberries, muskmelons, grapes, asparagus, celery, radishes,
cucumbers, carrots, beans, lima beans, peas, beets, cabbage, corn, pumpkins, and
potatoes—and kept cows, hogs, and chickens. George, the third of seven children
living at home in 1855, found himself planting, hoeing, weeding, making beanpoles,
fixing fences, and putting up a chicken coop that spring and early summer. He
also helped to build the main barn, which would supplement the granary and "cow
hovel" already on the property.

Barn building began on May 30. George recorded in his diary that he helped
with the initial phase of the project, stating: "We laid the square for the barn which
is to be 40 ft square. . . . I obtained the rule for making a square namely, measure
6 feet on one side of the angle 8 ft on the other and then measure 10 feet across
from point to point."[1] Construction materials were obtained on-site or from local
sources. George hauled stones for the foundation, and sand for the mortar was

drawn, perhaps from the banks of the nearby Hudson River. The Buckmasters had to purchase gravel for the mortar from a Mr. Hasbrouck, and the essential ingredient, lime, came from the Amos Soap Factory. The family bought planks for scaffolding and lumber for doorframes in nearby Newburgh.

Labor for the project was provided by a Mr. Turner, who brought knowledge of construction, family members, and at critical points a number of other men whose names George recorded in his diary. George wrote about his own work in late May and early June digging the trench for the foundation and building the stone foundation walls. By June 21 and 22 George's older brother Robert and Mr. Turner were transforming the chestnut trees that would form the frame of the building into squared logs. On July 3 George noted, "I was busy making mortar nearly all day we have run up two sides about four foot high and got the lot ready for the third side." On the sixth a rainstorm halted the operation until the following Monday, when, upon returning from a rare relaxing morning at the river, George and Robert helped "lower the timbers," marking the near completion of the shell of the structure. The following day George recorded his last diary entry, using the remainder of the book for accounting rather than day-to-day descriptions of activities.[2]

George's short journal, running from April 13 to July 10, 1855, provides a rare personal glimpse of the barn-building process in the 1850s, something that is foreign to most of us in the twenty-first century. Yet the knowledge George gained by participating in this construction project is significant for anyone trying to understand old barns. Materials, construction methods, and even decorative techniques inform us about the time, place, and people that made these buildings possible. By examining saw marks on wood, for example, we can better determine when a building was constructed. Some materials, such as cobblestone (Figure I.1), provide evidence of regionally distinct resources and trade networks, while others, like ceramic silo tile (Figure I.2), demonstrate the widespread distribution of both building materials and construction plans.[3] Decorative elements, such as distinct animal figures painted on red barn doors (Figure I.3), help delineate the chronology and geography of farming practices. The observation of physical characteristics and what they can tell us serves as a starting point for further analysis of any vernacular architecture.

Without our knowing much about the intended use of the Buckmaster barn, George's descriptions of its construction still provide important information and help situate it in the place and time in which it was built. Like other farm buildings of the mid-nineteenth century, it was constructed by family and a small group of other people with building experience, and it was made of materials available locally. The main structure was wood, but stone, found on the property, was used on the lower level to provide protection from the moisture of the ground. Because of the reliance on local materials, the Buckmaster barn also illustrates another characteristic of older New York State barns: they varied in appearance from region to region. These variations are perhaps most noticeable in buildings constructed at least in part

Figure I.1. Cobblestone Barn, ca. 1840, Town of Marion, Wayne County. Stone that has been rendered round by the action of water or glaciers is known as cobblestone. Cobblestones were used as a decorative building material in the area surrounding the Great Lakes and stretching as far south in New York as today's Route 20. Here large squared stones are used to create the corners of the original section of this barn, and cobblestones are laid in even courses across the façade. (Photograph by Cynthia Falk, June 2010.)

of stone, which diverges in appearance in the different geological regions within the state, and which, because of its weight, was seldom transported long distances (Figure I.4).

Only with the use of new materials in the twentieth century was local stone supplanted as the dominant material for foundations and other masonry construction. The authors of a 1922 book for those planning to build a barn noted, "For practical purposes, concrete, brick, and tiles are fully as economical, and are more easily handled."[4] As a result of these mass-produced materials, barns began to appear less regionally distinct. At the same time, literature on barn building, often made available through federally funded agricultural experiment stations and cooperative extension services, brought a new level of professionalism and uniformity to barn design, and new machines like the gasoline engine changed the way farming was practiced. Although barns built during the early twentieth century shared a similar overall form and function with those the Buckmasters would have known years earlier, change was occurring rapidly and on a broad scale, especially when it came to building materials.

This is not to say that barn building before 1900 had not been influenced by new technologies as well as changing agricultural practices and markets. The age of a farm building can often be at least roughly ascertained simply by observing how

Figure I.2. Barn with attached milk house and twin tile silos, Lima area, Livingston County. The twentieth century brought a variety of new barn building materials, farm technologies, and health concerns. The structural clay tiles used to construct these silos could be used instead of wood to create silos that would not be damaged by the moisture inherent in storing silage. The construction of a separate milk house addressed issues of sanitation that were especially important in the dairy industry. (Photograph by Cynthia Falk, June 2010.)

Figure I.3. Carriage barn, Sloansville vicinity, Schoharie County. In an area centered on Schoharie County, barn door decoration became popular in the nineteenth century. This elaborate example includes silhouettes of horses, an appropriate motif for a carriage house. (Photograph by Cynthia Falk, May 2010.)

Figure I.4. Stone agricultural building, ca. 1882, Canadarago Lake area, Otsego County. The builder of this multiuse farm structure used carefully shaped blocks of local stone to form the front of the building, which could be seen from the road, and less refined fieldstone for the side and rear walls, which were not as visible to passersby. (Photograph Cynthia Falk, April 2010.)

Figure I.5. Adze and timber hewn by Ernest Vroman, Howes Cave, Schoharie County. A metal-bladed tool was essential for turning trees into lumber to be used in barn building. (Photograph by William Schwerd, Archive of New York State Folklife, New York State Historical Association Library, Cooperstown, 72–0056.0033.)

Figure I.6. Mortise and tenon joinery, Windfall Dutch barn, ca.1800, Salt Springville, Montgomery County. Mortise and tenon joints, seen here in a New World Dutch barn, provide a way to connect wooden members without using nails. An empty mortise hole near the center of the picture is evidence of a missing horizontal member. (Photograph by Ronald Soodalter, Archives of New York State Folklife, New York State Historical Association Library, Cooperstown, 72–0205.)

Figure I.7. Saw marks on the framing of the Herkimer summer kitchen and woodshed, 1810–1840, formerly located in the Schuyler Lake vicinity, now at The Farmers' Museum, Cooperstown, Otsego County. Straight, parallel saw marks like these indicate that this beam was cut by an up-and-down saw at a water-powered sawmill. (Photograph by Cynthia Falk, January 2010.)

the wooden elements were prepared and joined together. In traditional structures such as the Buckmaster barn, wood for framing was hewn square with a broad ax or a metal-bladed tool known as an adze (Figure I.5). Wooden elements were joined together with mortise and tenon joints: a tenon, a rectangular projection at the end of one piece of wood, was inserted in a mortise, or hole, in another and pegged into place (Figure I.6).

Lumber for exterior cladding, roof shingles, and flooring was most often cut with an up-and-down, or sash, saw at a water-powered sawmill if one was located nearby. Eventually even large framing members could be cut, rather than hewn, by an up-and-down saw. Straight, parallel saw marks on framing lumber, clapboards, and flooring in some farm buildings provide evidence of the use of this technology, which helped replace human power with power from water turning a waterwheel or turbine (Figure I.7).

By the second half of the nineteenth century, up-and-down saws began to be replaced by circular saws, which left arched saw marks on the wood they cut (Figure I.8). At about the same time, builders started using mortise and tenon joints less frequently in farm buildings. A light frame, or balloon frame, consisted of smaller studs nailed at the top and bottom to sills and plates. It proved more efficient for residential buildings and smaller agricultural structures that were not subject to strong forces or heavy loads. Even in larger barns, builders began to rethink the use of heavy timber frames joined with mortise and tenon joints. One early-twentieth-century author reported, "With the scarcity of heavy timber and consequent cost it is time farmers who are to erect barns should give some study to the new methods of framing, where no timber is thicker than two inches, and from six to eight inches wide."[5] When the additional strength provided by larger posts and beams was needed, multiple pieces of dimensional lumber could be joined together to do the job; roofs could be framed with trusses composed of many pieces of lumber spiked or laminated together (Figure I.9).[6]

In wooden structures, the nails and other metal fasteners used to join pieces of lumber can also be good indicators of the age of a building. Even early barns with heavy timber frames had siding and often flooring that was nailed in place. Builders working in the seventeenth and eighteenth centuries used nails created individually by blacksmiths. Known as wrought nails, these had shafts that tapered on all four sides. Nail heads were hand hammered and sometimes resembled a flower with petals; for this reasons wrought nails are often referred to as rosehead nails (Figure I.10).

By the late eighteenth century, nail making was beginning to be mechanized as nails were cut from iron stock. Cut nails have shafts that taper on only two sides (Figure I.11). In the first decades of the nineteenth century, nail heads still had to be hammered by hand. Eventually that process was mechanized as well. Although handmade wrought nails could still be used in the nineteenth century, and even today, manufacturing nails with machines made them cheaper and more readily available. Wire nails, with round wire shafts and round heads, began to be used in the late nineteenth century (Figure I.12). While they never completely replaced cut nails for all applications, evidence of their use helps date repairs or building campaigns.

At the beginning of the twentieth century, as a half century earlier when the Buckmasters were building their barn, new barns in New York had stone foundations, wood frames, and wood cladding. "An Up-to-Date New York Barn" singled out in a book of barn plans was praised for its cement floors, a recent innovation.[7] The rest of the sizable building, owned by C. E. Colburn of Portlandville, was very traditional in its use of materials (see Figure P.5). The foundation was fieldstone, and the principal components of the frame were heavy timbers, which were held together with mortise and tenon joints. The exterior was clad in vertical wooden boards, and the gambrel roof was finished with wood shingles. The two round silos were constructed from wooden staves held in place with iron bands. Colburn's Hillside Stock Farm was "up-to-date" in terms of its facilities for efficient feeding, breed-

Figure I.8. Framing members with circular saw marks, Shaker barn, 1916, Shaker Heritage Society, Colonie area, Albany County. The new barn built for the Shaker Watervliet Church family in the early twentieth century was constructed from timbers cut with a circular saw, which left telltale arched marks on the wood. (Photograph by Emily Holmes, 2006.)

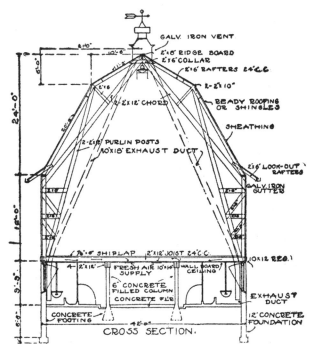

Figure I.9. Light frame construction as illustrated in a 1917 guide for barn builders. (Herbert Shearer, *Farm Buildings: With Plans and Descriptions* [Chicago: F. J. Drake and Co., 1917], 11.)

Figure I.10. Barn door, The Farmers' Museum, Cooperstown, Otsego County. Hand-headed nails are sometimes referred to as "rosehead" nails because the blacksmith's hammer leaves marks that resemble petals. (Photograph by Cynthia Falk, January 2010.)

Figure I.11. Fence, The Farmers' Museum, Cooperstown, Otsego County. Cut nails were made by machines that cut the shaft and fashioned the head from sheet iron. (Photograph by Cynthia Falk, January 2010.)

ing, and processing, but its concrete floor with mangers and manure gutters was the owner's primary foray into modern materials.

All this was about to change. In the 1920s the authors of a book on barn planning noted the new developments in barn building in the previous decade. In terms of materials, the authors devoted chapters of the volume not only to wood but also to concrete and structural clay tile. Concrete was used for floors, especially in dairy barns, and for foundations, silo walls, and fence posts, as well as for making concrete blocks, stucco, and mortar. Clay tile could be used for floors and walls, and, when

Figure I.12. Wire nails used for hanging equipment in an agricultural outbuilding, Canadarago Lake area, Otsego County. (Photograph by Cynthia Falk, April 2010.)

created in curved sections, for silos (see Figure I.2).[8] A new emphasis on sanitation encouraged the use of materials such as concrete and glazed tile in areas where foods, especially milk and feed, were stored. The use of the new materials had other advantages as well, including protection from fire and rot.

Wood did not disappear as a building material, but other materials did take its place for some applications. Wood shingles, for example, were still the most common cladding for barn roofs in the 1920s. Asphalt, galvanized metal sheets, slate, and composite cement shingles were also being used, however, and asphalt and metal roofing would become the standard as the twentieth century progressed.[9] Cupolas, which were built on barn roofs to help facilitate air circulation, were replaced with modern metal ventilators (Figures I.13 and I.14). As farmers were advised:

> The object of the cupola is to protect the opening of the flue from the elements, keep out birds, prevent back drafts as far as possible, and assist in drawing foul air from the barn. The well-designed steel ventilator accomplishes these objects. The home-built wood cupola accomplishes none of the objects satisfactorily. For any other purpose than ornamentation, the wood cupola should be replaced with the modern steel cupola.[10]

Even the decision to paint a barn or leave it unpainted came under scrutiny in the transitional years of the early twentieth century. In 1900 Isaac Phillips Roberts, the director of the College of Agriculture at Cornell University, noted that

Figure I.13. Farmstead, Madison vicinity, Madison County. The wooden cupola on top of the main barn bears the date 1885. At this time traditional building materials, chiefly wood and stone, were the predominant materials used in the construction of farm buildings. (Photograph by Cynthia Falk, June 2010.)

many unpainted barns were still in a good state of repair although they had been subjected to the weather for years. He concluded, "When the barns are well removed from the house and virtually hidden by trees, they may be left unpainted, but where they are conspicuous they should be painted, that the barn may not mar the beauty of the home."[11] In other words, painting was optional, done primarily for aesthetic reasons. A survey of Otsego County barns conducted in the 1960s suggests that Roberts's advice reflected common practice: 56 percent of barns remained unpainted.[12]

By the 1920s, however, paint was increasingly recommended. As the author of a farmers' bulletin put out by the U.S. Department of Agriculture explained, "although a coat of paint adds greatly to the appearance of a building or piece of farm machinery, the chief purpose of painting on the farm is to preserve houses, barns, and implements from the effects of the weather." New materials, such as tinned sheet iron for roofs or yellow pine lumber, did not hold up as well without paint as the more durable kinds of wood used previously, and ready-mixed paints made the task of painting easier and the results more predictable. The bulletin advised, "New wooden buildings should have a priming coat of paint as soon as the weather permits; their finishing coats should be put on within the next month or two. Tinned roofing should be painted as soon as it has been laid."[13]

Figure I.14. Farmstead, near Pompey Center, Onondaga County. Innovations such as concrete silos, concrete blocks for foundations, steel for ventilators and roofing, cylindrical wire mesh corncribs, and, most important, tractors and trucks with gasoline engines all influenced the way farmers have made a living over the past century. (Photograph by Cynthia Falk, June 2010.)

Wood framing, metal fasteners, concrete floors, paint, and other building materials represent the ingredients for barn building. Some were optional, and others were introduced only after a certain date. But all have distinct histories that speak to changes in construction practices and the manufacture and transportation of building supplies. For farm families like the Buckmasters, raising a barn was a fairly traditional craft facilitated by local labor and natural resources. Although the Buckmasters lived in a period when barn design was changing to accommodate new ideas about how animals should be housed, building materials remained fairly constant. In the early twentieth century, the introduction of new materials such as concrete brought about yet another series of changes in the appearance of the barn. In both periods, and throughout the history of barn building in New York, the intended use of farm buildings, based on agricultural practices of the period, and the availability of building materials have gone hand in hand in inspiring the appearance of the barns we appreciate as part of the rural landscape today.

Often the study of architecture, even vernacular architecture, is based on conclusions about how a building fits within a progression of academic styles, such as the Greek Revival or the Queen Anne style. Like building materials, the style of a building

Figure I.15. Gothic Revival barn, ca. 1850, South Livonia, Livingston County. Built for the Coe family, this barn was designed in one of the historical revival styles popular in the mid-nineteenth century. At a time when many barns were practical buildings with little decorative embellishment, pointed arch windows, ornate bargeboard, and a patterned slate roof set this Gothic Revival building apart. Unfortunately, the elaborate structure was lost to fire in early 2009. (Photograph by Paige Miller, Rochester, 2008.)

provides clues to when it was built. It can also provide evidence of influences—where the builders got their ideas—as well as what they hoped their buildings would convey. As the art historian Jules Prown argues, "objects reflect cultural values in their style," and barns, as very large objects, visually and tactilely embody the culture of the time period in which they were built through their plan, materials, and construction as well as through their style.[14]

Unfortunately, it is often hard to describe barns in terms of the styles that typically characterize other types of buildings, but the importance of aesthetics should not be overlooked. In the nineteenth century particularly, Americans embraced a wide variety of architectural styles utilizing historic European or exotic design elements. Barns that incorporated such architectural motifs most often took the form of carriage sheds or stables in New York villages. Sometimes, however, farmers incorporated architectural details such as Italianate brackets or Victorian bargeboard on larger farm buildings. In South Livonia, in Livingston County, a barn with pointed-arch windows, pierced bargeboard, and a patterned slate roof epitomized the Gothic Revival style that was popular when it was built circa 1850 (Figure I.15).[15] An unusually bold example, it attests to the fact that farmers were not unaware of popular aesthetic trends, even if they seldom went to this extreme.

Figure I.16. Barns, Esperance vicinity, Schoharie County. Paint was one means of decorating agricultural buildings. In an area centered on Schoharie County, a regional aesthetic featuring barn doors decorated in contrasting
colors is still a recognizable element of the landscape. (Photograph by Cynthia Falk, May 2010.)

Often stylistic elements are a more subtle part of barn design. Most barns were
constructed with utility in mind; they had to be conveniently sited, efficiently ordered, and economically erected. When they were painted, the color red, traditionally
made from iron oxide pigment, proved especially popular because it was inexpensive, readily available, and long lasting. Yet farmers were not always satisfied with
plain, unadorned farm buildings and in some cases could not resist using the barn
as a creative outlet. In central New York, in an area centered on Schoharie County,
for example, more than seven hundred barns with decoratively painted doors have
been documented (Figure I.16). The largely geometric motifs, which include arches,
diamonds, sections of circles, triangles, and an occasional horse, date to the second
half of the nineteenth century. What sparked this trend is not known, but the urge
to paint barns and highlight the doors in a contrasting color certainly caught on in
this one locality, creating a local aesthetic that is hard to ignore.[16]

In an earlier period, cutouts in the exterior cladding on Dutch and English barns
in New York similarly served as a vehicle for both creativity and regional variation
(Figure I.17). These vents allowed for air circulation, much as cupolas and ventilators would do later. In addition, the cutouts, sometimes referred to as martin holes or
owl holes, allowed birds access in and out of the building. Farmers encouraged birds
to live in or around the barn, as they provided insect and pest control. Although the

Figure I.17. Sweet-Marble barn, ca. 1803, originally from Mount Vision, Otsego County, now at The Farmers' Museum, Cooperstown, Otsego County. Early New York barns often featured cutout holes in the siding to provide access for birds, which would eat pests such as mice and bugs. Often these cutouts were decoratively shaped, in this case echoing the silhouette of the barn itself. (Photograph by Cynthia Falk, 2008.)

Figure I.18. *Horace Tuttle's Livery Stable,* artist unknown, oil on canvas, 18 1/4" x 24 1/4". As this painting attests, Horace Tuttle advertised the nature of his business in text on the walls of his stable and through the large horse-shaped weathervane located above the structure. (Fenimore Art Museum, Cooperstown, N0284.1961. Photograph by Richard Walker.)

holes could have taken any shape, farmers often created elaborate geometric forms that added visual appeal to barn walls. On Dutch barns some forms are typical in a certain area; a triangle with a smaller inverted triangle on top, for example, is a local-ized expression southwest of Middleburg in Schoharie County.[17]

Whether barn decoration is limited to doors or martin holes, or takes a more elab-orate form, it should not be overlooked in the study of New York's farm buildings. Like the use of building materials, barn decoration evolved over time and arose from the needs and desires of the agricultural community. For some barn owners, embel-lishment was combined with another important function: advertising. Barns could be labeled with important information including the name of the farm or the name of the owner, sometimes in conjunction with the date when the barn was constructed or the farm was founded. Individual buildings might advertise what was inside, such as horses for sale or exchange (Figure I.18). They could be adorned with information about the owner's affiliation with farming associations, or quality breeds, products, or equipment (Figure I.19). With the advent of automobile travel, farmers continued to advertise their own products but also allowed outside companies to rent the side of

Figure I.19. Barn door near Cortland, Cortland County. The owner of this building used the façade to advertise memberships, accreditation, equipment, breeds, and reading material. (Photograph by John Collier, October 1941, Library of Congress, Prints & Photographs Division, FSA-OWI Collection, LC-USF34- 081220-D.)

Figure I.20. Mail Pouch tobacco advertisement, Schuyler Lake vicinity, Otsego County. (Photograph by Amy Frey, spring 2009.)

a barn located near a busy roadway for use as a billboard. The best-known campaign was for Mail Pouch tobacco (Figure I.20), but barns advertised everything from patent medicines to macaroni (Figure I.21).[18]

While barns could be used to promote goods for sale, they also boasted the success of the farm on which they were found and the farmers with whom they were associated. One of the functions of buildings is that they make others aware of the financial means of those who build them. In many instances these economic resources are thought to correspond with other admirable qualities. One mid-nineteenth-century author repeated an adage about the prosperous farmer: "When you see his

Figure I.21. Barn, Portlandville area, Otsego County. Warner's Macaroni advertised its product on both ends of this barn, strategically located in a curve on a busy north-south route along the Susquehanna River. (Photograph by Cynthia Falk, June 2010.)

Figure I.22. Fenimore Farm, 1916–1918, Cooperstown vicinity, Otsego County. The new buildings designed by Frank P. Whiting for Edward S. Clark included, from left to right, a creamery, dairy barn, and herder's cottage. (Photo, Ward files, New York State Historical Association Library, Cooperstown, ca. 1919.)

barn larger than his house, it shows that he will have large profits and small afflictions." In case the point had not yet been driven home, he continued, "When his hogpen is boarded inside and out it shows he is 'going the whole hog' in keeping plenty inside his house and poverty out."[19] Large, well-maintained agricultural buildings were signs of a successful farm. And successful farms were considered the product of the labors of hardworking, honest farmers.

The Jeffersonian agrarian ideal, which ties farming to civic virtue, has influenced New Yorkers for centuries. Even the Vanderbilts, Rockefellers, and Roosevelts created country estates where they could manage farms dedicated to breeding high-performing animals and plants. According to an architect who specialized in designing farms for wealthy gentleman farmers, "the country has always attracted man as a place in which to rear his habitation and no matter how complex are his urban interests there is in the human heart a lurking desire sooner or later to revert to the soil."[20] In Cooperstown, the current site of The Farmers' Museum was farmed in the past by author James Fenimore Cooper, Supreme Court Justice Samuel Nelson, and lawyer and Singer sewing machine financier Edward Clark and his grandsons and heirs Edward Severin Clark and Stephen C. Clark. From 1916 to 1918 Edward Severin Clark converted Fenimore Farm to a modern dairy farm, including a large stone barn as well as an accompanying creamery and herdsman's cottage all designed by architect Frank P. Whiting (Figure I.22).[21]

For Clark and Whiting, the new buildings at Fenimore Farm provided a means to express a reverence for tradition, as well as a respect for modern methods of farming. In a period of abrupt transformation in barn-building techniques, the two men used both materials and decorative embellishments that expressed their relationship to other farmers, past and present. They chose local stone, an old-fashioned material, but used it lavishly for the walls of the structure rather than just the foundation. Concrete floors and metal support posts and stanchions were hidden behind the decorative historical elements of the façade.

As a gentleman farmer, Clark could afford to be mindful of how the buildings he created reflected his priorities and, over time, the era and place in which he built. But even farmers like the Buckmasters, who did not have such luxuries, made choices that inform us today about what they valued and how they worked. Farm buildings, through physical characteristics such as size, shape, materials, construction technique, floor plan, and finish, have much to tell about farmers and farming in New York State. By studying the tangible attributes of farm buildings, we can uncover more about the work that went on inside, the people and communities that made them possible, and the eras in which they were built and used. New York State's agricultural history can be studied through statistics about products produced, acres farmed, and income earned, but it can also be appreciated through the buildings left on the rural landscape.

Chapter One

Diversity, Dairying, and Designing the Main Barn

Sunday 1st April 1861. Try to turn over a new leaf by rising at 5 a.m.
take grist provender (28 bush[els]) to Fall mill & draw 3 l[oa]ds wood—
turn out & put up cattle again on a/c of snow storm.

Orville M. Slosson, Pompey, Onondaga County

In 1859 *Moore's Rural New-Yorker* held a contest to find the best barn, one recognized for "not only the beauty of the structure, but the greatest amount of convenience, cheapness, and adaptation to all the wants of the majority of farmers." In announcing the winners, the selection committee noted, "We can but remember the few years ago when through the whole country one barn was the counterpart of another, 30 by 40 feet, with a bay on one side and a stable and granary on the other, covered with unseasoned, rough boards, open and uncomfortable; and it is gratifying to all well wishers of the farming interests that this era is fast passing away."[1] While this sentiment greatly overestimates the sameness of early barns in New York State, it does capture the spirit of change that was sweeping the region in the mid-nineteenth century. Old barns were relatively small, both in footprint and because of their single-story design, and inside, hay, grain, and animals were separated by only a few feet. New barns, like the Sweet family's in Pompey, Onondaga County, which placed first in *Moore's* contest, offered something different. They were large, multistory structures conveniently arranged with distinct spaces for grain, hay, horses, cattle, and sheep (Figure 1.1).

The Sweet barn and farm in Pompey were clearly exceptional. In the 1860 census, brothers Homer and Wheaton, who continued their father, Horace's, business after he died, were recognized as having property worth a substantial $12,000. The ideas

Figure 1.1. Horace Sweet & Son's barn, ca. 1859, Pompey, Onondaga County. The Sweets' three-level barn was awarded first premium by *Moore's Rural New-Yorker*. The ground floor contained an open shed, tool room, stabling, and a bay for hay; the first floor a horse stable, grain bins, and threshing floor; above that storage for hay, grain, clover, and straw. Other up-to-date features included board and batten siding and rolling barn doors. ("Rural First Premium Barn," *Moore's Rural New-Yorker* 10, no. 6 [February 5, 1859]: 45.)

and practices that informed the construction of their new barn, however, were not theirs alone. The Slosson family, who lived just across the road from the Sweets, had a farm worth roughly half as much. The diary of thirty-one-year-old Orville Slosson shows that despite his lesser means, he was also a participant in the transformation of upstate New York agriculture in the mid-nineteenth century. Orville loaded hay into the upper level of the family's barn with a hay fork, used a mechanized scythe to reap grain, bought and sold beef, eggs, and butter, and even attended two days of the Onondaga County Fair, noting that after his first visit he had to milk the cows by moonlight when he came home.[2] As Orville's experience shows, new technologies, new means of distributing information at venues such as county agricultural fairs, and an increase in the buying and selling of farm produce and supplies changed agricultural practices. The resulting new customs and procedures required new types of buildings. Although we do not know just what the Slosson barn looked like, it is safe to assume that while not as extravagant as the Sweets', it did incorporate some of the same features.

In the mid-nineteenth century, as in the periods before and after, the rural built environment both reflected and made possible agricultural production. Perhaps nowhere is this clearer than in the main barn. Multipurpose Dutch and English barns, built by New Yorkers of European descent through the early 1800s, were already considered old-fashioned in the mid-nineteenth century, at least by some farmers and the farm journals they read. But when originally constructed, they testified to the ingenuity of the settlers who had made the New York wilderness their home.

By the time the Sweets were building in the late 1850s, the desire for more function-specific spaces guided the creation of multistory barns that allowed for the separation of animal feed, animals, animal products, and animal waste. The so-called basement barn, which appeared in the first half of the nineteenth century and persisted with minor modifications for the next one hundred years, is a testament to both the change and continuity experienced by New York farmers. While some experimented with round or polygonal barn forms that were designed to foster increased efficiency, and gentleman farmers commissioned architect-designed farm complexes, most farmers, like Orville Slosson, turned over a new leaf through a commitment to their animals and crops, beginning in the barn before sunup and ending, at least on occasion, under the light of the moon. The experiences of these farmers were seldom recorded in published farm journals or manuals but are documented in the barns they built and used.

Today, many of New York's farmers have turned to still newer types of agricultural buildings, such as freestall barns on dairy farms, to further improve product quality and profitability. Older barns have become "monument[s] to the old style of farming," but this does not mean they have to become "decayed relics," as writers for *Moore's* imagined many years ago.[3] An increased appreciation for what barns tell us about past farm practices strengthens the case for their continued use, even if that requires sensitive conversion to new purposes. Farming has never been a static enterprise, and agricultural buildings evidence continual change as well as the persistence of traditional approaches.

Early Diversity

In the seventeenth and eighteenth centuries, as people of European descent arrived in the area that is now New York State, they brought with them ideas about what a barn should look like and how it should be built. They adapted barn types they had known in Europe to suit conditions in their new environment, making changes according to available building materials, agricultural production, and even weather. As settlement continued in the years after the American Revolution, people brought new barn forms from other regions within the new United States. The New Englanders who settled in upstate New York, for example, often constructed the type of "Yankee" barns they had known in Massachusetts and Connecticut.

Barns built through the early nineteenth century tended to reflect the background of their builders or users. Dutch and English barns were especially common, but some people of German descent also built distinct barn types. Later immigrant groups continued to infuse new ideas about agriculture and barn style. As the nineteenth century progressed, however, ethnic barn types became less desirable and less distinct. Standardized and specialized forms proved more useful as farmers increasingly pursued market-oriented agricultural strategies, especially related to dairying.

Dutch Barns

From about 1613 until 1664, settlements in what is now New York were part of the Dutch colony of New Netherland. Dutch barns, built by early Dutch settlers and their descendants, were most commonly found in the Hudson, Mohawk, and Schoharie valleys of eastern New York State, as well as on Long Island.[4] Those who study these distinct buildings often refer to them as New World Dutch barns (Figure 1.2), a term that distinguishes them from their counterparts in Europe, referred to as Old World Dutch barns. Dutch immigrants brought their traditional building skills with them when they settled in New Netherland but also made some adaptations to fit their new environment. In the timber-rich New World, for example, Dutch barns were typically framed, clad, and floored with long, straight pieces of wood and roofed with wood shingles. In Europe, barn builders often utilized other materials such as stone piers, brick nogging, earthen floors, or thatch roofs. Often Dutch farmers in Europe combined agricultural and residential functions in one multipart building, the house-barn, a form much rarer in the New World (Figure 1.3).[5]

The ceding of control of New Netherland from the Dutch to the English in 1664 did not necessarily lead to a change in cultural practices such as agriculture or barn building. In the middle of the eighteenth century, almost a century after England gained political power, a Swedish botanist named Peter Kalm traveled throughout North America. In New York, Kalm observed a particular type of barn, which he associated with people of Dutch descent, as well as the German-speakers who settled near them in the colony's river valleys. He briefly described the unique characteristics of this building form in his later writings:

> The *barns* had a peculiar kind of construction in this locality, of which I shall give a concise description. The main building was very large almost the size of a small church; the roof was high, covered with wooden shingles, sloping on both sides, but not steep. The walls which supported it were not much higher than a full grown man; but on the other hand the breadth of the building was all the greater. In the middle was the threshing floor and above it, or in the loft or garret, they put the unthrashed [*sic*] grain, the straw, or anything else, according to the season. On one side were stables for the horses and on the other for the cows. The young stock had also their particular stables or stalls, and in both ends of the building were large doors, so that one could drive in with a cart and horses through one of them, and go out the other. Here under one roof therefore were the thrashing [*sic*] floor, the barn, the stables, the hay loft, the coach house, etc.[6]

At one time there were as many as 50,000 to 100,000 Dutch barns like the ones Kalm described in New York and New Jersey, the principal areas of Dutch colonial settlement in the seventeenth century. Today it is estimated that a mere 650 survive.[7]

Figure 1.2. Johannes Decker barn, 1750, Shawangunk, Ulster County. New World Dutch barns typically have a footprint that is almost square, with access via main doors on the gable ends of the building. A pentice roof above the doors provides protection from the weather. (Photograph by D. M. C. Hopping, 1970, Historic American Buildings Survey, NY, 56-SHWA, 3A-1.)

Figure 1.3. House-barn, ca. 1760, originally in Zeijen, Drenthe, now at the Open Air Museum (Openluchtmuseum), Arnhem, Netherlands. This Dutch building included not only space for its human inhabitants but also stalls for cows and calves and a sheepfold. The steeply pitched roof is finished with thatch, and the walls are half-timbered. (Photograph by Jeroen Van Den Hurk, 2003.)

Figure 1.4. Windfall Dutch barn, ca. 1800, Salt Springville, Montgomery County. Geometric holes in the siding near the peak of the gable end allowed ventilation as well as access for birds, which helped control rodent and insect pests. (Photograph by Cynthia Falk, June 2010.)

While there are several variations on the Dutch barn, some dating as late as the 1880s, the classic, most recognizable form was commonly built between approximately the 1630s and the 1830s. It is nearly square, rather than rectangular, in footprint, with an average width between forty-two and forty-eight feet and average length between thirty-six and fifty-six feet.[8] Walls tend to be between twelve and fifteen feet tall and sided with horizontal boards.[9] Doors were located on the gable ends of the barn, not along the long side walls, as was common in most other types of barns. The main door at either end was typically tall and designed as a "Dutch door," with upper and lower sections that could be opened independently. When the top section was open and the bottom closed, animals could be kept either within or outside the barn while still allowing for ventilation. Often, a smaller door was located on either side of the main door, allowing access to the side aisles where the animals were housed. A pentice, or small projecting roof, might cover the main door, providing some protection from the weather.[10]

Despite Kalm's observation that the roofs were not steep, compared to those found on later agricultural buildings, the roofs on Dutch barns are indeed sharply pitched. Especially steep roof pitches, forming an acute angle at the peak, suggest an earlier date, often before the American Revolution. The steep roof allowed increased storage for grain and grass crops in the loft above the main floor. At the top of the gable-end walls, small cutouts in the cladding, often in stylized geometric shapes (Figure 1.4), provided ventilation and pest control, the latter by allowing birds access to the building.[11]

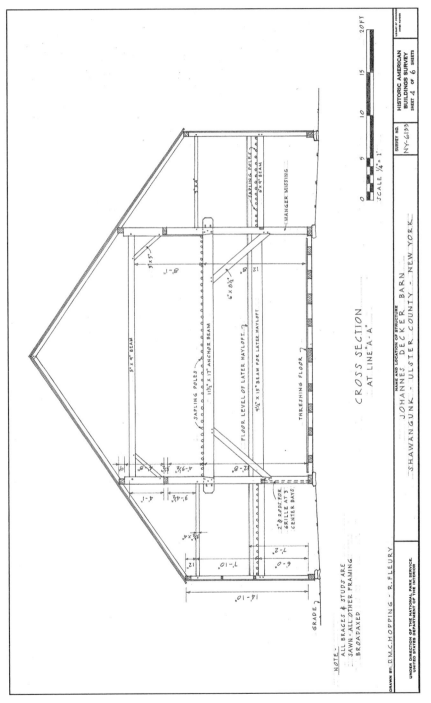

Figure 1.5. Johannes Decker barn, 1750, Shawangunk, Ulster County. The H-bent framing, clearly visible in this cross-section of a barn interior, divided the New World Dutch barn into three distinct spaces: a central area with a plank floor for threshing grain, and aisles at either side for housing animals. (Drawing by D. M. C. Hopping and R. Fleury, Historic American Buildings Survey, NY-6133.)

Figure 1.6. Interior of the Alex Stevens barn, Alplaus, Schenectady County. The rounded end of one of the anchor beams projects through the mortise hole in one of the posts. Together the anchor beams and posts form the H-bent configuration typical of New World Dutch barns. (Photograph, Historic American Buildings Survey, NY, 47-ALP, 4–2.)

On the inside, evidence remains of how builders constructed Dutch barns. A series of H-bents—composed of vertical posts and horizontal anchor beams, often of oak, pine, or occasionally basswood, held together with mortise and tenon joints—extended down the length of the barn, from gable end to gable end, typically creating three or four bays, although two-, five-, six-, and seven-bay examples are known.[12] The posts stood roughly ten feet from the exterior side walls between the central threshing floor and the side aisles (Figure 1.5). This interior post configuration differentiated Dutch barns from other types of barns whose support posts were typically integral to their exterior walls. The rounded ends of the tenons of the anchor beams generally extended through the mortise hole and beyond the post, creating a unique framing characteristic (Figure 1.6).[13]

Barn builders constructed Dutch barns to accommodate the multiple tasks that went on inside them. The floor plan of most Dutch barns was composed of three main sections: a large center driveway and two aisles that ran along either side, from gable end to gable end.[14] Grain could be threshed in the center aisle on the strong

Figure 1.7. Alex Stevens barn, Alplaus, Schenectady County. This New World Dutch barn was altered by later farmer-owners to include a door on its long side. The extension to the right is also a later addition to this iconic New York barn type. (Photograph, Historic American Buildings Survey, NY, 47-ALP, 4–1.)

wooden floor. Along the outer aisles, animals and equipment could be housed. According to Kalm, the horses and cows were kept on separate sides of the barn.[15]

Dutch barns were commonly altered to accommodate changing agricultural practices throughout the nineteenth and twentieth centuries. Extra bays were added, increasing the length of the structures. Additions were also commonly attached, drastically changing the original appearance (Figure 1.7). Doors were typically added on the sides parallel, rather than perpendicular, to the roof peak, and some original gable-end doors were covered over with siding. Cement floors and stanchions were added to barns that were converted to house cows on later dairy farms.[16]

New barns built in the early nineteenth century could combine the H-bent configuration of Dutch barns with an entrance on one or both of the long side walls, representing a hybrid form combining elements from both Dutch and English barn building traditions. In the mid- to late nineteenth century, Dutch framing characteristics were occasionally used on barns built as multistory structures. The emblematic Dutch barn with its three-aisled square floor plan and gable-end doors fell out of favor by 1840, however.[17]

Dutch barns are not nearly as common a sight in New York today as they were in the eighteenth century. With increasing frequency, Dutch barns that have outlived

their usefulness as farm buildings are being demolished or removed from their original sites. In some cases they have been reconstructed under private ownership in places
as far away as Texas to serve as houses, garages, or community centers. Some historic
sites in New York have moved original barns to their museums in order to add an
agricultural component to locations that were once farms but have long since lost their
own farm buildings. Although these barns have been removed from their original
context, they, along with examples restored or adaptively reused in situ, are being preserved for future generations to see.

English Barns

English barns, also called Yankee or Connecticut barns, can be found throughout
New York State. They were most common where people of English descent settled
before the mid-nineteenth century, including eastern Long Island and much of the
central and western parts of the state.[18] Many were constructed by the New Englanders who arrived in New York State following the American Revolution.

Like Dutch barns, English barns were typically one-story buildings with a loft.
A steeply pitched gable roof maximized interior space (Figure 1.8). English barns
usually were constructed from heavy timbers with the use of mortise and tenon
joints. To clad the exterior of the barn, logs from locally available pine, hemlock, and
on occasion basswood trees were sawn to create boards. The English barn structure
accommodated either vertical or horizontal cladding. While English barns rarely
had windows, small vent holes, which facilitated air circulation and insect control by
birds, were often cut into the siding at the top of the gable-end walls.[19]

English barns, which are typically longer than they are wide, differed from
Dutch barns in shape. Near the end of the eighteenth century, these rectangular
buildings averaged roughly twenty feet wide by thirty feet long; later examples were
typically about thirty feet by forty feet.[20] The interior of an English barn was usually
divided into three bays, or mows, enclosed by the framing bents (Figure 1.9). Usually English barns had four framing bents, one at each end of the barn and two that
were offset from the center, creating the three separate bays. If additional bays were
needed, farmers would add more bents.

Central doors led to the threshing floor, also known as the driveway or runway,
in the center of the barn with mows on either side. This central driveway served two
purposes: it allowed for easy entrance and exit of teams of animals, and it provided
farmers with a place to thresh, or separate, their grain (Figure 1.10). Threshing often
occurred during the winter, when farmers had fewer other tasks. Bundles of wheat
were placed on the threshing floor and beaten, usually with a tool known as a flail.
Once the seed was separated from the straw, or stalk, farmers opened the opposing
doors to allow for a cross-breeze. Using a winnowing basket, they tossed the grain
and its husks, or chaff, into the air and back into the basket, or let the mixture fall to
the floor. The cross-wind blew the chaff and dust away, and the grain settled back
into the basket or onto a piece of cloth on the barn floor.[21]

Figure 1.8. Detail, *Residence of T. B. Townsend/Pamelia, N.Y.,* 1870–1899, by George K. Townsend (1832–1900), pencil on paper, 27 1/4" x 32 1/4". The barns built by settlers of English descent through the early nineteenth century were typically one-story wood-frame structures with steep roofs, like New World Dutch barns. They might even have similar cutouts for ventilation and pest control high on the gable-end walls, in this case in a diamond shape. They differed from Dutch barns because of their rectangular footprint and the location of the main doors on the long side. (Fenimore Art Museum, Cooperstown, N0014.2008. Photograph by Richard Walker.)

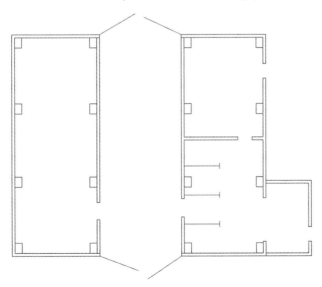

Figure 1.9. Floor plan, English barn, near Whig Corners, Otsego County. Documented as it stood in 1965, this barn included three main sections, which historically would have been used, from left to right, for hay storage, a threshing floor, and animal stabling. The left-hand bay was later converted to a shop. (Floor plan based on drawing by Henry Glassie, "The Variation of Concepts within Tradition," *Geoscience and Man* 5 [1974]: 183, fig. 5a.)

Figure 1.10. Brooks barn, ca. 1790, originally in South New Berlin, Chenango County, now at The Farmers' Museum, Cooperstown, Otsego County. The doors on the long side of an English barn opened onto a central area used for threshing grain. Typically a set of doors on the opposite side of the barn allowed a cross-breeze to help in the winnowing process. (Photograph by Cynthia Falk, 2008.)

At either end of the barn, one mow typically served as the granary, while the opposite bay served as livestock stalls. With loft space above the stabling and a removable scaffolding system over the central runway, farmers increased the amount of storage in the barn (Figure 1.11). In these lofts, small hand tools or hay would have been stored, with larger implements stored in the runway when it was not being used for threshing.[22] In providing for grain processing and storage, animal housing, and other tasks in one building, the New Englanders who developed this type of barn combined into a single structure various elements of the traditional English farm complex, which typically included many different buildings, each serving its own function. Like the Dutch, they also substituted building materials to make use of available natural resources, relying heavily on wood, rather than stone or thatch, for both walls and roofing.[23]

The new form of English barn that New Englanders brought with them to New York remained largely unaltered until the mid-nineteenth century, when Empire State farmers, increasingly attuned to the market and the needs of dairy production, began to raise their barns onto taller foundations, creating a basement level, which provided

Figure 1.11. Sweet-Marble barn, ca. 1803, originally in Mount Vision, Otsego County, now at The Farmers' Museum, Cooperstown, Otsego County. The interior of an English barn was designed to maximize storage. A loft over the animal stalls and sometimes even portable scaffolding above the threshing floor provided additional space for both hay and tools. (Photograph by Cynthia Falk, 2008.)

stabling for animals separate from crop storage.[24] Found throughout New York State, the once common English barn was adapted and expanded to facilitate new agricultural practices. As people migrated westward from New York and New England, the English barn form also traveled with them and can be found as far west as Utah.[25]

German Barns

German barns, and the so-called Pennsylvania barns that developed from them, never became common in New York. Today only a handful survive in the state. Nevertheless, because of the familiarity of the Pennsylvania barn, it is important to understand the distinctions between English and Dutch barns, Pennsylvania German barns, and the barn forms that would later become common in New York in the nineteenth century. In 1858 *Moore's Rural New-Yorker* actually recommended barn plans based "partially on the plan of the famous Pennsylvania barns"[26] (Figure 1.12). Yet New York farmers did not readily adopt the distinctive elements of this form, most notably the second-story projection known as a forebay.

Figure 1.12. "A Pennsylvania Barn," 1858. This barn plan, published in *Moore's Rural New-Yorker,* was adapted from the Pennsylvania barn form credited, at least in part, to Pennsylvania's German settlers. A typical Pennsylvania barn feature is the forebay protruding into the barnyard. Less common among Pennsylvania barns is the entrance on the shorter side of the building and the unusual gambrel roof. ("A Pennsylvania Barn," *Moore's Rural New-Yorker* 9, no. 42 [October 16, 1858]: 333.)

As a result of two separate waves of immigration of German-speaking people, German farmers settled in two areas of New York State. The smaller, lesser-known group immigrated after the War of 1812. These settlers arrived not from Europe but from Pennsylvania, establishing roots in New York's Erie County, especially in the towns of Clarence and Lancaster.[27] They were preceded in New York by German-speakers from Europe who had arrived more than a century earlier. These colonial period farmers settled in the Hudson, Schoharie, and Mohawk valleys.[28] Many of the settlements in this area were destroyed during the Seven Years' War and the Revolutionary War. Few buildings survive from the early eighteenth century, and even documentary sources about vernacular architecture are scarce. Extant colonial barns in the valleys are New World Dutch barns, although a suggestive nineteenth-century illustration of a barn on a German farm near the Mohawk River indicates a different form that does not conform to common Dutch, English, or Pennsylvania German barn models (Figure 1.13).[29]

Much of what is known about German barns in the United States is based on surviving examples in Pennsylvania. The first German-speaking settlers there constructed simple, small to medium-sized log, frame, or stone structures that stood one

Figure 1.13. *The BARN in the rear of Gen.l Herkimers Dwelling,* by Rufus Grider (1817–1900), watercolor and ink, dated August 10, 1895. Grider's image, produced years after Nicholas Herkimer, son and grandson of German immigrants to New York, died during the American Revolution, seems to show a banked building with a porch-like overhang on the uphill side and an asymmetrical roofline. An adjoining building has another, smaller over-hanging projection on the downhill side. Though not of a typical Pennsylvania German barn form, Herkimer's barn may have been influenced by a Continental European prototype. (Rufus Grider Collection, SC23932, vol. 3, fol. 33. Courtesy New York State Library, Albany.)

or sometimes two stories tall.[30] During the late eighteenth and early nineteenth centuries, as agricultural and livestock production grew, people of German descent in Pennsylvania increasingly turned to a barn form that had two levels rather than one. Barn historian Robert Ensminger has convincingly demonstrated that the two-story bank barn form, with its second level projecting beyond its lower level on one side, emerged in German-speaking Continental Europe but that its appearance was a synthesis of multiple barn-building traditions, and it continued to evolve in the New World.[31] It was this composite barn type with Germanic roots that the Pennsylvania Germans who came to Erie County, New York, reproduced.

In these multistory buildings, the projection of the upper level beyond the lower level on the downhill side of the barn created what is known as a fore-bay (Figure 1.14). To facilitate access to both floors, the structure was often built into a bank, either natural or created. The main doors were placed on the uphill side, while a row of several smaller doors on the lower level was protected from

Figure 1.14. Erisman barn, Lancaster, Erie County. The forebay, or overhang projecting from the upper level, provided increased space on the second floor and also sheltered the doors leading to the animal stabling on the lower level. (Detail of "Res. of A. Erisman Esq., Town of Lancaster, Erie Co.," *Illustrated Historical Atlas of Erie Co. New-York: From Actual Surveys and Records* [New York: F. W. Beers & Co., 1880], 81.)

the elements by the forebay.[32] Roofs on forebay banked barns were gabled and could be centered on either the main structure of the barn or a combination of the main structure and the forebay. Construction materials included stone, used for the lower level and sometimes gable-end walls, and wood framing for the upper level and forebay.[33]

Inside the barn, stables occupied the lower floor, while mows for hay, straw, grain, and fodder filled the second level. The latter also often included a threshing floor. The forebay, as a continuation of the second level, afforded extra storage space; it also provided additional shelter for animals, which entered and exited the stable area through the doors on the ground level.[34] While a multistory barn form would become common later in the nineteenth century in New York, its origins were distinct from those of the Pennsylvania barn. For most New Yorkers, it was not until the mid-nineteenth century that two-story barns became desirable, and when they did, they did not have the characteristic forebay design so recognizable on Pennsylvania German examples.

The Basement Barn and Dairying

In its various forms, the basement barn is the most common type of barn found throughout New York State. The prevalence of the form is based in part on its longevity. The basement barn was first used in the decades before the Civil War, and it continued to be a model for a hundred years. Geographically, basement barns are found in every region of the Empire State, although the highest concentrations are in central and western New York.[35] The iconic look, especially of the gambrel-roofed basement barn, is so easy to recognize that it has become synonymous with the American farm. The stereotypical image of a two-story red barn with white trim, perched on a stonework foundation could easily have been modeled after a New York basement barn.

Several factors combined to make the basement barn a desirable form for such a long period over such a wide geographic area. Its introduction is generally associated with the rise of dairy farming, which in places like central New York began in the 1830s and expanded through the remainder of the century. Dairying, however, was one element of a more general shift toward intensified production of crops for market and was often part of a strategy of mixed or diversified farming. The historian Thomas Summerhill considers the year 1850 a watershed in this regard and claims that by 1860 there had been a "capitalist transformation of upstate New York." A growing market and cash orientation, coupled with new machinery for tasks such as threshing, and new transportation networks, led to increased production and the need for different types of buildings, like the Sweets' award-winning barn that was singled out in *Moore's*.[36]

Despite its longevity, the basement barn form was not static, and basement barns of the 1840s have as many differences as similarities with those built in the 1870s or 1920s. In the late nineteenth and twentieth centuries, local and state organizations began regulating the physical environment where milk was produced, leading to greater public scrutiny of dairy farms.[37] Increased production, as well as state and federal regulations, defined the interior arrangement of dairy barns and the way waste was managed. Conditions were dictated not only by farmers' needs but also by policies created by outside agencies to protect the interests of consumers. In addition to new regulations, other factors such as new materials, new building techniques, and new farming equipment also helped determine the appearance of the basement barn by the late nineteenth century and into the twentieth.

What unites basement barns and distinguishes them from the English and Dutch barns that were built during earlier periods is the functionality of their two stories. The lower level, or basement, was used primarily for housing livestock and related equipment, while the upper level was used for threshing wheat and storing grain and large farm equipment. The basement level was frequently constructed of stone or, later, concrete, while the upper level was wood frame. The exterior of the upper story was often clad with horizontal clapboard, though vertical boards were also used as sheathing (Figure 1.15). By the middle of the nineteenth century, some farmers turned to board and batten cladding. Thin wooden battens covered the gap between sawn boards applied vertically, creating a tight seal to keep out the cold winter weather.[38]

Figure 1.15. Mordecai and Agnes Carmen barn, Mecklenburg, Schuyler County. A stone basement level provided increased space for and separation of animals and field crops in the Carmens' basement barn. (H. B. Pierce and D. Hamilton Hurd, *History of Tioga, Chemung, Tompkins, and Schuyler Counties* [Philadelphia: Everts and Ensign, 1879], after 620.)

By building a multistory basement barn rather than a single-level barn, farmers were able to double their usable barn space without expanding the footprint. Basement barns could be built into a hillside, allowing natural access into both the upper and lower levels. An alternative was the construction of a wooden bridge or artificial earthen bank. In either case, on early examples, the main double doors to the upper level of a basement barn swung on hinges. As early as the 1840s, some authors advocated a new type of door that slid on rollers along a metal track.[39] As time went on, ground-level doors to the second story, as well as banks and bridges, were avoided altogether, as access to upper levels was achieved via an interior staircase and an exterior pulley system that allowed crops to be lifted from the ground rather than rolled in on a wagon (Figure 1.16).

Figure 1.16. Barn, near Bouckville, Madison County. No bank or bridge gave access to the upper level of this barn, as hay and other crops could be mechanically lifted into the large doors on the gable end of the building. The gambrel roof provided increased storage space, and the hay hood helped protect the track and equipment used to elevate the crops. (Photograph by Cynthia Falk, June 2010.)

Basement barns are sometimes referred to as "raised barns" because of their multiple stories, in some cases created by elevating an older one-story barn onto a new basement level. Farmers made space for their dairy herds by raising the barn and building a masonry foundation underneath. A number of one-story English barns were adapted in this way. Dutch barns could also be remodeled to create two levels (Figures 1.17, 1.18).

Even when basement barns were constructed from scratch, they often echoed the rectangular shape of the one-story English barn. For this reason, early basement barns are sometimes termed English bank barns or side-hill English barns.[40] As agricultural production increased, however, larger barns were needed. English barns were typically between twenty and forty feet long.[41] Basement barns could be double or triple the size of the old single-level barns, averaging sixty to one hundred feet in length. In an age of increased production of farm goods to be sold off-site, the extra space for storage and animal housing was important.

Despite their increased size, many basement barns were, like English barns, oriented with access on the long side of the building. Basement barns, however, could also take on different local variations. In some areas basement barns were sited perpendicular to a hill or slope with access to the upper level on the gable end. In

Figure 1.17. Raised English barn, Cherry Valley area, Otsego County. As the different types of masonry that make up the foundation suggest, this barn was literally lifted to create a more substantial basement level that could be used to house livestock. (Photograph by Cynthia Falk, July 2010.)

Figure 1.18. Adapted Dutch barn, Wemple farm, Dunnsville, Albany County. An earthen ramp and wooden bridge provided access to a second floor created within this New World Dutch barn. (Photograph by Nelson E. Baldwin, Historic American Buildings Survey, NY, 1-DUNV, 1A-1.)

Figure 1.19. *Bank Barn II,* by Jessica Dalrymple, oil on canvas, 14" x 18". Delaware County is known for its bridge barns, and the one featured in this painting is located in Bovina. Barn bridges, wooden structures not unlike the covered bridges used to span waterways, could be located on the gable end or long side of a barn. Typically a space below the bridge provided extra covered storage, and the structure itself kept the barn doors protected from rain and snow. (Courtesy Jessica Dalrymple.)

Oneida County this arrangement has been credited to Welsh settlers, who began arriving in the early nineteenth century.[42] In other areas, such as Delaware County, wooden bridges proved an especially popular feature for accessing the upper level (Figure 1.19).[43]

Although basement barns took on slightly different forms in different parts of New York State, it is also important to recognize variations based on when they were constructed. The most noticeable change in barn design during the nineteenth and early twentieth centuries involved the roof shape. Early basement barns had gable roofs. In the last quarter of the nineteenth century, barn builders made the transition to a gambrel roof, which allowed for increased storage capacity in the upper level (Figure 1.20).[44] The 1920s saw the use of yet another roof form, variously known as rainbow, arched, or Gothic (Figure 1.21).[45] The new roof, made out of laminated lumber trusses, marked the advent of standardization and mass production in barns, as well as the widespread adoption of new technologies for both construction and farm work. Often basement barn roofs were topped with wooden cupolas or, in the

Figure 1.20. Barn with gambrel roof, West Winfield area, Herkimer County. (Photograph by Cynthia Falk, June 2010.)

Figure 1.21. Barn with "rainbow" roof, east of Seneca Falls, Seneca County. (Photograph by Cynthia Falk, June 2010.)

twentieth century, steel ventilators to facilitate air circulation in buildings that were becoming increasingly tightly clad.[46]

Basement barns in their various forms were the most common type of barn built in New York from the mid-nineteenth through the mid-twentieth century.[47] Many continue to be put to good use today. The basement barn was developed to support multiple functions, including the housing of animals and the storage of grain, hay, and farm equipment. In this respect it was similar to earlier barn types found in New York. Unlike its predecessors, however, the basement barn provided for the separation of functions and for an increased scale of production. In an era that saw a rise in dairying and the cultivation of other crops for market, both factors were important. Despite the variations in roof shape, ventilation strategies, building materials, and orientation to the hillside, the overall form of the basement barn, divided horizontally into two different zones, one for animals and another for field crops, made it a lasting feature of the New York State rural landscape.

Cows and Manure

The lower level of a basement barn was devoted to animal husbandry. Farmers housed cattle, especially milking cows, and other animals there. A door opening into a pasture area provided the farmer with an easy way to let the cows out in good weather. Commonly, stalls or stanchions flanked an aisle down the center length of the lower level of the barn (Figure 1.22). Stanchions, introduced in the mid-nineteenth century, secured the heads of the cows and maintained their position without requiring the space and materials necessary to construct individual stalls (Figure 1.23).[48] After the introduction of stanchions, box stalls were usually reserved for horses.[49]

The arrangement of the cows, typically facing the exterior wall of the barn, facilitated feeding, milking, and waste removal.[50] A gutter, or trough, ran behind the cows and was used to collect manure (Figure 1.24). The gutter sloped away from the cows and shifted the waste downward for easy removal into a cart from the center aisle.[51] Manure was a waste product for dairy farmers but one that could be put to good use. Distributed over the fields with a manure spreader, animal waste enriched the soil and improved crop quality (Figure 1.25). Agricultural literature of the mid-nineteenth century advised that manure lost much of its potency as a fertilizer when left uncovered and suggested alternative storage solutions, which more progressive and wealthier farmers often followed. These included storing the manure inside the barn or carrying the waste out to a separate shed.[52]

Spaces dedicated to manure storage inside the barn were often enclosed rooms either on the ground floor or in a subterranean cellar. On the exterior, barns with manure cellars had a door at the lowest level, which allowed the farmer to go down a ramp with a cart to collect the waste to use on the fields as fertilizer (Figure 1.26).[53] Farmers with larger herds and therefore bigger barns sometimes installed trapdoors in or alongside the gutters and dropped manure into the cellar below.[54]

Figure 1.22. Basement floor plan, 1853. The lower level of this model mid-nineteenth-century barn included stalls for five horses and six cows with an aisle between. The aisle was recommended because it allowed for feeding "with much less trouble and less risk of being kicked." The area labeled A could be used to store a carriage, wagon, or straw for bedding. ("Plan of a Side-Hill Barn," *Moore's Rural New-Yorker* 4, no. 12 [March 19, 1853]: 93.)

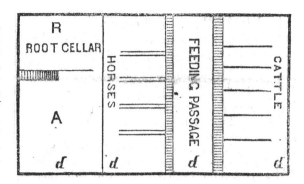

Figure 1.23. Stanchions at the Hayt farmstead, Patterson, Putnam County. (Photograph by Rob Tucher, Historic American Buildings Survey, NY, 40-PAT, 2-G-7.)

Farmers who utilized distinct spaces for manure storage moved them farther and farther from the animals and even out of the main barn altogether as the nineteenth century progressed. Barn builders shifted manure cellars, once directly under the cows, away from the animals to the opposite end of the barn.[55] Fears about odor traveling to the upper floors and other sanitation issues eventually encouraged the transition to alternative types of storage. With the acceptance of germ theory in the last decades of the nineteenth century, the connection between infectious disease,

Figure 1.24. Lower level of a dairy barn, Warren area, Herkimer County. A sunken manure gutter, formed from concrete, runs behind the stalls. The cows, in typical fashion, face the outside barn walls. (Photograph by Cynthia Falk, November 2009.)

Figure 1.25. *Earl Chase,* 1941, by Arthur J. Telfer (1859–1954), dry collodion plate, 5–07488. Chase used a tractor equipped with tracks for winter use to pull a manure spreader. By applying manure to his snow-covered fields, he put the animal waste to use as fertilizer even in the off-season. (Fenimore Art Museum, Cooperstown.)

Figure 1.26. "A New York Dairy Barn," 1875. After visiting dairy farms in Westchester County, New York, re-
porters for the *American Agriculturalist* published this illustration of the general style of the barns found on large-
scale dairy farms producing milk for the New York City market. The manure cellar is located under the center
of the barn and is accessible via an exterior door "large enough to back a wagon into." ("A Dairy Barn," *American
Agriculturalist* 34, no. 4 [April 1875]: 139.)

disease-causing microorganisms, and unsanitary physical conditions became a scientific fact. For dairy farmers, the increased emphasis on the relationship between
excrement, germs, and disease required that cows and manure be kept separate in
order for the milk supply to remain untainted.[56]

By 1916, the United States Department of Agriculture, the Department of Health
of the City of New York, and the Agricultural College at Cornell University had all
created scorecards to rate New York dairy farms. To maintain the highest standards,
manure had to be removed from the barn at least once per day, and it had to be taken
to a location a certain number of feet from the barn where it could not be accessed by
cows.[57] After the 1930s, guidelines further stipulated that the gutter located behind
the animals had to be constructed of concrete rather than a more porous material to
ensure that waste could be completely removed.[58]

As a result of the new standards, by the 1920s, manure sheds, which stood one
hundred to three hundred feet away from the barn, were recommended for storage
rather than cellars.[59] For these purely functional buildings, one writer advised farmers: "You might easily run up a cheap shed, covered with boards or slabs, on each side
of the barn yard. If you had these sheds, most of the manure would be dropped under

Figure 1.27. Manure shed, 1916, Church family farmstead, Shaker Heritage Society, Town of Colonie, Albany County. The Shakers used a covered track to transport a manure carrier from the dairy barn (left) to the manure shed (right). (Photograph by Cynthia Falk, August 2010.)

them, and . . . turned to the best account."[60] Probably on account of their cheap materials, which were prone to rot, early manure sheds rarely survive today. One example still stands at the Shaker Heritage Society in the Albany area (Figure 1.27). It was built for the Church family, a subgroup within the Watervliet Shaker community.

The Shakers designed barns meant to create a healthy environment for animals and make agricultural tasks as efficient as possible.[61] Unlike some other religious sects, Shakers were known for their innovations and for embracing modern technology. The new barn built for the Watervliet Church family in 1916 included not only roof ventilators and sliding doors on protected tracks but also a dairy wing featuring a concrete slab floor molded to create mangers and a curb for pipe stanchions. Manure was collected in a manure carrier suspended on a track that ran along both sides of the barn. The carrier was located behind the cows, allowing a farmer to shovel in the contents of the gutters. A track attached to the ceiling connected the barn to the manure shed and transported the carrier (Figure 1.28). An underground pipe pumped liquid manure collected in the barn's gutters into the shed. The design of the manure shed addressed the problem of retrieving manure by providing a covered passageway for wagons to back up to the pit.[62]

For New York farmers, especially those engaged in dairying, collecting and storing manure were matters that could not be ignored. Solutions changed over time as increased knowledge and concern about disease dictated how animal waste should

Figure 1.28. "Manure Carrier and Trolley," 1913. According to barn architect Alfred Hopkins, "the easy handling of the manure and its prompt removal from the cow barn is, perhaps, the most important thing to be considered in the plan and in the administration of that building." Hopkins recommended an elevated manure carrier and illustrated a farmhand pushing one along a manure track. (Alfred Hopkins, *Modern Farm Buildings* [New York: McBride, Nast & Co., 1913], photo plate between 60 and 61.)

be handled. Manure cellars located within the barn provided covered storage but little distance from animals and milk. Manure sheds moved animal waste outside the barn and away from cows. Today, manure lagoons and holding tanks continue to serve a similar function, allowing the storage of potential fertilizer away from cows in a contained environment.[63]

Grain and Hay Storage

While the lower level of a basement barn and its accompanying outbuildings, such as manure sheds, were devoted to animals and their needs, the upper level of the barn provided a large space for grain processing and storage. Initially, the central floor of this level was used for threshing and the side mows for storing grain and grass crops. With the invention of machines for threshing and new concerns about the effect of dust from the process on the health of cows, storage became the primary function. Wheat and other grains could be stored in enclosed granaries located within the barn, hay in larger open areas. In addition, large machinery could be kept on this level when not in use.

Hay provides nourishment for livestock that are unable to graze during New York State's unforgiving winter months. The process of storing hay, and therefore barn design, changed significantly during the second half of the nineteenth century

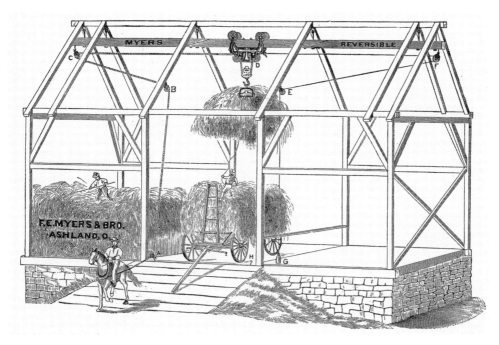

Figure 1.29. F. E. Myers and Brother's hay fork advertisement, 1887. Hay forks were mounted on a track at the peak of the barn roof. They helped make the work of unloading hay from a hay wagon easier by using horses to do the lifting. (*F. E. Myers & Bro. Manufacturers of Haying Tools, Force and Lift Pumps, etc. Proprietors of the Ashland Pump and Haying Tool Works* [Ashland, Ohio: F. E. Myers & Bro. Co., (1887)], 9. Trade Catalog Collection, Special Collections, New York State Historical Association Research Library, Cooperstown.)

with the invention of the hay fork (Figure 1.29). Through a system of ropes, pulleys, a trolley, and a track, the hay fork allowed farmers, with the help of horses, to lift hay from a wagon into the hayloft or a haymow on the upper level of the barn, making it easier to store hay inside rather than in haystacks in the field.

The track for a hay fork was made from a wooden or steel beam and hung with metal ties or hangers under the peak of the barn roof. The trolley, from which the pulleys and hay fork were hung, ran back and forth along the track. A horse or horses standing on the ground and connected to the trolley by a rope would be walked forward and backward to raise and lower the hay fork.[64]

Barn design had to change to accommodate the hay fork. The framing of gable roofs traditionally utilized a complex system of wooden posts and crossbeams for support (Figure 1.30). This roof framing made it difficult to use a hay fork: crossbeams running between the two roof planes prohibited the trolley and fork from moving along the track installed at the peak of the roof. As a result, individuals building barns with hay forks during the second half of the nineteenth century had to change the way they framed their roofs. One option was to incorporate support posts, which allowed the crossbeams to be relocated, creating room for the installation of a hay fork system (Figure 1.31). Gambrel roofs, as well as rainbow roofs, also became popular designs for barns utilizing hay forks. These new roof forms allowed

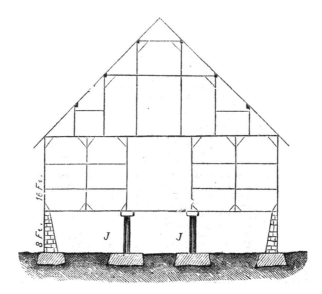

Figure 1.30. D. W. Clark barn, ca. 1871, Schuyler Lake, Otsego County. *Moore's Rural New-Yorker* touted Clark's barn as a model. The large structure included six bents and was framed traditionally with mortise and tenon joinery and crossbeams to support the roof. (A.G.M., "Model Farm Barn," *Moore's Rural New-Yorker* 23, no. 23 [June 10, 1871]: 361.)

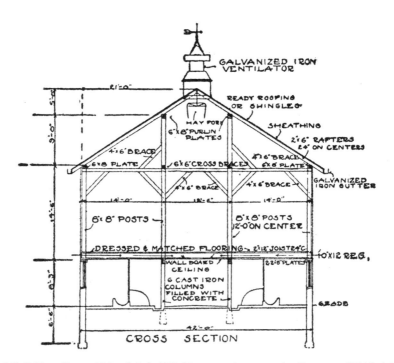

Figure 1.31. Gable roof barn with hay fork. In 1917, this cross section was used to illustrate an "Old Style Timber Frame Barn." The framing of this barn, with an open area under the peak of the roof, was designed to allow the use of a hay fork. (Herbert A. Shearer, *Farm Buildings with Plans and Descriptions* [Chicago: Frederick J. Drake & Co., 1917], 10.)

the framing of the roof to remain close to the outside of the structure, providing room for the hay fork system.[65]

The exterior of a barn offers clues to whether or not a hay fork was once used inside. A gambrel or Gothic arch roof is one indication, especially when combined with large haymow doors located on the upper level in the gable end of the barn. The doors allowed horse-drawn hay wagons to remain outside the barn while being unloaded. The hay fork track extended beyond the exterior wall so the hay fork could lift the hay from the wagon to the upper story. Often a hay hood covered the track and protected it from the weather (Figure 1.32). In some cases, because hay was loaded directly from a wagon outside the barn, there was no ramp, bank, or barn bridge providing vehicular access to the upper story.

In addition to marking the widespread adoption of the hay fork, gambrel and Gothic roofs signified a change in barn construction. While some early gambrel-roofed barns were made with traditional heavy timber framing, most were constructed from lightweight, machine-sawn lumber, which was assembled into a truss configuration and held together with nails rather than mortise and tenon joinery. The building materials needed for a gambrel roof, and later an arched roof, were often mass-produced, even available in mail-order catalogs.[66] The new roof types reflected national trends as well as the heightened importance of industrialization and technology in farming.[67]

Polygonal and Round Barns

Although most New Yorkers who constructed multilevel barns used a rectangular footprint, a few dozen New York farmers experimented with polygonal and circular floor plans. Intended to maximize efficiency in the utilization of space, materials, and labor, round and polygonal barns were constructed during the nineteenth and early twentieth centuries. After the First World War, the lack of adaptability to accommodate changes in agricultural technology diminished the popularity of non-orthogonal barns. The few remaining round and polygonal barns in New York bear testimony to a once novel concept that never gained full acceptance from most farmers and slowly faded from popularity.[68]

Whereas farmers in midwestern states such as Indiana, Illinois, Wisconsin, and Iowa constructed hundreds of round barns, only forty-three round or polygonal barns have been documented in New York. Of this total, approximately half still stand. Farmers built the majority of these barns in the dairy-rich central and western counties of New York, although round barns could be found in almost all regions of the state. Erie County and Montgomery County had four round barns each, more than in any other county in New York.[69] The Town of Greene in Chenango County may hold the record for the most extant round barns in a single township, with two examples standing a short distance from each other on Route 12 (Figure 1.33).

Figure 1.32. Barn, Colliersville area, Otsego County. This twentieth-century basement barn did not require wagon access to the upper level as hay wagons could remain outside the building to be unloaded with a hay fork. The hay hood helped shelter the hay track from the weather, and the decorated doors provided access to the interior of the barn. (Photograph by Cynthia Falk, June 2010.)

Figure 1.33. Bates round barn, 1928–1931, near Greene, Chenango County. Devern Bates built a round barn for his neighbor James Clifford Young between 1914 and 1916. In the late 1920s he opted for the form for his own dairy barn just up the road. (Photograph by Cynthia Falk, August 2010.)

The concept of round or polygonal buildings came to America with other European building practices during colonial times. Circular or polygonal hay barracks, used exclusively for hay storage, dotted the Dutch countryside in the sixteenth century and were used on a limited basis in England's northern counties and New York State in the 1700s. George Washington adapted the polygonal structure for large-scale agricultural use with his construction of a sixteen-sided grain-threshing barn at Mount Vernon in 1793. In the mid-1820s, Shakers in Hancock, Berkshire County, Massachusetts, built the first round barn to receive widespread renown. This unique structure, which later burned and was rebuilt in 1865, may have inspired the construction of New York's first polygonal barn twenty-five miles to the west in Coxsackie (Figure 1.34). Here, around 1832, James Bronck built a three-story thirteen-sided barn for hay storage. Bronck presented an early argument for the efficiency of such buildings through his handwritten notes, which show his calculation of the potential volume of hay storage within the polygonal structure.[70]

The 1848 publication of *A Home for All,* by phrenologist-turned-author Orson Fowler, spurred the first wave of octagonal building construction across New York State. While Fowler advocated the benefits of the octagonal form for houses and other domestic buildings, he offered little commentary regarding barns of this shape, leaving prospective builders to create their own floor plans. Like later proponents of

Figure 1.34. James Bronck thirteen-sided barn, 1832, Coxsackie, Greene County. (Photograph by Cynthia Falk, October 2010.)

round barns, however, Fowler advocated the efficiency of this design for agricultural use. He suggested having cattle face each other in two parallel rows, an arrangement necessitating fewer steps in feeding. The size and shape of such a barn would allow wagons to circle around the interior of the building without having to back out. Fowler also advised builders to consider large barns with two or three stories that could be used for other purposes in addition to dairying, such as threshing. While very few if any polygonal barns resulted from Fowler's writings, the book popularized the nontraditional shape and likely prepared New York farmers for the next phase of round barn building twenty-five years later.[71]

In 1874, farmer, editor, and professor Elliott W. Stewart constructed a two-story octagonal barn, eighty feet in diameter, on his farm near Lake View, Erie County. Highly satisfied with the merits of his new building, Stewart published details of his plans in respected periodicals such as the *Livestock Journal,* the *Cultivator and Country Gentleman,* and the *American Agriculturist.* Like Fowler, Stewart emphasized the efficient use of space within an octagonal structure, and he also detailed the economy of construction materials and the building's resistance to strong winds. He noted that an octagonal design provided more square footage while using fewer linear feet of wall than a rectangular design. Stewart took special pride in his barn's self-supporting roof, which he divided into eight panels joined by continuous rings of timbers around the walls. The lack of internal supports created an unencumbered

Figure 1.35. Baker octagonal barn, 1882, Canadarago Lake area, Otsego County. The Bakers sited their octagonal barn on a hill, allowing access from ground level to multiple stories of the barn. Recent owners received a New York State barn grant to help with repairs. (Photograph by Cynthia Falk, April 2010.)

haymow on the building's top level. "For convenience and cheapness," Stewart wrote, "there is nothing more to be desired."[72]

Construction of thirteen octagonal barns in New York can be dated to the 1870s through the 1890s, and most of these structures were based on Stewart's widely published design. The majority measured between thirty and sixty feet in diameter, a considerable difference from Stewart's massive eighty-foot building. Almost universally, these structures featured heavy timber framing, a lower level made from fieldstone, and vertical board siding on the upper floor. Most farmers opted to build their polygonal barns into a bank, thereby allowing easy entry into both levels. In spite of their shape, almost all of this era's barns maintained a floor plan of parallel cattle stanchions. As a result, the framing necessary to support a polygonal floor and long rows of stanchions created an awkward and irregular maze of beams and supports.[73]

Although most octagonal barns duplicated aspects of Stewart's design, every barn featured a slightly different structure and appearance. Each barn's roof and the roof's supporting structure varied according to the knowledge and concerns of the builder. Many builders utilized Stewart's support-free plan, while others, such as H. N. Baker of the Town of Richfield in Otsego County, chose to extend four supporting posts through each level of the building (Figures 1.35, 1.36). The shape and style of roofing also varied, but most builders chose to top their barn with a central cupola. Two contemporary polygonal, but not octagonal, barns—the sixteen-sided

Figure 1.36. Framing of the Baker octagonal barn, 1882. Whereas Elliott Stewart designed an octagonal barn with a self-supporting roof, the Bakers built theirs with four posts rising all the way to the cupola on top. (Photograph by Cynthia Falk, April 2010.)

McArthur barn built in Kortright, Delaware County, in 1883, and the thirteen-sided Hubbell-Parker barn, constructed in Schoharie County in 1896—abandoned the parallel stanchion arrangement in favor of a more efficient round design. The new plan had all cows facing a central circle around a haymow, thus requiring fewer steps for feeding. The circular stanchion layout also resulted in a far more efficient framing system in which all major beams were laid out in a circle.[74]

The third and final phase of non-orthogonal barn design and construction in New York involved dramatic changes to the interior and the adoption of a round, rather than a polygonal, footprint. The design, also conceived with efficiency and economy in mind, originated not in New York but in Wisconsin. In 1889 Franklin H. King of the University of Wisconsin's Agricultural Experiment Station designed and built a stone-walled "true-round" barn for his brother's farm. The enormous structure, ninety-two feet in diameter and two stories high, housed ninety-eight cows in two circular rows facing a common feeding alley. A six-foot-wide wagon drive behind each row allowed for the efficient removal of manure. King's barn, which utilized relatively inexpensive balloon framing, was built around a cylindrical wooden silo. The centralized location of the silo prevented its contents from freezing or spoiling and allowed for convenient loading on the uppermost floor.[75]

William H. Voorhees built New York's first true-round barn in Montgomery County in 1895 and published its design in *Hoard's Dairyman* in March 1897 (Figure 1.37). As with polygonal barns inspired by Stewart's writings, no two New York barns

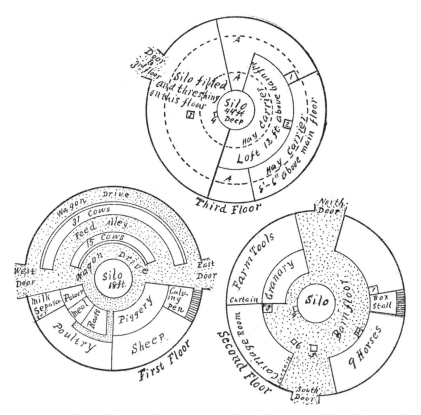

EXPLANATION OF FLOOR PLANS:—Nos. 1, 2, 3 are Feed Chutes; 4 is Silage Chute; 5 Door to Root Cellar; 6 Door to Meal Bins.

Figure 1.37. Vorhees "true-round" barn, 1895, Mill Point, Montgomery County. Influenced by Franklin King's plans, details of William Vorhees's completed barn were published in the Wisconsin journal *Hoard's Dairyman*. (F. H. King, "A Consolidated Type of Farm Buildings," *Hoard's Dairyman,* March 26, 1897, 103.)

modeled after King's plans were exactly alike internally or externally. Some true-round barns featured unique designs, such as the Kelly round barn in Halcottsville, Delaware County. Built in 1899, the two-and-a-half-story building incorporated a plank bridge in its top story, which allowed teams to draw wagons over the tops of the hayloft and silo. The outer walls of true-round barns were constructed of wood, clay tile, or poured concrete, while cones, domes, gambrel roofs, and even flat roofs crowned the new structures. Most farmers continued to build round barns into a bank to allow entry at multiple levels. The new round barns of the late nineteenth and early twentieth centuries generally had a much larger diameter than their octagonal predecessors.[76]

Despite their much-heralded reputation for efficiency, round barns waned in popularity in the years following World War I. Many prospective builders struggled to find carpenters willing and able to construct a large round structure, and most farmers preferred their traditional rectangular barns over an experimental form. Praise from respected agricultural organizations turned to criticism of the difficulty of adapting round barns to technological advances. Large mechanized machinery, especially tractors, could not easily be stored within a round configuration, and changes in dairying technology had altered the role of manual labor in a dairy barn. Small round barns were not economical to build, and large ones required a considerable financial investment. Once constructed, round barns could not be expanded without adding traditional rectangular wings. The weakness of America's agricultural industry in the 1920s precluded large monetary outlays for new farm structures, and finally the Great Depression brought barn construction to a standstill.

Estate Farms

For some New Yorkers, farming meant subsistence and survival; the latest innovations and model barns that were described in the agricultural press were far out of reach. At the other end of the spectrum were gentleman farmers, who created country estates across New York State. Working farms were an important part of these properties, and farming was viewed as a way for gentlemen to relax and become connected with the land. Gentleman farmers did not need to farm for a living. Because they were able to hire help or to engage tenant farmers, their role was that of manager. Even so, many estate owners kept a farm manager on their payroll.[77]

Despite their detachment from the experience of most farmers, it is important to examine the goals of those who created estate farms within the broader context of agricultural history. While their farms differed in scale and design, they often introduced new ideas for increasing quality and production. By experimenting with new materials for building and incorporating new technologies for tasks such as milking and removing manure, gentleman farmers helped to ensure the modernization of farming practices, especially in the pivotal years of the early twentieth century.

Estate farms were most common during the country place era, which began after the Civil War.[78] During this period, families from both old and new money were able to purchase large tracts of land, either as a whole or piece by piece. For the nouveaux riches, estates, with their picturesque grounds and grand residences, were a way to show off their wealth.[79] The country place era came to a close with the stock market crash of 1929, when new tax laws made ownership of such large estates less viable, even for the rich.[80] Estate farms were not, however, a new phenomenon. During the late eighteenth and early nineteenth centuries, gentleman farmers experimented with new crops on manor estates along the Hudson River. For example, Robert Livingston bred merino sheep and experimented with fruits and vegetables new to the United States at his property, Clermont.[81]

Barns and other buildings associated with farming were seen as a way of making an estate more picturesque. Unlike barns on subsistence or commercial farms, estate barns were often designed by an architect. Alfred Hopkins, who designed barns for estates throughout Long Island and the Hudson Valley, wrote his book *Modern Farm Buildings* as a guide to "the most approved ways of designing" various farm structures. In his opening chapter, Hopkins wrote about the aesthetic qualities inherent in farm buildings:

The various buildings necessary for their several uses are capable of such an infinite variety of groupings, that the requirements of the farm would seem to offer more scope to the architect than do the problems of the house. There are the tall towers for water or ensilage; the long, low creeping sheds for the storage of wood, farm implements and machinery; and the huge protecting and dominating structures required for the proper housing of the hay, grain and straw. With these buildings in effective combination and appropriately placed among the fields, the picture of the farm can be made so pleasing, and the idea of going back to Nature as the source of all sustenance so ingratiating, that it would be possible to build up an effective philosophy on the principle that the architecture of the home should be made to resemble the architecture of the farm, rather than the other way about.[82]

To Hopkins, barns were not lowly utilitarian structures to be hidden but were to be designed as a picturesque part of the landscape.

In New York State, estate farms were very diverse. Their owners came from different professions and levels of wealth, and they maintained varying degrees of involvement on their farms. Their motives differed, too; some were interested in experimental farming, some in raising certain animals or crops, and some simply in having a hobby in the country, away from their usual urban employment. While estate farms were especially concentrated in the Hudson Valley and on Long Island, there were estates all over New York, and estate barns reflected the varying geography, resources, and crops found in their locales.

Estate barns were set apart from barns on other farms because they were conceived as part of the "farm group." Whereas a subsistence farmer would add buildings to a farm as they were needed, without trying to create a coherent aesthetic, estate barns were often conceived as a singular architectural expression. Even if the buildings were not all constructed at the same time, they were usually designed in a similar style. In some cases, designers even devised barns to match a house or other building on the estate. For example, at Olana, the estate of the painter Frederic Edwin Church in Columbia County, the primary barn structure echoed the style of Cosy Cottage, a home designed by the firm of architect Richard Morris Hunt (Figure 1.38).[83]

Estate farms often featured new technology and farming practices, as well as experimentation with new breeds of animals and plants. In *Modern Farm Buildings,* Hopkins provided instructions for sanitary facilities for milking cows, ideal setups for the interior of barns, and even plans for the removal of manure. Edward Severin Clark's new stone barn at Fenimore Farm, built in the 1910s, was referred to by locals as the "cow palace," as it offered sanitary, modern facilities for eighty dairy cows (Figure 1.39).[84] Its architect, Frank P. Whiting, was clearly interested in many of the same ideas in farm design as Alfred Hopkins.

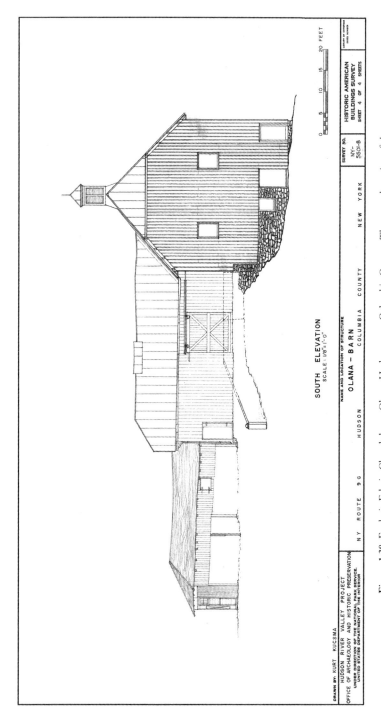

SOUTH ELEVATION
SCALE : 1/8"=1'-0"

0   5   10   15   20 FEET

Figure 1.38. Frederic Edwin Church barn, Olana, Olana, Hudson area, Columbia County. The central portion of the barn complex at Olana was built in the 1860s; a large multilevel dairy barn, seen to the right, was added to the west end in the 1890s. The clipped gables of the roofs echo a similar design on the nearby residence, Cosy Cottage, where the Church family lived before completing the grand Persian-style home that is the showpiece of this historic site. (Drawing by Kurt Kucsma, Historic American Buildings Survey, NY, 11-HUD, 1B-.)

Figure 1.39. Interior, main barn, Fenimore Farm, 1916–1918, Cooperstown area, Otsego County. Set up for a dinner, perhaps at its grand opening, Edward S. Clark's dairy barn featured the latest materials and technologies for housing dairy cattle. (Ward Files, Special Collections, New York State Historical Association Research Library, Cooperstown, "Lake Road—Fenimore Farm," PH-14.007.)

The size and use of materials further distinguished estate barns. William Simpson's barn, "McKinney," erected from 1907 to 1909, was built of concrete blocks made on-site (Figure 1.40). Concrete was chosen in response to a devastating fire in a previous barn on the property, which killed several prized racehorses.[85] The building measured 347 feet long by 50 feet deep, big enough for a center aisle that could be used for indoor equestrian exercise in the winter. The barn also provided space for forty stalls, a foaling room, office, and storage for fodder.[86]

Although estate farms were carefully planned so that all buildings contributed to a cohesive design, certain features, such as horse stables or dairy barns, were frequently the focal point. Many gentleman farmers had an interest in either riding or breeding horses for racing. At the Roosevelt home in Hyde Park, James Roosevelt, father of Franklin D. Roosevelt, chose the location in part because it already had ample pasturage, a horse track, and a stable he could use for raising trotting horses.[87] Cow barns and related structures, such as creameries, were also common on estate farms. Not only was milk a necessary staple for running an estate, but many gentleman farmers were interested in creating model farms, and aimed to improve sanitary conditions for cattle and increase milk production. Creameries in particular

Figure 1.40. William Simpson barn, 1907–1909, Cuba area, Allegany County. Named after the prize horse McKinney, Simpson's barn, built of concrete block with a tile roof, was not as susceptible to fire as wooden structures. (Postcard collection, "Cuba," Special Collections, New York State Historical Association Research Library, Cooperstown.)

Figure 1.41. Creamery, 1904, Camp Santanoni, Newcomb, Essex County. Great Camp Santanoni, the former estate of Robert C. Pruyn, was designed with the help of noted agriculturalist Edward Burnett. The creamery, a functional building associated with the dairy barn, resembled a quaint cottage. (Photograph by Mary Lord, September 2010.)

Figure 1.42. Farm Court, 1901, Frederick Vanderbilt estate, Hyde Park, Dutchess County. Unfortunately, much of this extensive barn complex, designed by Alfred Hopkins, no longer survives, having been destroyed by fire. (Photograph, Vanderbilt Mansion National Historic Site, National Park Service, Rodney McKay Morgan Collection, Farm Court.)

were seen as an opportunity for picturesque expression on the part of the architect. Examples at Fenimore Farm, Frederick Vanderbilt's Hyde Park in Dutchess County, and Robert C. Pruyn's Camp Santanoni in Essex County in the Adirondacks were designed to look like quaint country residences (Figure 1.41).

Throughout the Empire State, estate farms were created in one of two ways. On some estates, such as the Roosevelts' in Hyde Park, barns or barn complexes from previous landowners were reused, sometimes with little modification. Rather than build a new farm, the Roosevelts used an existing one, which they referred to as the "Home Farm," and added elements, such as a new silo, when they were needed.[88] Nearby at Frederick Vanderbilt's estate there was an attempt to use existing barns as well. In 1895 Vanderbilt hired the architectural firm of McKim, Mead, and White to repair existing barns, at a cost of $42,377. In 1901, however, he gave up on the older buildings and had a new complex built.[89]

On most estates across New York, new barn complexes were designed and built specifically for their locale. Some architects, such as Alfred Hopkins, specialized in the "barn group." Hopkins was known for his low-profile horizontal groups, which drew on historical styles, especially those of the English countryside. He was also very interested in efficiency, and his designs created efficient spaces with separate areas for work related to horses and cows. Examples of Hopkins's work are the new farm group on the Vanderbilt estate (Figure 1.42) and a large barn complex at Caumsett, the estate of Marshall Field III on Long Island (Figure 1.43).

Figure 1.43. Guernsey Farm, 1923–1925, Caumsett Manor, Marshall Field Estate, Lloyd Neck area, Suffolk County, designed by Alfred Hopkins. (Photograph, Historic American Buildings Survey, NY, 52-LOHA.V, 1-C-1.)

Hopkins was sometimes joined in his work by Edward Burnett. Burnett, who turned his own model farm in Massachusetts into a commercial operation, served as a farm "expert." He would work alongside Hopkins or another architect, aiding in the development of the farm, and then stay on for an introductory period as farm manager.[90] At Camp Santanoni, the Adirondack estate of Robert C. Pruyn in the town of Newcomb, Burnett was hired in 1905 to expand an existing farm complex probably designed by Robert Robertson.[91]

In the estate barn group, architects and wealthy landowners alike found a unique opportunity to mix the picturesque aesthetic, which was rooted in historical styles, with the values and ideas of a model farm, based on efficiency, cleanliness, and the use of modern devices. Although most farmers could not copy the size and grandeur of the barn complexes on estates, the modern farming techniques developed and practiced on estate farms during the country place era influenced contemporary farming techniques.

Barns Today

Throughout most of New York's history, agriculture constituted the largest segment of the state's economy. Today it is still a vital economic driver. In fact, as recently as 2009, the top five counties in agricultural sales—Suffolk, Wyoming, Cayuga,

Figure 1.44. Marks Farms, freestall barns, Lowville area, Lewis County. Marks Farms makes use of multiple freestall barns in its large-scale dairy operation. (Photograph by Cynthia Falk, October 2008.)

Genesee, and Wayne—accounted for more than $4.4 million in receipts. At close to $2 million in sales statewide, dairy products are by far the most valuable agricultural commodity.[92] The importance of dairy production to the state is central to our understanding of the types of barns being built in New York today. While historic barns are a striking part of the landscape, active dairy farms with modern dairy barns and equipment demonstrate the continued importance of agriculture to an ever-changing economy. Among the buildings most commonly found on dairy farms is the freestall barn, the standard barn for dairying across the country today (Figure 1.44).

Freestall barns were introduced to the dairy industry in the late 1970s, bringing a revolution in dairy farming. Unlike barns built in the past, which were primarily designed to foster ease and convenience for the farmer, freestall barns are designed with the comfort of the cows in mind. The revolutionary concentration on "cow comfort" creates spaces inside the barn that allow for easy movement, rest, and access to food, as well as excellent ventilation and harmonious traffic patterns for both animals and operators, that is, the farmers. The freestall, from which the barn takes its name, is the primary distinguishing characteristic.

Freestalls provide heifers space to lie down, sometimes on a mattress filled with sand, woodchips, organic material, or water. Most freestall barns are designed in one of four configurations—two-row, three-row, four-row, or six-row—depending on the size of the herd and the size and breed of the cows. One unifying feature of each of these configurations is the feed delivery driveway. It runs along the center of the barn, from gable end to gable end, providing an easy way for farmers to get a

Figure 1.45. Danmark Farm, Newport area, Herkimer County. The fans of the ventilation system are clearly visible on the gable end of this single-story cow barn, an addition to an older dairy farm complex. (Photograph by Cynthia Falk, August 2010.)

fresh supply of food to the animals. The rows of freestalls are located on either side of the feed delivery driveway—one, two, or three on each side, depending upon the configuration of the barn. The freestall rows are separated further by freestall alleys that divide the herd into groups of heifers on the same milking schedule. Animal waste is typically removed from the freestall barn alleys by scraping with a tractor or automated system or flushing into a liquid manure lagoon.[93]

Freestall barns are generally part of a larger class of buildings developed in the first half of the twentieth century and referred to as pole or pole frame barns. A pole barn is a one-story building with a concrete slab or dirt floor. Framed with vertical posts running from the floor to the roof, a pole barn generally features wide spaces between the posts and a low-pitched roof.[94] Pole barns, which can be constructed of wood or metal, became popular after World War II. In freestall barns, the exterior walls of the pole barn may be removable or eliminated altogether to allow for more light and ventilation. The primary purpose of the structure is to provide shade in the summer and protection from the harshest winter weather.

Freestall barns are a radical departure from basement barns of the past because they have no basement or loft. They have entrances at one or both gable ends and are relatively long in proportion to their width. Many freestall barns that are enclosed with exterior walls have visible ventilation systems either at one gable end or running the length of the building (Figure 1.45). Freestall barns can be found as stand-alone

Figure 1.46. Cooperstown Holstein Corporation, milking parlor, Cooperstown area, Otsego County. (Photograph by Cynthia Falk, November 2009.)

buildings among a larger complex of dairy buildings or, in the case of many older and smaller operations, as additions to basement barns. In either case they serve to separate the animals from food and grain storage and the milking parlor.

Freestall barns also reflect the increased specialization of agricultural buildings. Farmers of the late nineteenth and early twentieth centuries began to shift from all-purpose barns to specialized forms. Architects such as Alfred Hopkins promoted the specialization of rooms within barns and of whole buildings, specifically for dairying. Such innovations did not catch on immediately, however. In 1928 a publication from the Agricultural Experiment Station at Cornell discouraged the use of one-story cowsheds. Describing the new building type, the report noted, "On many farms where certified milk is produced, the cows are kept in a one-story barn, with hay storage in another barn." Even though the type of single-story cow barn described was typically attached as a wing to the hay barn, the author concluded, "This arrangement necessitates much additional labor in feeding and thus raises the cost of milk production."[95] While advances in science, which documented the effect of bacteria and dust on the health and milk production of the heifers, prompted a shift to single-use buildings, only later mechanization made them feasible for most farmers.

As units of larger late-twentieth-century and twenty-first-century dairy facilities, one-story freestall barns have become just one part of the modern farm complex. An adjacent milking parlor, designed to maximize the efficiency of the dairy, is central to production and profitability. Milking parlors are located near and generally connected to the freestall barn to minimize the walk for the cows. The size of the milking parlor is determined by the performance goals of the dairy and the equipment in the facility, which can range from milk tanks, chillers, and generators to employee locker rooms and showers (Figure 1.46). Milking parlors are rectangular or circular in plan, with various configurations of milking equipment and stalls to allow for efficient milking on the basis of herd size and available labor.[96]

Because of the expense associated with adding or renovating dairy buildings, farmers have become increasingly concerned with materials and methods used in barn building. Quality of construction is an issue because of the lack of builders who understand the unique needs of dairies and the unique physical strains that dairying puts on buildings. Because of these considerations, some farmers have turned to prefabricated buildings.[97]

Prefabricated agricultural buildings have been available since the early twentieth century and have only grown in popularity with time. Several companies cater exclusively to the dairy industry. Their buildings are designed to the specifications of the individual farmer. They can be delivered and set up by the company or assembled by a private contractor. Prefabricated freestall barns share many identifiable characteristics with freestall barns built on-site, particularly in their interior arrangement, though they are often built on a much larger scale and may resemble greenhouses, with galvanized steel framing and removable sidewalls.

Freestall barns represent the continued evolution of the dairying industry. New trends include a focus on the importance of animal comfort, but old concerns, such as ease of movement for both the herd and the farmer, continue to influence barn design. Though perhaps not as picturesque as barns of the past, modern freestall barns, in their response to contemporary farm needs, represent a resilient, essential, and ever-changing industry.

Chapter Two

SHELTERING THE FLOCK, PROCESSING THE PRODUCT

Ice 6½" on Brown Pond.
Our Ice house at Dairy wont be ready before Saturday night
Ordered 10 tons Furnace Coal at $4.90
Teams commenced hauling it in afternoon.
Killed 10 hogs today for Tarrytown butchers.
Wrapping pipes in cellar at House.
Starting on fixing brooder house.

Grasslands Farm Journal, Tarrytown,
Westchester County, December 19, 1900

When the new farm manager arrived at Grasslands, the Westchester County estate of William Cochran, on October 20, 1900, he immediately set to straightening up the cottage where he would live, unpacking his trunks, and even hanging pictures. The next two months, documented in a daily diary, were full of activities more directly related to the farm. While the Cochran property was unusual among New York State farmsteads because of its scale, the variety of activities that went on there was not atypical. In a single day, the new manager reported working on an icehouse for cooling milk, repairing the brooder house, and slaughtering hogs, activities that reflect the variety of animals that Cochran kept, including dairy cows, chickens, and swine. Other entries indicate that horses, kept in a horse barn, were among the mix.[1] Rarely did New York farmers—from gentlemen like Cochran to non-landowning tenants—limit themselves to one type of animal, and this diversified strategy, particularly when large in scale, often required specialized types of buildings.

The earliest Dutch and English barns in New York provided shelter for livestock as well as space for storing grain and hay. Basement barns likewise housed cows and horses and sometimes other animals such as sheep, pigs, and even poultry, in addition to serving other functions. Although a farm's main barn could be used to accommodate a wide variety of animals, some farmers, particularly those who specialized in animal husbandry, chose to erect additional buildings—from horse stables to pigpens to sheepfolds to chicken coops—designed to meet the needs of specific breeds. In form and finish, each type of building catered to its animal inhabitants, as well as to the people who cared for them and benefited from their meat, eggs, milk, wool, and work.

Like animal housing, the processing of animal products led to the creation of a distinct array of buildings. Nowhere is this more apparent than in the dairy industry. Even before the advent of twentieth-century sanitary regulations, farm families understood that milk required cool temperatures and clean conditions for effective storage and processing, and farmers built specialized buildings to create the required environment. In an age before liquid milk could be easily transported, farm women turned it into butter or cheese in dairies on farmsteads. By the mid-nineteenth century, dairy factories allowed for increased production, using milk from cows on multiple farms.

The shift of processing from the individual farm to more centralized locations affected more than just dairy farmers. Slaughtering historically occurred outdoors on the farmstead without the benefit of a specialized building. Meat was preserved by smoking it in a smokehouse on the farm property. With improvements in transportation, butchering moved off the farm and even, in many cases, out of New York State, to slaughterhouses built specifically for that purpose. The widespread availability of mechanical refrigeration in the twentieth century replaced smoking as the preferred method of preservation. Changes in the processing of meat—like changes in dairy farming, animal housing, and agricultural work in general—were reflected in the increased specialization of rural building types. In the colonial period, subsistence farms were the site of multiple steps in the production of a diverse array of farm goods. As time has passed, many farmers have opted to use services available beyond the farm for processing and distribution. Farm buildings demonstrate this trend toward both the specialization of design and the centralization of processing.

Structures for Dairying

The terrain and climate of New York are well suited for dairying, and many farmers have chosen dairy products as a staple crop, both in the past and today. In the colonial period, farmers produced limited quantities of milk, butter, and cheese for their own use and for sale. But by 1840, New York farmers were already responsible for over $10 million in dairy products annually, more than three times the total for any other state. Milk from more than a million dairy cows yielded over 90,000 pounds of butter and roughly 39,000 pounds of cheese in 1855, and farmers, especially those close to cities, had also begun selling whole milk to meet the growing demand from urban dwellers.[2]

As the nineteenth century progressed, New York's dairy industry continued to grow. In the 1870s, agriculturalists debated whether milk was more profitable sold fresh by the quart or converted into butter or cheese. The sale of liquid milk, transported in milk cans, often by railroad, was a new phenomenon. Farmers were warned that in hot weather, milk could be kept "sweet" for only twenty-four to thirty-six hours when stored in cans sterilized with boiling water and transported, ideally, in milk cars "arranged to keep ice."[3] Milk not destined to be consumed in liquid form continued to be converted into butter and cheese as new dairy "factories" largely supplanted farm-based enterprises. Today, New York is still a major dairy producer. It boasts over five thousand dairy farms, and the state ranks third in production of dairy products in the United States.[4]

The farm buildings that support the dairy industry have taken various forms over the years. Dairying first and foremost requires a space for cooling milk to keep it fresh and to facilitate the separation of cream. Changes in production practices and sanitation laws have influenced the design of dairy buildings and the materials used to construct them. Through much of the nineteenth century, farmers relied on water, or sometimes ice, for cooling; today refrigerated tanks serve a similar function. Whereas in the past, the same building often provided space to cool milk and process dairy products such as butter and cheese, the ability to transport milk as a liquid has since allowed for processing plants to be located off the farm some distance from the dairy herd.

Springhouses

Milk needs a cool place to be stored until it is either consumed or processed. Cooling also facilitates the separation of cream from milk, an essential first step in making butter and processing skim cheese. Before the advent of mechanical refrigeration, much dairy production occurred in a springhouse, usually a small, rectangular building of masonry construction with a gable roof (Figure 2.1). The site of the springhouse was determined by the location of the spring used to cool it. If possible, the springhouse was located at the base of a slope or built into a hill to take advantage of the cooling properties of the earth as well (Figure 2.2). In some springhouses, water flowed along a masonry course on the floor or through an elevated wooden trough. Milk pans were placed in the water to cool (Figure 2.3). One hundred square feet of water surface could accommodate the milk from twenty cows.[5] Butter churning and cheese making could take place in the room where the spring was located, in an adjacent room designed for that purpose, or at another nearby location.

Figure 2.1. Springhouse, near Garrison, Putnam County. Located on the grounds of Boscobel, a relocated early-nineteenth-century Hudson River Valley mansion, this sizable springhouse was built of cut stone blocks and included fashionable details such as the fan over the door. (Photograph courtesy Boscobel.)

Figure 2.2. Springhouse, Town of Richfield, Otsego County. Low to the ground and hugging the hillside, this small stone springhouse likely provided a space to cool milk so the cream would rise, but did not include much additional workspace for processing butter from the resulting cream. (Photograph by Cynthia Falk, December 2010.)

Milk Houses

A milk house is typically a small, one-story rectangular structure attached to a dairy barn or built as a separate structure near the barn (Figure 2.4). Like springhouses, milk houses provided facilities for cooling milk; often they included additional space for farm women to process dairy products. Before the advent of mechanical refrigeration, water, drawn from a well or a pump into channels or troughs, typically provided the means for chilling the milk.[6] As an alternative, milk houses could combine the functions of a dairy and an icehouse, using ice as the coolant (Figure 2.5). These combination structures might have two adjoining rooms, one for the storage of ice and the other for processing dairy products, or they could be two stories, with ice stored above the dairy room (Figure 2.6).[7] The interior of a milk house had a cooling trough for milk pails or pans and space for the small-scale production of

Figure 2.3. Springhouse interior, 1906. A trough of water around the outer edge of the space provided a cool place to set filled milk pans so that the cream would separate. (Bryon David Halsted, *Barn Plans and Outbuildings*, rev. ed. [New York: Orange Judd, 1906], 281.)

butter and cheese. At the end of the nineteenth century, electric cooling vats began to replace water or ice as the refrigerant, and milk houses primarily became storage places for milk before it was shipped to the city for consumption or to the factory for production.

Increasing federal, state, and local regulations in the twentieth century—particularly after outbreaks of typhoid and other diseases from contaminated unpasteurized milk during the World War I era—regulated the construction and use of milk houses.[8] In New York City, for example, the Department of Health issued a series of regulations regarding milk shipped from farms outside the city. These concerned not only the care, feeding, and milking of the cows but also the physical layout and condition of the farm buildings. The regulations required a milk house to be located on elevated ground at least one hundred feet from any hog pen, privy, or manure pit and separate from the farmhouse and barn. It had to have watertight floors, a window sash that opened for ventilation but was screened to keep out flies, water for cooling (preferably running water), and space to expose milk pails and other equipment to sunlight or steam for sterilization.[9]

Figure 2.4. Thayer farm milk house, ca. 1910, Town of Springfield, Otsego County. This separate structure, built of wood with a concrete floor, was located near the dairy barn. It provided a place for milk to be processed away from the odors, flies, and dirt found in the barn itself. (Photograph by Cynthia Falk, June 2010.)

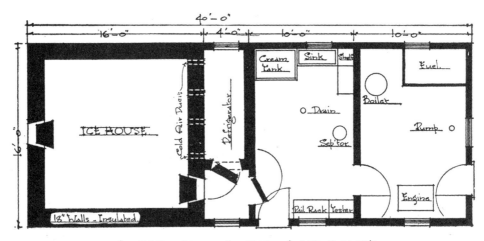

Figure 2.5. Floor plan for a combination dairy-icehouse, 1925. In an age before the widespread use of mechanical refrigeration, ice was a convenient cooling device, even chilling the "refrigerator" in this dairy building. (R. M. Washburn, *Productive Dairying*, Lippincott's Farm Manuals series, ed. Kary C. Davis [Philadelphia: J. B. Lippincott, 1925], 295.)

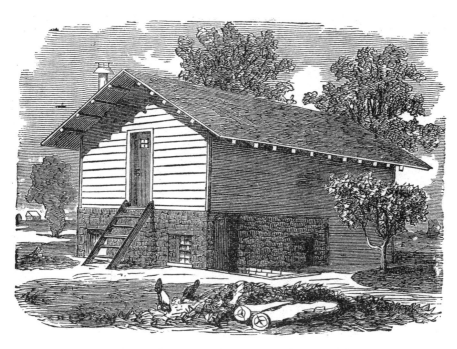

Figure 2.6. Combination milk and icehouse, 1906. This two-story building included a dairy in the lower stone part of the building and an ice house above and to the rear in the portion of the structure sided with clapboard. Wood walls constructed of two-inch planks spaced ten inches apart with the intermediate spaces filled with tanbark helped insulate the ice. (Byron David Halsted, *Barn Plans and Outbuildings*, rev. ed. [New York: Orange Judd, 1906], 261.)

During the early twentieth century, the appearance of milk houses became increasingly standardized in response to the new regulations. Concrete became the preferred construction material both for floors, where it provided the required watertight surface, and for walls. Concrete block walls could be kept clean and served as a more permanent barrier than wood-frame walls. Windows provided ventilation and light, and they could be fitted with screens. Though often attached to the dairy barn, milk houses were physically separate and were entered through an exterior door. Proper partitions between the cow barn and milk house protected the milk from dirt, disease, and stable odors. Today's milk houses are still often concrete or concrete block and are located adjacent to a dairy barn (Figure 2.7). A single door leads to the interior, which is dominated by a large refrigerated storage vat.

Cheese Factories

Jesse Williams of Rome, New York, is generally credited with establishing the first cheese factory in the United States, in 1851.[10] Williams relied on the cooperation

Figure 2.7. Milk house addition, Town of Otsego, Otsego County. Concrete blocks became the material of choice for milk houses among farmers who needed to conform to new dairy sanitation rules in the twentieth century. (Photograph by Cynthia Falk, September 2010.)

of neighboring farmers who joined him in supplying fresh milk to the factory in order to produce cheese on a large scale. In this factory system, sometimes referred to as associative dairying, the milk suppliers and the cheese maker shared the profits. Before the advent of cheese factories, cheese was manufactured on the farm, usually by women, in a milk house, springhouse, or similar outbuilding. The factory system was profitable, and by 1866 there were 424 cheese factories in New York located all over the state. Cheese factories were especially numerous in the counties of Allegany, Cattaraugus, Chautauqua, Chenango, Herkimer, Jefferson, Lewis, Madison, Montgomery, Oneida, Onondaga, Oswego, Otsego, and St. Lawrence.[11]

Cheese manufacturers converted unused buildings into cheese factories and built new buildings specifically to serve that function (Figure 2.8). In the nineteenth century, a cheese factory usually included four distinct spaces: the delivery area, processing room, press room, and a dry house for curing. Early cheese factories were located next to a spring or other source of water, as plentiful water supplies were needed for production. A new structure built in 1860 to process the milk of six hundred cows cost about $3,000.[12] Equipped with rows of windows for light and ventilation, the model cheese factory included a story-and-a-half building for manufacturing and a two-story wing for curing. On the inside it was roughly finished. Flagstones lined the floor of the processing room to accommodate the water

Figure 2.8. *Milk Delivery to International Cheese Plant,* 1912, by Arthur J. Telfer (1859–1954), dry collodion plate, C-5–01967. (Fenimore Art Museum, Cooperstown.)

Figure 2.9. Cooperstown Cheese Company, Milford area, Otsego County. Today small manufacturers continue to hand-produce specialty cheeses in New York State. (Photograph by Cynthia Falk, October 2010.)

Figure 2.10. Ridge Mills Creamery, ca. 1875, near Rome, Oneida County. A facility of the American Dairy and Commercial Company, the sizable Ridge Mills Creamery produced both butter and cured cheese, the latter made with skim milk supplemented with added fat from oleomargarine. (Xeres Addison Willard, *Willard's Practical Butter Book* [New York: Rural Publishing Company, 1875], 166.)

and waste from manufacture. Vats, presses, sinks, and pumps equipped the factory. Stricter health regulations enacted just after World War II forced the pasteurization of milk used in most cheese production, adding pasteurization machines to production equipment. The majority of the cheese produced in New York today is manufactured by large companies such as Kraft, but smaller cheese plants are still in operation, primarily producing artisan and specialty cheeses. Modern cheese factories are often constructed from concrete blocks or metal panels for purposes of sanitation (Figure 2.9).

Creameries

Before the existence of large factories and milk distributors, many farm families chose to use the cream from excess milk to make butter because it was easier to produce than cheese and could be sold in towns and cities for a small profit. Farmwives and daughters produced the butter in springhouses or milk houses, peppering the New York countryside with cottage industries. The quality of butter produced by these hardworking women was inconsistent, and the standardization desired by merchants could be better achieved by new factories.

The architectural specifications for a creamery, also known as a butter dairy or buttery, were similar to those of a cheese factory. In fact, many cheese factories produced butter as well, often in a separate wing or rooms with extra cooling vats, cream vats, and churns (Figures 2.10 and 2.11). Milk collected at night cooled, and

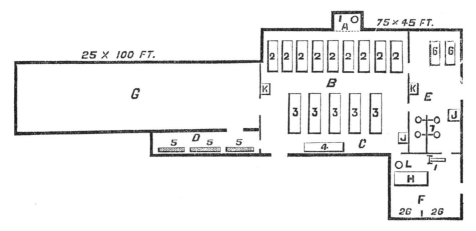

Figure 2.11. Floor plan for Ridge Mills Creamery, ca. 1875, near Rome, Oneida County. Milk was received in room A; cheese made in sections B and C, pressed in section D, and cured in section G; butter production occurred in section E. (Xeres Addison Willard, *Willard's Practical Butter Book* [New York: Rural Publishing Company, 1875], 163.)

Figure 2.12. Butter dairy, 1906, New York State. Even in the early twentieth century, books devoted to farm planning included information about buildings designed for manufacturing butter on the farm. In this example, the churns were powered by horses on a treadmill located just outside the building. (Byron David Halsted, *Barn Plans and Outbuildings*, rev. ed. [New York: Orange Judd, 1906], 264.)

the cream, which naturally rose to the top, was skimmed from it in the morning. The cream was churned into butter while the remaining milk was processed for a skim cheese or added into the morning's whole milk for a partial skim cheese. Some smaller factories chose to produce only butter and used the skim milk as nutritious fodder for farm stock.

Smaller butter factories were one-story rectangular structures with gable roofs and were heavily plastered or built of stone for insulation (Figure 2.12). Similar in construction to the combination icehouse–milk house, small butter factories contained three rooms: an ice room, a milk room, and a churning room. Today butter manufacturing has been separated from cheese manufacturing, and butter is produced in large factories that struggle to compete with a growing range of butter substitutes such as margarine.

Horse Stables

Until the advent of the automobile and steam- and gasoline-powered engines, horses provided transportation for farmers and their crops as well as power for farm equipment. Although large farms might have a separate stable or horse barn, many farms incorporated stalls for horses in another building such as the main barn. In the 1860s and 1870s, with multi story barns the norm, farmers debated whether horses should be kept on the basement level or the upper floor. Some agriculturalists disliked the dampness in the basement, while others were concerned about the colder temperatures on the upper level in the winter. Wherever horses were housed, it was important that they be able to get to the stalls easily. Storing wagons adjacent to the horse stalls was recommended so the horses could be hitched and unhitched under cover.[13]

The ideal was always to separate the horse stalls from areas used by other livestock. Even in multipurpose Dutch barns, eighteenth-century traveler Peter Kalm observed, "on one side were stables for the horses and on the other for the cows."[14] This separation continued through the nineteenth century, and by the twentieth century it was mandated by a scoring system for dairy farms that penalized producers who kept a horse among their milking cows.[15] One barn designer recommended sliding doors, which could be opened only when necessary for cleaning, to isolate horses—or, more important, horse manure—from dairy cows (Figure 2.13).[16]

Barn planning books from the early twentieth century made various additional recommendations for building a barn or a section of a barn for horses. One recommendation was to install box stalls so that horses had adequate space. A box stall, or double stall, is a large, enclosed stall that houses one horse. The recommended size of the stall was at least eight feet square, but if space allowed, eight-by-ten or ten-by-twelve-foot box stalls were ideal.[17] The extra space that a box stall provided allowed the animal to move around as well as lie down easily. As William Radford speculated in his planning guide: "Nothing looks so comfortable for a good horse as a roomy box stall. If the horses had their way about it, there would be more box

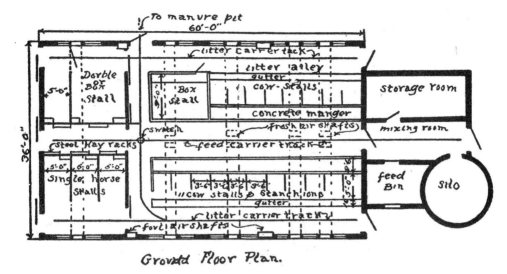

Figure 2.13. Floor plan for a dairy barn and horse stable, 1917. Horses were housed at one end of the barn, away from the cows, in single or double stalls. Sliding doors physically separated most of the stalls from the dairy cows, although one box stall with a separate door was located adjacent to the cow stalls. It may have been used to isolate a sick cow or young stock rather than a horse. (Herbert A. Shearer, *Farm Buildings with Plans and Descriptions* [Chicago: Frederick J. Drake & Co. Publishers, 1917], 18.)

stalls."[18] Box stalls take up a lot of floor space, so barns often had only one or two box stalls as well as several regular stalls. These were narrower, consisting of two partitions extending from the wall. The advantage of these smaller stalls was that the barn could accommodate more of them.

Other recommendations for creating buildings to house horses included having plenty of windows for ventilation and light as well as providing adequate feed boxes. More attention was given to the comfort of horses than to that of most other animals on a farm. Their value and the work they provided in terms of both power and transportation were important factors in determining how to care for and house horses.

On horse farms where a large number of horses were bred and trained, accommodations could be almost palatial. Adolphus Busch, co-founder of Anheuser-Busch, owned property near Cooperstown, in Otsego County, where, in addition to growing and processing hops for brewing, he also raised horses. The famous Clydesdales would not become associated with the company until 1933, at the end of Prohibition, but even before then horses were important to the Anheuser-Busch enterprise and were well housed and tended at the Cooperstown property.[19] According to Adolphus Busch, "there was no good reason why an animal as cleanly, as orderly, and as free from destructive disposition as a horse, should not be housed as comfortably and with as much regard for sightliness as a human being" (Figures 2.14 and 2.15).[20]

In rural villages where artisans and professionals relied on horses for transportation, the animals were often stabled in carriage houses (Figure 2.16). These structures

Figure 2.14. *S. Uhlman (Busch Stables), 1902,* by Arthur J. Telfer (1859–1954), dry collodion plate, 5–2133. The prominence of hops in central New York made the region important to the Anheuser-Busch company, and in 1904 Adolphus Busch purchased property from Simon Uhlmann on the west shore of Otsego Lake near Cooperstown in Otsego County. (Fenimore Art Museum, Cooperstown.)

Figure 2.15. *Interior Stable, Busch Carriage House,* by Arthur J. Telfer (1859–1954), dry collodion plate, 5–2133. The Busch stables offered well-appointed accommodations to the horses they housed. (Fenimore Art Museum, Cooperstown.)

Figure 2.16. Carriage house, ca. 1870, Hamilton Place, originally in Campbelltown, Steuben County, now relocated to the Genesee Country Village and Museum, Mumford, Monroe County. John Hamilton's house, the rear of which is seen at the far right, and carriage house demonstrated his prominence in his community. The carriage house was designed to match the style of the main house and to provide space for horses, carriages, and the storage of hay. (Photograph by Cynthia Falk, June 2010.)

had enough room for a few horses as well as one or two carriages. Overhead was a loft where hay was stored. These buildings were often more decorative than rural barns and were sometimes designed to match the main house. Today many of these carriage houses have been converted into garages for automobiles or even apartments.

In urban areas, horses were and still are kept in stables that almost blend into the cityscape. In New York City, horses have played an important role in commercial, public, and private transportation since the city's founding. The mounted unit of the New York Police Department was established in 1871 "to prevent fast and reckless driving" in the area around Central Park.[21] Today mounted police officers can still be seen in the city, and visitors can take a ride in a horse-drawn carriage, at a slower pace, through the park.

For those who want more excitement, horses bred for their speed race at several New York State tracks. The most famous are on Long Island at Belmont and in the Hudson Valley at Saratoga. Though not exactly agricultural in nature, horse racing does require a large number of stables. Racehorses are typically housed in barns with long rows of box stalls. An overhanging roof protects the horses and their keepers from the weather (Figure 2.17). These buildings differ in form from the stables found on most farms, and from the carriage houses found in urban areas, because of the large number of horses they are meant to house; nevertheless, like horse stalls

Figure 2.17. Sanford Court stables, 1901, Saratoga Springs area, Saratoga County. Located near the track, the Sanford Court barns were designed to accommodate numerous horses during the racing season. (Photograph by Cynthia Falk, October 2009.)

in basement barns and stables on farms and in larger communities, they attest to the importance of these animals to those who have relied on them for power, transportation, and prestige.

Sheepfolds

In 1837 Elam Tilden of Columbia County provided a sketch for the readers of *The Cultivator* illustrating a sheep barn he had recently built in New Lebanon (Figure 2.18). The barn could house seven hundred sheep and store eighty to one hundred tons of hay and 2,500 bushels of rutabaga, both of which were used as feed.[22] Tilden's sheep barn was far from ordinary, but it provides one example of the sizable specialized structures that were erected as some New York farmers turned to large-scale wool production in the early nineteenth century.

Sheep had been a part of the agricultural landscape of New York since the early colonial period. They were valued for their fleece, which could be transformed into warm woolen textiles, and they were also used for meat. Sheep in early New York were generally either stabled in multipurpose farm buildings (Figure 2.19) or left to roam free. Farmers who chose the latter option risked damage to the fleece when sheep strayed into wooded areas, as well as attacks by wolves or dogs.[23] A few real estate advertisements for prosperous eighteenth-century farms mention sheep houses, but provide little additional information about what they looked like or how they were constructed. By the 1840s, agricultural reformers insisted that sheep needed at least "the protection of roofed sheds" so they were not subjected to winter snow or spring rain and sleet.[24]

As domestic textile production increased in the new United States, sheep and their wool became more valued. By 1850 New York was home to over 3.4 million sheep, which produced in excess of 10 million pounds of wool annually.[25] Some specialized farms like Tilden's included buildings constructed specifically as sheep barns. A "shearing floor" provided an indoor space to shear the sheep, and a "wool-room," finished on the inside with plastered walls, served as a repository for the wool. The lower level of the building housed the sheep, which had access to attached yards. Multiple doors could be closed in winter and opened in warmer weather to help regulate temperature, and windows provided ventilation. Feed, in the form of hay and root vegetables, was kept in the same building, a well with a pump supplied fresh water, and sheep manure was collected and stored for fertilizer.[26]

By the beginning of the twentieth century, the number of sheep raised in New York had dropped to below 1 million.[27] Books and journals advocating a modern approach to shepherding continued to emphasize the need for ventilation, dry earthen floors, natural light, and fresh water in sheep barns, as well as convenient grain and root storage. Additional recommendations included separate lambing pens for ewes and their young—with artificial heating—and feeding racks to prevent sheep from

Figure 2.18. Tilden sheep barn, 1837, New Lebanon, Columbia County. Elam Tilden reported that he had a flock of one thousand Saxony sheep in 1837. This barn held seven hundred sheep on the lower level, eighty to one hundred tons of hay above, and 2,500 bushels of root crops in a cellar. (E[lam] Tilden, "Sheep Barn—Ruta Baga," *The Cultivator* 4, no. 5 [July 1837]: 84.)

Figure 2.19. Sheep and lambs in the Sweet-Marble barn, The Farmers' Museum, Cooperstown, Otsego County. An English threshing barn, the Sweet-Marble barn provides space for feeding and bedding sheep as many multi-use barns did in the past. (Photograph by Cynthia Falk, July 2010.)

pulling hay onto the floor, where it would be trampled (Figure 2.20). As one author conceded, however, "almost any kind of barn, providing it is waterproof, roomy, well drained and well ventilated, will answer the purpose of a sheep barn."[28]

Pigpens

Pigs, also referred to as hogs or swine, are hardy animals that can survive with minimal human care. They are omnivores and use their highly sensitive snouts to locate and uncover food. Their natural diet includes fungi, roots and bulbs, fruit, snails,

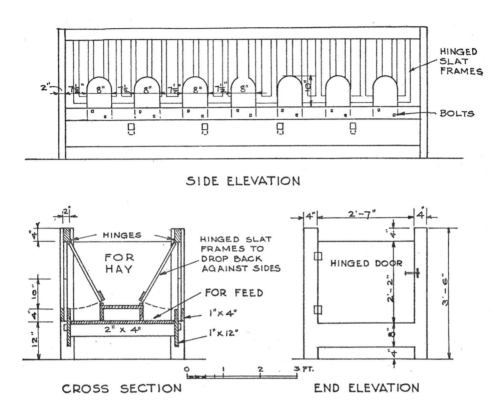

Figure 2.20. Plans for a sheep feeding rack, 1913. Alfred Hopkins recommended that sheep pens be created by partitioning a larger space with feeding racks. He devised plans for feeding racks that allowed the sheep to fit its head between two tombstone-shaped dividers so it could eat without pulling hay onto the floor. (Alfred Hopkins, *Modern Farm Buildings* [New York: McBride, Nast & Co., 1913], 192.)

earthworms, reptiles, birds, and rodents.[29] For settlers in colonial New York, hogs were the ideal low-maintenance livestock, and most people kept some swine for their own consumption. It was common practice to turn the animals loose in the sur-rounding woods to forage on their own. They required no shelter or feeding, but if trained to receive a ration of domestic refuse, they would remain nearby.[30]

By the late 1700s, New York farmers began to assume a more active role in the raising of pigs. They devised and built structures for the purposes of keeping their animals close at hand and protecting them from predators. For some, the need to create enclosures was mandatory. In 1770 an act forbade colonists from allowing swine to run at large in New York City and the counties of Westchester, Queens, Kings, and Richmond.[31] Pigs were valued for meat as well as lard, which was used in cooking and for making soap and candles.[32] The multiple products derived from swine made them important possessions, even if they could not roam free.

Because pigs have a natural tendency to gnaw and root, any structure for con-taining them had to be constructed in a way that would withstand their destructive behavior. A description of appropriate swine housing published in Massachusetts in

Figure 2.21. Pigsty with shelter, The Farmers' Museum, Cooperstown, Otsego County. This reconstructed fenced area includes a basic shelter for hogs at one end. (Photograph by John Emery, 2006.)

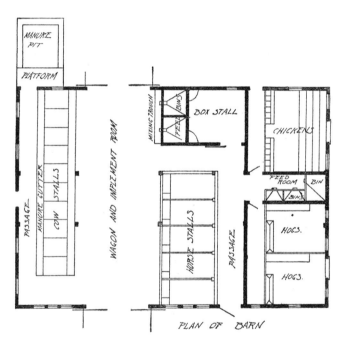

Figure 2.22. "Barn for a Small Farm—A160," 1909. These barn plans include room for ten cows, five horses, fifty chickens, and "a couple of breeding sows." For farms that did not specialize in raising hogs, it was not uncommon to shelter a few swine in a general-use barn. (William A. Radford, *Radford's Practical Barn Plans* [Chicago: Radford Architectural Company, 1909], 183.)

1797 advocated framed and boarded construction of hardwood to retard gnawing. Floors were to be made of either tight planks or large stones that could not be overturned.[33] Typical accommodations included common feeding troughs built of heavy wood and set on wide platforms so they could not be upset by the animals.

Historical records from the early 1800s to the present show a variety of universal designs for swine structures. Although no evidence points to any distinct building style peculiar to the State of New York, census records certainly reveal the regional importance of hog farming in the state. Counties in close proximity to major population centers, especially New York City, and along major transportation routes had the largest numbers of hogs. Between 1845 and 1875, Dutchess, Columbia, Ulster,

Figure 2.23. Hog house, Mt. Vision, Otsego County. A long, low building divided into pens proved useful on farms that raised a large number of pigs and required better control of their environment. (Photograph by John Emery, 2006.)

Orange, Monroe, Jefferson, and Onondaga were New York's leading hog-producing counties.[34]

Pigsties varied from specialized structures to simple enclosures to portions of larger barns. The earliest and most basic pigpens were corrals large enough for one pig or several, which were fenced with logs or sawn planks. Typically a low covered shelter made of wood was erected in the pen to protect animals from the elements (Figure 2.21). On small farms with diverse livestock, hogs could be kept in the same barn with other animals. One plan book from the early 1900s featured a barn for a small farm designed to accommodate ten cows, five horses, fifty chickens, and room for "a couple of breeding sows"[35] (Figure 2.22). Pigs served an ecological function on the farm; their natural tendency to root was often put to practical use for mixing horse or cow manure on farms with diverse animal stock.[36]

Raising hogs for market typically necessitated the most elaborate buildings. One or more long, low wood-frame buildings served larger operations with more pigs (Figure 2.23). The interiors of these buildings were typically divided into pens. Low doors on the sides allowed the animals to move outdoors to pasture. Some farmers who bred and raised a larger number of animals might build a more elaborate structure, known as a farrowing house, for sows and their litters. These were typically enclosed one-and-a-half- or two-story buildings adjacent to a corral with indoor pens for mother pigs and their piglets. Since hogs could grow to market size faster when their forage diet was supplemented with cooked grain, model piggery designs featured grain storage and cooking facilities in conjunction with shelters (Figure 2.24).[37]

Surviving pigsties on historic farmsteads in New York are not common. By the late 1800s Chicago had become the nation's primary hog market, which curtailed large-scale pig farming in the Northeast. For many farmers raising pigs returned to being a subsistence endeavor. Since a few of the hardy creatures could survive well on a farm without elaborate buildings, minimal effort and expense were invested in

Figure 2.24. Piggery at Alasa Farms, Alton, Wayne County. The lower stone level of this two-story building provided shelter for hogs. The upper story is designed with built-in corncribs around two of the outer walls. A cooker on the uphill side of the building could have been used to boil grains to fatten the hogs and then again when it was time for slaughtering. (Photograph by Cynthia Falk, June 2010.)

constructing their shelters. Today on New York farms where hogs are raised for the meat market, modern pole barns often serve the purpose quite well.

Facilities for Processing Meat

Meat processing on the farm frequently took place outside, away from the farmhouse, because of the odors it produced and the pests it attracted. Tools needed to butcher animals included skinning knives, sticking knives, butcher knives, meat saws, cleavers, and, very important, a chain hoist to lift the carcass. On farms where an enclosure was built for slaughtering, a hoist, a large wooden wheel and pulley system, was an integral part of the design.[38] Farm families tried to use every possible part of the animals they butchered, leading to creations such as blood sausage and Jell-O, invented in LeRoy in Genesee County.[39]

Although many animals were butchered for consumption on the farm or in the local community, some farmers raised animals such as hogs or beef cattle on a larger scale to sell their meat commercially. As early as the late 1600s professional drovers assumed the role of middle men who walked or used limited water transportation to take livestock longer distances to market. With improved transportation networks in the early 1800s, production began to shift westward to places such as Cincinnati and Chicago. Drovers transported live animals, or merchants shipped packed meat to southern and eastern markets.[40]

Railroads, and particularly refrigerated railroad cars, introduced in the 1870s, furthered the geographic shift. Railroads could transport fattened cattle expediently in cattle cars, and refrigerated cars provided an easy year-round way to ship meat without fear of spoilage. Large-scale commercial processing plants, such as those made infamous by Upton Sinclair in *The Jungle,* were created in places with ready train access for shipping cattle in and dressed meat out.[41]

While Chicago and other western cities dominated the meat processing industry, butchering continued on the farm on a much smaller scale to meet family and local needs. Albert E. Parker of Appleton in Niagara County, for example, helped neighbor Earnest Sahr kill two hogs on December 6, 1907, and six days later Sahr returned the favor, assisting Parker in slaughtering two eight-month-old pigs weighing 250 and 225 pounds. Over the next few days, Parker cut up the pork, salted the hams and shoulders, and then packed them. On December 26 he sold some of the meat, as well as butter, to another neighbor.[42] In Lorraine in Jefferson County, H. H. Lyman remembered a similar process in earlier times, noting that butchering was winter work that required extra hands. A fire was started before dawn "not a great way northeast from the hog-pen," and the animals "were brought out of the pen, killed and scalded, and the bristles taken off." The family used the resulting lard and pork, and additional "meat brought a good price and was an important part of the income of the farm."[43]

As the twentieth century progressed, although some slaughtering continued to take place on the farm, meat processing facilities in New York came to serve two specialized functions. Despite the competition, some New York farmers, especially those who lived in proximity to New York City, continued to find a market for meat. To this day, New York State metropolitan processors supply hotel and restaurant needs. At the same time, small rural processors serve the needs of farmers and hunters. By the twentieth century, rural slaughterhouses were built with concrete floors and drains to deal with offal and blood. These structures are typically boxy in appearance, made of concrete block, and painted white (Figure 2.25). They may offer their customers meat storage in refrigerated lockers in addition to butchering services.[44]

Smokehouses

Well established by 1890, mechanical refrigeration revolutionized the meatpacking industry and eventually home meat preservation. Before its advent, as one farmer reported, "in hot weather very little meat was used or had. In the cool weather of the

Figure 2.25. Slaughterhouse, near Richfield Springs, Otsego County. Twentieth-century rural slaughterhouses were typically unadorned buildings constructed from cement block, often painted white. (Photograph by Anneke Nordmark, 2006.)

spring, fall and winter, there was always plenty of it."[45] Smokehouses were historically built to preserve meats such as ham, beef, turkey, and fish for family consumption or sale. With the rise of refrigerators and freezers, the need for and therefore the construction and use of smokehouses declined. Today smoking is primarily used to add flavor to the meat.[46]

Smoking can be done in a variety of structures including pits in the ground, barrels, fireplaces, and freestanding buildings (Figure 2.26).[47] Wood was frequently recommended as a building material for smokehouses in nineteenth- and early-twentieth-century agricultural literature, and it is easy to believe that many smokehouses were made of wood. Building with wood was quick and inexpensive but left the resulting structure susceptible to fire when in use and to rot after discontinuation of use.[48] The majority of surviving smokehouses in New York State are of more durable materials, including stone, brick, or a combination of the two. In Delaware County, slate was also used for construction.[49]

Because of the danger of fire, smokehouses were typically freestanding structures. Rather than being sited near the farmyard, they were located to the side or rear of the farmhouse, typically within twenty to forty feet. Generally square in plan, they varied in height and width, and therefore in capacity. In larger smokehouses, a full-size door provided access to the interior; in smaller houses, a window-like open-

Figure 2.26. Keown Farm Smokehouse, South Valley, Cattaraugus County. (Anthony Cucchiara, Architecture Details Slide 2, Archive of New York State Folklife, 77–0074, New York State Historical Association Research Library, Cooperstown.)

ing with a solid wooden shutter served the same function (Figure 2.27). Often the smokehouse door was located in the gable end of the building facing the house.[50] The interior of a smokehouse, blackened from creosote, the coating created during the smoking process, attests to its use.

Poultry Houses

Beginning in the 1820s with the introduction of Mediterranean and then Asiatic breeds, American farmers began to recognize the potential in raising fowl, especially chicken, as a source of food.[51] The female birds provided eggs, while both males and females could be used for meat. The animals also provided feathers, which were used to create soft, warm bedding. By 1840 New York State had become the leading producer of poultry of all kinds.[52] For some farm families of the nineteenth and

Figure 2.27. Brooks smokehouse, originally from South New Berlin, Chenango County, now at The Farmers' Museum, Cooperstown, Otsego County. Built of durable brick and a relatively flat slate tile roof, this smokehouse is small in scale. (Photograph by Cynthia Falk, March 2008.)

twentieth centuries, poultry brought additional income through the sale of eggs, which was often overseen by the farmwife or children.[53] In the early twentieth century, some farmers invested heavily in poultry, with eggs or broilers raised for meat among their chief products.

Buildings used to house chickens, and to a lesser extent roosters, were at first rudimentary, consisting mainly of coops that provided a protected place for nesting and kept the birds safe from predators. Advances in technology in the late nineteenth and early twentieth centuries, and the increase in demand for poultry and its by-products, gave rise to specialized architectural forms such as colony, brooder, and laying houses. The development of the heated incubator, electric lights, and chicken cages further influenced the types of buildings found on poultry farms as greater control of the flock became desirable, especially among large-scale producers.

Chicken Coops

The chicken coop, also known as a henhouse or poultry house, was the basic structure used to house chickens and laying hens (Figure 2.28). Ideally a henhouse was

Figure 2.28. Poultry house, Hayt farmstead, Patterson, Putnam County. The shed roof allowed for more exposure on the warm south-facing side and less on the cold north-facing side. The windows on the south elevation provided for warmth and light from the sun as well as ventilation. (Photograph by Rob Tucher, February 1989, Historic American Buildings Survey, NY, 40-PAT, 2-L-1.)

Figure 2.29. Nesting boxes and roosting poles, chicken house, The Farmers' Museum, Cooperstown, Otsego County. (Photograph by Cynthia Falk, January 2010.)

Figure 2.30. Chicken house with chicken door, The Farmers' Museum, Cooperstown, Otsego County. (Photograph by Cynthia Falk, March 2008.)

warm, well lit, sufficiently ventilated, and easy to clean. The interior of the house generally included roosts, a dropping board for catching manure, and nesting boxes. (Figure 2.29). Most houses had small square doorways at the base of a wall to allow fowl to exit into a connected outdoor run with a scratching place where the chickens could peck at the ground and at grain fed to them (Figure 2.30). Ideally henhouses were elevated or located on high ground to provide drainage, ventilation, and protection from predators.[54]

Henhouses were designed to allow for maximum heat and light. The south side of a henhouse characteristically was taller than the north and was fitted with numerous windows to take full advantage of sunlight. The wall on the north side, usually no more than four feet in height, allowed roosting hens' body heat to warm the house further (Figure 2.31). Because of the differing wall heights, chicken coops can often be identified by their shed roof or asymmetrical gable roof—high on the south side, low on the north side. Window openings on the south wall were glass paned

Figure 2.31. Model chicken house, 1888. The two levels of windows on the south wall take full advantage of the sunlight. (T. M. Ferris, Mason Cogswell Weld, and P. H. Jacobs, *Profits in Poultry: Useful and Ornamental Breeds, and Their Profitable Management* [New York: O. Judd Company, 1888], 23.)

or covered with muslin. The latter allowed for ventilation without drafts, and both muslin and glass permitted the building to access heat from the sun.[55] Historically, hot water pipes, a small stove, or electric lights provided additional heat to henhouses during harsh winters.

Colony Houses

By the turn of the twentieth century, some poultry farmers began to increase the size of their flocks, making their businesses dependent on specialty breeding and the production of eggs, meat, or feathers.[56] When large numbers of chickens were housed together, however, the potential for spreading disease increased. Consequently, farmers attempted to separate their large flocks into smaller colonies. The colony house was a portable structure, typically on skids, which allowed farmers to divide their flocks by age or size. The interior was similar to that of a henhouse.

The colony plan was popular on farms that specialized in breeding. A twelve-foot by twelve-foot colony house could shelter 250 to 350 chicks. The houses were usually dispersed over a large grassy area (Figure 2.32). Experts in poultry farming recommended that they be moved every three weeks by a team of horses or a tractor, although reportedly many farmers left their colony houses in the same spot during an entire summer season, rotating locations year to year.[57]

While the colony system was typically employed on larger poultry farms, a single colony-style henhouse could be used in rural, as well as suburban or urban, locations

Figure 2.32. Colony houses, ca. 1910, Bonnie Brook Poultry Farms, Saratoga Springs, Saratoga County. Colony houses allowed flocks to be divided and spread out around a farm property. (*The Bonnie Brook Poultry Farms, Saratoga Springs, New York* [Saratoga Springs: Bonnie Brook Poultry Farms, ca. 1910].)

for raising a small number of chickens for eggs or meat. A 1914 advertisement from an Elmira firm targeted those who intended to raise chickens as "a recreation" or "to provide an addition to the present income" (Figure 2.33). The plans, available by mail, showed how a two-part coop, with an enclosed area for laying and an outer penned area, could reportedly be made in an hour for as little as twenty-five cents.

Brooder Houses and Incubators

On larger poultry farms where the colony system was in place, animals were often divided on the basis of age. Young chicks were the most susceptible to harsh weather and fluctuations in temperature. Intended to approximate the conditions provided to chicks by a mother hen, a brooder house offered a heated space, often including a compact compartment known as a hover, a feeding area, and room to exercise.[58] Prior to the development of electric heating methods, hot water pipes or kerosene or gasoline burners were used to heat brooder houses (Figure 2.34).[59] Larger brooders, part of the landscape of poultry farms using the colony system, were sometimes referred to as colony brooders.

In 1879 Charles Hearson invented the modern incubator, which automatically regulated the temperature of eggs with a heating device. It allowed farmers to incu-

Figure 2.33. Advertisement for a chicken coop, 1914. In the early years of the twentieth century, raising chickens was still a way to earn extra income. ("A Living from Poultry" *Cosmopolitan Magazine* 58, no. 1 (1914): 118, Widener Library, Harvard University.)

bate eggs artificially during seasons when hens were less likely to hatch eggs, further industrializing poultry farming.[60] Until the invention of electric incubators in the late nineteenth century, egg temperatures were regulated with a combination of oil lamps, gas flames, and warm water (Figure 2.35).[61] In general, incubators on large poultry farms are placed in separate structures near the brooder house where the chicks are moved after they hatch.

Barracks, Range Houses, and Batteries

The high demand for chicken and eggs during the First and Second World Wars brought an increased emphasis on poultry farming. Protective tariffs helped American farmers compete by keeping the price of foreign eggs, often imported from

Figure 2.34. Brooder house, 1927. Designed to house young chicks, brooder houses typically had some form of heating, in this case provided by hot water pipes. (William Adams Lippincott, *Poultry Production,* 4th ed. [Philadelphia: Lea & Febiger, 1927], 350.)

Fig. 14. Brindley's Incubator.

A A. Temporary Artificial Mother for newly-hatched Chicks.
B B. Lamp and Reservoir.
C. Egg Drawer.
F. Hot-water Boiler.

Figure 2.35. Brindley's incubator. In this example, a gas jet or paraffin lamp warmed water, which was circulated through a series of metal pipes to approximate the warmth provided by a mother hen. (Lewis Wright, *Practical Poultry Keeper: A Complete and Standard Guide to the Management of Poultry, Whether for Domestic Use, the Markets, or Exhibition,* 5th ed. [New York: Orange Judd, n.d.], 205.)

Figure 2.36. Poultry cooperative chicken house, Liberty, Sullivan County. Documented by a Farm Security Administration photographer in 1936, this large chicken house was part of a cooperative venture by Jewish farmers in the Catskills. (Photograph by Paul Carter, April 1936, Library of Congress, Prints & Photographs Division, FSA-OWI Collection, LC-USF341-011034-B.)

Figure 2.37. Barrack-style brooder, 1929. Although authors of early-twentieth-century manuals on poultry farming expressed concerns about the profitability and environmental conditions of permanent long brooder houses, such buildings could provide shelter for large numbers of chicks. This one was designed to accommodate fifteen thousand. (Louis M. Hurd, *Practical Poultry-Farming* [New York: Macmillan, 1929], 104.)

China, high.[62] Large poultry farms focused on raising either broilers for meat or egg-laying hens. In the New York market area, leghorns, which produce white eggs, were the most popular breed.[63]

The large farms typically procured sizable tracts of land in rural areas. Sizable henhouses, or laying houses, could be one or often more stories tall. They usually had continuous rows of windows on the south side to provide heat from the sun and ventilation, as in smaller chicken coops (Figure 2.36).[64] Increasingly in the twentieth century, however, artificial heating, ventilation, and even air conditioning, combined with insulation, better regulated temperatures. Mechanization also affected building design. Large farms specializing in egg production often confined fowl in hen batteries, or laying cages, either individually or in small groups, and utilized technological advancements such as conveyor-belt feeders and automatic egg collectors.[65]

The buildings for housing new chicks varied. While some poultry farms used colony brooding houses to divide and shelter their young flocks, by the 1920s others turned to larger buildings. A long brooder, or barrack, was a building divided internally into units where chicks spent their early days. A long brooder looked much like a laying house and was often used as one once the chicks were hardy enough to be moved outside (Figure 2.37).[66] Range houses, portable open structures for roosting that were located in the fields, provided shelter for the young domestic chickens, or pullets, once they could tolerate a less controlled environment (Figure 2.38).[67]

Figure 2.38. Range houses, 1935. Clarence Lee, onetime head of the Poultry Department of the New York State Institute of Applied Agriculture, recommended open range houses, rather than confined brooder houses, for raising young birds to broiler age. (Clarence E. Lee, *Profitable Poultry Management,* 8th ed. [Cayuga, N.Y.: Beacon Milling Company, 1935], 41.)

Figure 2.39. Chicken batteries, 1935, Beacon Poultry Research Farm, Cayuga, Cayuga County. The Beacon Poultry Research Farm recommended batteries like these designed for individual laying hens rather than groups of chickens. They allowed for close monitoring of feed consumption and egg production, and prevented cannibalism. (Clarence E. Lee, *Profitable Poultry Management,* 8th ed. [Cayuga, N.Y.: Beacon Milling Company, 1935], 67.)

Figure 2.40. J. Hallock's Atlantic Duck Farm, 1924, Speonk, Suffolk County. Long Island has been known for its duck farms since the early nineteenth century. In 1922 the owners of the Atlantic Duck Farm estimated an output of 140,000 birds. (John H. Robinson, *The Growing of Ducks and Geese for Profit and Pleasure* [Dayton: Reliable Poultry Journal Publishing Company, 1924], 158.)

The battery system of brooding provided another option for raising chicks by the late 1920s. Unlike colony brooding houses and barracks, which allowed chicks to move about freely in small groups, battery brooders confined chicks to chicken crates. The exterior appearance of the building in which the batteries, or cages, were located was less important than the interior conditions, which had to be warm and well ventilated. Batteries could house one or several chicks, and were stacked from four to six tiers high (Figure 2.39).[68]

Other Poultry Houses

Various architectural forms are essential in raising and maintaining flocks of chickens, and although some farmers keep a small number of other fowl such as turkeys, ducks, and geese without the benefit of specialized buildings, commercial production requires dedicated structures. Since the early nineteenth century, Long Island has been known for its duck farms, often located near the water's edge. Long Island duck farms were and are commercial operations, with ready access to the New York City market and transportation networks. In 1922 Long Island farmers raised roughly 2 million ducklings, about the same number they produce today.[69] By the early twentieth century, a commercial farm made use of incubators, brooding houses, and fattening sheds for its stock. Many of these buildings looked similar to the structures used to house chickens (Figure 2.40). Large duck farms also had separate facilities for butchering, plucking, and packing the ducks before sending them to market.[70]

Figure 2.41. Turkey wattle, The Farmers' Museum, Cooperstown, Otsego County. This round structure with a thatch roof and woven wooden walls provides shelter from the coldest winter weather. While currently used to house turkeys, it could have sheltered other poultry flocks. (Photograph by Cynthia Falk, March 2008.)

On general farms or farms that specialized in other crops, ducks could be kept in small numbers to supply meat, eggs, and feathers. Ducks could also be employed to control pests, weeds, and algae on land and in waterways.[71] They required little care but needed plenty of clean water and a warm, dry laying shelter. One how-to book directed, "Any available shed or a part of the poultry house may be utilized for this purpose."[72]

Turkeys have also been used in pest management in New York, as farmers have employed them since the mid-eighteenth century to control tobacco hornworms and grasshoppers.[73] By the turn of the twentieth century, farmers raised turkeys particularly for the Thanksgiving and Christmas markets, as well as for their feathers. In 1890 New York farms were home to over 400,000 turkeys, with the largest numbers in St. Lawrence, Onondaga, Monroe, Steuben, and Erie counties. Turkey raising was often delegated to the farmwife as a way to earn additional income. Hardier than chickens, turkeys require few specialized structures (Figure 2.41). A small number of young turkey poults, which are more susceptible to cold and wet weather than mature birds, could be moved into almost any agricultural building temporarily. Only on larger farms were turkey sheds, rectangular buildings ideally ten feet wide by twenty or more feet long, built to shelter the young turkeys.[74] While today turkey

Figure 2.42. Ridgecrest Turkey Farm, Brockport, Monroe County. Similar in exterior appearance to a freestall dairy barn, this modern building houses turkeys raised for the Thanksgiving market. (Photograph by Jennie Davy, 2009.)

husbandry is largely the domain of big multinational corporations, some farms in New York still raise smaller flocks (Figure 2.42).[75]

Geese have never been raised in large numbers in the United States but are sometimes found on small farms, where they are utilized for their weeding abilities and watchdog personalities. They require rudimentary shelter and are fairly self-sufficient, but need plenty of space because they are messy, loud, and protective when nesting.[76]

The animals raised by New York farmers were valued by their owners and by consumers for a wide variety of reasons. They provided transportation, wool for warm clothing, feathers for soft bedding, lard for soap and lighting devices, and meat, milk, and eggs to eat. They also helped eliminate pests, turn manure, power equipment, and even entertain. The buildings that provided shelter for farm animals or served as a place to process animal products met specific needs. While some animals could be housed in a multipurpose barn or left to roam free, distinct structures corresponded with requirements for sunlight or drainage or durable gnaw-proof materials.

As farmers moved from subsistence to market-oriented production, agricultural buildings were adapted and adopted to suit different scales, technologies, and breeds. In many cases, processing moved off the farm to rural factories, and farm buildings became more specialized. New York farmers who raised large numbers of sheep in the early nineteenth century might invest in a sheep barn; those who lived near a metropolitan area might construct a farrowing house for their sows and piglets. In the twentieth century, chickens—raised in both small and large numbers—required poultry houses, which could range from makeshift chicken coops to industrial-scale barracks. Dairy farmers altered their older milk houses to accommodate refrigerated vats for storing liquid milk to be shipped away in tanker trucks. The resulting farm buildings, often less striking than the main barn and harder to reuse adaptively as agricultural needs shifted, attest to the ingenuity of farmers and the importance of their animal products to New York's culture and economy.

Chapter Three

From Haystacks to Silos

Friday, 23 [July]. Robert, Alex & Uncle John worked in hay spreading & drawing in & raked, hand led horse fork & cocked hay.

Saturday, 24 [July]. Alex helped to make a bridge at east doors of big barn & draged, I helped to make the barn door bridge, chored to Supper time & then mowed in 4 acre lot.

E.L. McFetridge, Sparta, Livingston County, 1869

In mid-July 1869 Edward McFetridge was getting ready to hay. His parents, Archibald and Jane, were Irish immigrants who had established a sizable farm in Sparta, in Livingston County. Twenty-nine-year-old Edward, still single and living at home, was becoming a farmer in his own right, and he recorded his activities in a daily log. On July 14 he documented a noteworthy event: he bought a "grab and hook" for a hay fork, a device that would use the power of a horse to raise the hay into his family's "big barn." By that evening he was cutting holes at the barn so the hay could be lifted from a wagon into the hayloft. After experimentation with the hay fork, more modifications were required, including the construction of a "bridge" at the barn door to provide access for the equipment. Apparently all the work was worthwhile since Edward was able to add to the farm's income in December by selling a ton of hay for eight dollars.[1]

For the McFetridges, hay was one of several crops produced either for market or for home use. In 1865, when the New York census taker visited the farm, the family had five milk cows and reported producing 850 pounds of butter the previous year; by 1875 the number of milk cows had risen to nine and butter production had increased to one thousand pounds. Nevertheless, as on most dairy farms during this period, dairying was part of a diversified strategy that included other products for sale, for family use, and for feed for the animals, which at the McFetridges' included horses, swine, sheep, and chickens in addition to cattle. Edward and his family grew a variety of cereal and vegetable crops: wheat, oats, barley, buckwheat, Indian corn, potatoes, peas, and beans. The coupling of grain and hay cultivation with animal husbandry was especially common in Livingston County and throughout much of New York State.[2] When animals could not be put out to pasture, hay and grain were essential fodder; furthermore, some crops, such as buckwheat, provided farm-grown sustenance for members of the household, while, as the McFetridges' case suggests, others were marketable commodities.[3]

When storing the grain and hay used to feed people and animals, farmers must protect their harvested crops from the weather and from pests such as rats, mice, and birds. Today, corn, oats, and hay can all be preserved in various types of silos. Silos work to keep the crops moist in an airtight environment, enabling fermentation and the creation of a nutritious fodder for cows and sheep. Yet silos and the moist storage they create are relatively recent innovations, dating in the United States to the 1870s. Prior to that time, farmers concentrated on keeping grains and hay dry, often, like the McFetridges, in a multipurpose barn, in order to ensure preservation.

The wheat, rye, oats, and barley that the McFetridges grew are all classified as grains. The grain itself is found in the seed of the plant, and in order to be consumed by humans, it must be separated from the stalk, leaves, and tough seed covering. Once it is harvested, grain is threshed—or beaten—to loosen the seed covering and finally winnowed to separate the grain from the chaff. Today a combine cuts, threshes, and winnows grain crops, though traditionally threshing and winnowing were done on the threshing floor of the main barn. Then as now, after the initial processing, grain had to be stored in a farm building to protect it from moisture and pests.

Corn, sometimes referred to as maize, is also a cereal, but it requires slightly different processing and storage space than does a crop such as wheat. Corn can be harvested with the stalk, cob, and husk for silage, or the kernel can be separated from the other plant material and used as a grain (Figure 3.1). When corn is used for silage, it is harvested while still green. Corn grown for grain is allowed to dry in the field before farm workers collect the cobs. Corn harvested for its kernels must continue to dry and is therefore stored differently from other grains. Wet or green corn will become moldy, and consequently corncribs are designed to facilitate air circulation. At the same time, farm buildings used to store corn cannot be too open or the corn will be devoured by rodents and birds.

Like grains, hay needs to be protected from the weather. The term "hay" refers to grasses, like ryegrass or alfalfa, sometimes mixed with clover, which are harvested for use as feed when fresh grasses are not available or not desirable. Ideally, hay was—and still is—stored in haymows or haylofts within the main barn, where it was kept dry and easily accessible. It could also be stored without benefit of a building by gather-

Figure 3.1. Shucking corn, near Cortland, Cortland County. Captured on film in 1941, this group of men talk politics while husking corn. (Photograph by John Collier, October 1941, Library of Congress, Prints & Photographs Division, FSA-OWI Collection, LC-USF34-081217-D.)

ing it in a haystack. When hay had to be kept outside, some early New York farmers turned to a distinct type of structure known as a hay barrack or hay cap. Developed from Old World models and tied to New York's Dutch heritage, hay barracks, open on the sides, provided some shelter for piles of hay stored in the field. Beginning with these simple structures, New Yorkers have devised a variety of agricultural buildings to help protect their grass and cereal crops for future human and animal use.

Granaries and Other Grain Storage

In the colonial era, New York farmers and merchants developed a prosperous international trade in grain and flour. The governor in 1678 reported the export of sixty thousand bushels of grain. In the early eighteenth century, a report prepared for London officials noted of New York: "The Staple Commodity of the Province is Flower & Bread which is sent to all Parts of the West Indies we are allowed to trade with. . . . Several of our Neighbors upon the continent can not well subsist without our assistance as to Provisions for we yearly send Wheat & Flower to Boston & Rhode Island as well as to South Carolina." Throughout the colonial period, most of the grain and resulting flour shipped from New York City was grown nearby in the Hudson Valley and on Long Island.[4]

In the nineteenth century, the regional basis of grain cultivation shifted as new transportation networks and new settlers opened up rich lands farther west. In 1845, when agricultural census statistics were collected on a county-by-county basis, wheat and oats were harvested in every county in New York, including New York City. Barley and rye were only slightly less common crops. A new geographic pattern was becoming evident, however. Columbia County in the Hudson Valley harvested a significant quantity of oats and rye, but farmers in Ontario and Monroe counties, just south of Lake Ontario, were responsible for more wheat. Farms in central New York had the largest countywide yields of barley.[5] In the twentieth century, this pattern became further exaggerated. Wheat continued to be a major crop south of Lake Ontario and into the Finger Lakes region, while rye cultivation dropped precipitously in the Hudson Valley.[6]

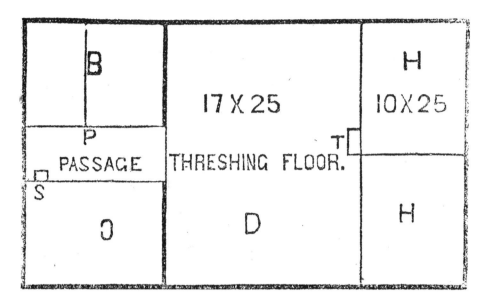

Figure 3.2. Floor plan for the upper level of a basement barn, 1853. The large center area is the threshing floor (D) with a trapdoor (labeled T) providing access to the lower level. Other spaces include cribs for corn and other grains (B, C), places for storing hay and oats (H), and a passage (P) with stairs (S) to the lower level. ("Plan of a Side-Hill Barn," *Moore's Rural New-Yorker* 4, no. 12 [March 19, 1853]: 93.)

Dutch barns, English barns, and multilevel basement barns were all designed to facilitate the processing and storage of grain as well as the housing of animals. When the botanist and author Peter Kalm described Dutch barns he had seen in the mid-eighteenth century, he noted, "In the middle was the threshing floor and above it, or in the loft or garret, they put the unthrashed [*sic*] grain, the straw, or anything else, according to the season."[7] Straw is the by-product of processing grain, the stalk of the plant which is not fit for human consumption but can be used for animal bedding, as part of winter animal feed, and even as the raw material for thatch roofs. In essence, Kalm was describing the Dutch barn as a multifunctional facility for collecting the harvested crop, processing it to release the grain, and storing at least one of the end products until it was needed.

The Dutch were not alone in this design idea. In fact English barns from the same period are sometimes referred to as three-bay threshing barns because their large center bay was created for threshing; on at least one side, mows provided storage for the crop.[8] A published "Plan of a Side-Hill Barn" from 1853 demonstrates how the same use and arrangement of space carried over into new multiple-level barn types; the center bay is labeled "threshing floor," and spaces to either side are designated as storage for oats, corn, and other grains (Figure 3.2). The location of a granary or grain bins within the barn near the threshing floor proved convenient in an era when farm goods had to be transported without the aid of elaborate machinery. Trapdoors in the floor provided an easy way to get feed and bedding to the animals below with the help of gravity.[9]

Figure 3.3. Cuyle farm granary, Unadilla, Otsego County. In order to keep out pests, granaries and corncribs were typically elevated. (Photo, Valerie Ingram, Archive of New York State Folklife 77–0018, New York State Historical Association Research Library, Cooperstown.)

Although valuable grain could be kept inside the main barn, ideally in an enclosed, protected space designed to keep out pests, farmers also found other storage solutions. Despite the added expense, some farmers chose to build a separate structure. Freestanding granaries were generally wood framed and tightly clad with wooden boards. Access was limited to one door on the gable end, and small vents high on the gable-end wall helped with air circulation. The interior was divided into bins for storage. Farmers needed the granary to protect grain crops from the weather, especially excess moisture that would cause spoilage, and also from rodents and insects. As a result, the ideal granary was elevated on stone, brick, or concrete piers (Figure 3.3). Metal or stone discs installed between the top of the piers and the flooring could help further defend against pests.

At least one inventive farmer, G. B. Johnson of the Brewerton area in Onondaga County, found a way to combine a "grain barn" with shelter for his sheep. He built the structure into a hill, providing a sheep stable on the ground level and grain storage above. In reporting on the building to the readers of *Moore's Rural New-Yorker,* Johnson boasted that "the granary . . . is like most granaries, except it is *proof against mice and rats,* is *lighted,* by a full-sized window, and the front of each bin can be taken out of the slides if necessary."[10] Combining grain storage with another function was typical in the nineteenth century, and though locating the granary within the main barn was the most common solution and highly advised in the agricultural press, freestanding granaries and other combination structures were not unknown.[11]

Figure 3.4. Depression-era grain storage bin, ca. 1930. Beginning in the late nineteenth century, metal grain bins began to replace wooden granary buildings. ("A 500-bushel portable bin of corrugated metal, mounted on skids," in U.S. Department of Agriculture, *Farm Bulk Storage for Small Grains,* Farmers' Bulletin no. 1636 [Washington, D.C.: Government Printing Office, 1930], 39; original Illinois State Library.)

With the coming of the twentieth century, the use of new equipment such as the combine, which completed the work of threshing and winnowing outside the barn, storing grain in the main barn began to loose favor. A series of inventors patented new types of structures for grain storage, making use of modern materials, specifically sheet metal (Figure 3.4).[12] In comparison to wood granaries, the structures, usually made of steel, had the advantage of offering more protection against weather,

Figure 3.5. Steel grain bins, Davy Farms, Albion, Orleans County. (Photograph by Jennie Davy, 2009.)

moisture, animals, and insects. Furthermore, in the event of a fire, steel would not burn and could even help prevent the spread of flames from the granary to other farm buildings.[13] The structures these inventors imagined, often round or polygonal in form, set the stage for the corrugated steel grain storage bins used on farms today (Figure 3.5).

Freestanding granaries and grain bins served the needs of farmers who grew and used their own grain, but when farmers produced grains for distant markets, more centrally located storage was also desirable. The grain elevator, invented in Buffalo in 1842 by Joseph Dart, was designed not for New York farmers but for merchants and transporters who oversaw the loading and unloading of grain from large ships on the Great Lakes to smaller boats using the Erie Canal. Grain elevators were designed to make the work of storage and distribution of grain easier by mechanizing lifting and consolidating location (Figure 3.6). By 1899 Buffalo, the major transfer point for grain grown in the Midwest, had forty-one grain elevators with a capacity of over 21 million bushels of grain.[14]

Grain elevators are recognizable by their height and location. Grain elevators are not found on farms but rather were located near major transportation routes such as canals and railroads (Figure 3.7). In some cases they operated in conjunction with

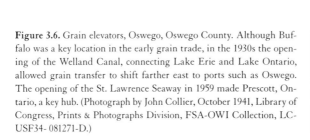

Figure 3.6. Grain elevators, Oswego, Oswego County. Although Buffalo was a key location in the early grain trade, in the 1930s the opening of the Welland Canal, connecting Lake Erie and Lake Ontario, allowed grain transfer to shift farther east to ports such as Oswego. The opening of the St. Lawrence Seaway in 1959 made Prescott, Ontario, a key hub. (Photograph by John Collier, October 1941, Library of Congress, Prints & Photographs Division, FSA-OWI Collection, LC-USF34- 081271-D.)

Figure 3.7. "Buffalo, New York. View from the pilot house of a grain boat from Deluth unloading wheat into a grain elevator on the Erie Canal," 1943. The FSA photographer who photographed this complex during the Second World War noted that in order to unload the ships, "'legs' are lowered into the hatches and draw grain into towers on endless belts of buckets." (Photograph by Marjory Collins, May 1943, Library of Congress, Prints & Photographs Division, FSA-OWI Collection, LC-USW3- 029165-C.)

mills at which grain was ground into flour. Originally grain elevators were made of wood and used buckets on a mechanized conveyor to transport grain. By the late nineteenth century, less fire-prone materials such as concrete and steel came into use.[15] Today, although Buffalo is no longer a major shipping port, and grain elevators there have largely been abandoned, Ogdensburg, New York, and Prescott, Ontario, on opposite sides of the St. Lawrence River, are major participants in the international grain trade.

Corncribs

Even before European settlers arrived in what would become New York State, corn was an important staple in American Indians' diets. European explorers noted that Iroquois groups along the Hudson and St. Lawrence Rivers raised maize. The legend of the "three sisters," recorded among the Mohawk years later, explained the system of planting corn in hills together with beans and squash, which the explorer Samuel de Champlain had observed in the early seventeenth century. Once harvested, corn

Figure 3.8. Baker farm corncrib and wagon shed, ca. 1882, Canadarago Lake area, Otsego County. The second floor of this stone building served as a corncrib with a slatted section providing for air circulation. The lower level was a wagon house with chutes from the crib above allowing for easy loading. (Photograph by Cynthia Falk, April 2010.)

was stored either in the upper level of Iroquois houses or in lined subterranean pits. When traveling along the Mohawk River in December 1634, for example, one European observed of the Mohawk people, "The houses were full of corn that they lay in store, and we saw maize; yes, in some of the houses more than 300 bushels."[16]

By the middle of the nineteenth century, New Yorkers, largely of European descent, on Long Island, in the Hudson Valley, and in the counties surrounding the Great Lakes and Finger Lakes grew more corn than those in other parts of the state. In Monroe County alone, over 900,000 bushels were harvested in 1864.[17] Corn could be kept in a designated area within a multiuse barn just like other grains. It could also be stored in a relatively small specialized structure known as a corncrib or a larger building known as a corn house. In some cases, corncribs were combined with other functions to create a multiuse building such as a corncrib–wagon house with chutes for transferring the corn from the upper level to the cart below (Figure 3.8).[18]

Like granaries used to store other grains, corncribs or corn houses were usually elevated to keep pests out. One agricultural writer noted, "To get a fine living, such as a well filled corn crib affords, rats will sometimes jump three feet high, hence a building, to be secure from their depredations, should have its lower floor three feet from the ground." The posts on which the corncrib sat—whether made of wood or masonry—could be capped with a metal disc to make it even harder for rodents to enter.[19]

Figure 3.9. Corncrib, 1869. As the agricultural press recognized, the typical basic corncrib had board slats and a shed roof. ("Corn Cribs Again," *Moore's Rural New-Yorker* 20, no. 43 (October 23, 1869): 677.)

Farmers usually constructed the walls of a corncrib from board slats applied over a wood frame either horizontally or vertically (Figure 3.9). Sometimes small round logs or poles were used instead (Figure 3.10). Regardless of building material, spaces left between the logs or boards allowed air circulation.[20] This open construction differentiates corncribs from granaries for other grains such as wheat, which were tightly clad.

The simplest corncribs had a single-pitch roof known as a shed roof, often made of boards. Larger examples had gable roofs with two corncribs, one down each side (Figure 3.11). The aisle between the two cribs could provide room for a wagon loaded with corn to be unloaded and then stored when not in use. It additionally served as a covered space where corn could be husked and shelled.[21] Regardless of roof type, eaves extended beyond the corncrib walls to help keep rainwater off the valuable crop.

For farmers who wanted even more protection from the weather, the side walls of a corncrib could be slanted so there was more room at the top of the crib than at the bottom (Figure 3.12). This helped further protect the corn from water shed from the roof. Additionally, it aided in unloading the corn from the bottom of the crib. *Moore's Rural New-Yorker* reported that a corncrib with slanted sides, vertical slats on the exterior, a gable roof, and an alley between two parallel cribs was "quite common in Western New York."[22]

Figure 3.10. Corncrib, Cattaraugus Reservation, ca. 1910. With a long history of growing and storing corn, the Seneca living on the Cattaraugus Reservation were using this crib, constructed of small logs, in the early twentieth century. (Arthur C. Parker, "New York State Museum Bulletin 144: Iroquois Uses of Maize and Other Food Plants," *Education Department Bulletin,* no. 482 [November 1, 1910], plate 7, published in University of the State of New York, *Indians of New York,* vol. 4 [Albany: University of the State of New York, 1897–1912].)

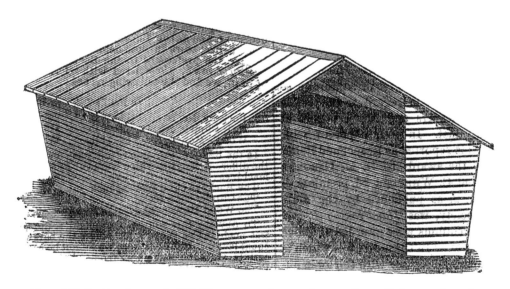

Figure 3.11. Double-crib corncrib, 1866. The open space between the two cribs provided a covered area for shucking as well as wagon storage. ("A Convenient Corn Crib," *Moore's Rural New-Yorker* 17, no. 40 [October 6, 1866]: 317.)

Figure 3.12. Corncrib, Migel estate and farm, Monroe, Orange County. Though quite sizable, this corn crib is of a typical form, with a pentagonal gable end, which kept water shed from the roof away from the dry corn inside. (Photograph by Rob Tucher, Summer 1997, Historic American Buildings Survey. NY, 36-MON, 2E-3.)

The difference between a corncrib and a corn house was one of scale as well as exterior finish and air circulation. Generally, corn houses were larger buildings tightly covered in boards, similar to granaries used for the storage of wheat or other cereal crops (Figure 3.13). In 1859 a farmer from North Rush in Monroe County asked fellow newspaper readers to suggest plans for a corn house. He explained: "Since the farmers of Old Monroe have been compelled to abandon wheat-growing, there is, consequently, more corn produced. . . . The curing in small cribs will do, but is not convenient for storing it after it is dry." The building he desired would keep out rodents, prevent mold and mildew, and include a small granary. Three responses to his inquiry all detailed sizable buildings, ranging from twenty to twenty-eight feet in length by ten feet or more in width. One, recommended by a farmer in Cadiz in Cattaraugus County, was raised on a full foundation rather than piers. Two readers specifically referred to their designs as corn houses, while the third described his variously as either a corncrib or a corn house. He concluded with a telling remark about corn storage: "A granary should be a separate building, for the simple reason that a crib should be made open, and a granary tight."[23]

Figure 3.13. Corn house, 1859. Though both were typically elevated on posts, a corn house was tightly clad, while a corncrib had open slats to allow air circulation. ("Design for a Corn House," *Moore's Rural New-Yorker* 10, no. 12 [March 19, 1859]: 93.)

Figure 3.14. Corncrib, Town of Warren, Herkimer County. Wire mesh helps hold the corn in place in this crib. (Photograph by Cynthia Falk, November 2009.)

Figure 3.15. Corncribs, near Weedsport, Cayuga County. These five corncribs show the variations in size, structure, and roof shape among twentieth-century circular cribs with wire mesh sides. Some patent applications show perforated sheet metal as another option for wall material. (Photograph by Cynthia Falk, June 2010.)

Corncribs constructed more recently have wider spaces between the boards, as wire mesh is used in addition to the slats to hold the corn in place (Figure 3.14). Circular corncribs, made with walls of metal wire mesh or even perforated corrugated sheet metal, provided alternatives to wooden corncribs beginning around 1900 (Figure 3.15).[24] As the twentieth century approached, however, silos began supplementing corncribs as places to store corn crops intended for animal consumption. By the 1930s, most acreage planted in corn in New York was harvested not for its grain but as silage or fodder, generally to be consumed by dairy cows.[25] As a result, it could be stored in closed silos as well as open cribs. Today, New York ranks behind only California, another top dairy-producing state, in the production of corn for silage. Corncribs, while still an identifiable feature of many farmsteads, are less essential than they once were.

Storing Hay

Hay barracks were introduced in the New World by Dutch settlers to New Netherland, and the form continued to be used even after the English took control of New York. Used to cover stored hay, these simple open-sided structures consisted of four or more wooden posts supporting a roof, usually of thatch, which could be raised or lowered to protect hay stacked beneath (Figure 3.16). Some hay barracks had a permanent location on a farm; they might have a stone foundation or posts set into

Figure 3.16. Reconstructed hay barrack, Herkimer Home State Historic Site, near Little Falls, Herkimer County. With a roof that could be raised or lowered, hay barracks protected the hay they covered from the worst weather. (Photograph by Cynthia Falk, February 2006.)

the ground. Other barracks were portable, set on skids so they could be moved to wherever they were needed.

The initial use of hay barracks is associated with New York's Dutch settlers, but the form was adopted by New Yorkers of other ethnicities as well. Hay barracks were erected from Long Island to western portions of the state. They were most common from the seventeenth through the early nineteenth centuries, although contributors to the agricultural press advocated for their construction as late as the second half of the nineteenth century (Figure 3.17), and some older structures were still in use into the twentieth century.[26]

Hay, the grass crop the barracks protected, can be grown on hilly terrain and in heavy soils that are not well suited for grain or other crops. Before the advent of the automobile and the decline of horse-drawn vehicles, hay was harvested throughout New York State, with high concentrations in the Hudson Valley to provide feed for horses and other animals in the city.[27] More recently, hay production has fallen off in the region surrounding New York City. The counties with the most acreage in hay are in the Adirondacks and Southern Tier, while the highest average yields per acre are found on the rich farmland of western and central New York.[28]

Figure 3.17. Hay barrack design, 1867. Although hay barracks are associated with Dutch settlement, they continued to be recommended and used on New York farms long after the colonial period. (*Moore's Rural New-Yorker* 17, no. 21 [May 25, 1867]: 165.)

Through the nineteenth century, hay was routinely cut by hand with scythes. Once cut, it was raked into small piles, or haycocks, and left to dry, or cure, in the field. New York farmers of the mid-nineteenth century were encouraged to cover their haycocks with hay caps made of fabric sheeting to protect them from dew and rain.[29] Farmers began using horse-powered mowers to cut grass crops in the second half of the nineteenth century. Hay rakes, also drawn by horses, created long rows of cut grass, known as windrows, in which hay could cure.[30] In the twentieth century, tractor-mounted mowers and rakes became the standard equipment for harvesting the hay crop.[31]

Once cut and cured, hay could be stored in three different ways: stacked or baled in open fields, sometimes with the protection of a hay barrack; loose in sheds or the haymows of barns; or in small bundles or bales in hay-drying sheds or in barns. Keeping as much hay as possible dry was the goal, as well as the reason for New York's early hay barracks. When kept outside in haystacks, the hay on the outside of the stack was damaged by moisture; the inside of a well constructed haystack, however, would stay protected for a number of years (Figure 3.18). Loose or bundled hay stored in a barrack, shed, or barn remained undamaged, so long as the roof did not leak, and remained fit for animal consumption for up to three years.[32]

The invention of the hay fork, a device used to transfer hay from wagons into haymows or lofts within the barn, made storing loose hay inside easier. A grasping device suspended from a track along the inside of the barn roof was lowered into a hay wagon, where the farmer loaded it with hay. Horses, guided by another person, provided the power to lift the hay up into the hayloft of the barn, where it could be stored until needed (Figure 3.19). One of the early patents for a hay fork, or hay

Figure 3.18. Haystack, The Farmers' Museum, Cooperstown, Otsego County. While the outer hay might be damaged by moisture, in a properly constructed haystack the interior hay can remain in good condition. (Photograph by Amy Gundrum Greene, 2006.)

BEARDSLEY'S HAY ELEVATOR, OR HORSE POWER FORK.

Figure 3.19. Barn with hay fork, 1861. Sometimes referred to as hay elevators, hay forks were powered by horses. They were lowered into the hay wagon and then lifted, loaded with hay, to the barn loft. (*Moore's Rural New-Yorker* 12, no. 12 [March 23, 1861]: 93.)

elevator, was filed by C. E. Gladding in 1858. The 1859 edition of *Moore's Rural New-Yorker* praised the invention:

> [We] were highly pleased with its operation. . . . It unloaded about a tun [*sic*] of hay, placing it in the loft of a livery stable, (the wagon standing in the street,) and pitching through a small door, doing its work in a very perfect and expeditious manner. From this test, in a difficult place,

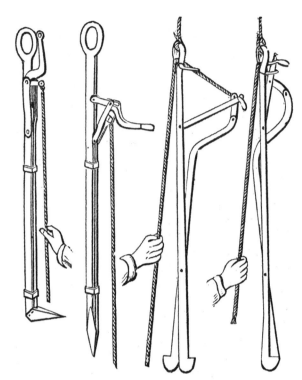

Figure 3.20. Harpoon-style hay fork, 1880. (Park Benjamin, ed., *Appleton's Cyclopedia of Applied Mechanics: A Dictionary of Mechanical Engineering and the Mechanical Arts,* vol. 1 [New York: D. Appleton and Co., 1880], 27.)

we are satisfied that the Elevator is a valuable labor-saving invention—the best machine for the purpose within our knowledge—and therefore commend it to the attention of all interested. It must prove a decided acquisition in the haying season.[33]

In the 1860s the hay fork became a popular agricultural tool, one that farmers continued to use at least through the end of the 1930s. Hay fork designs included the harpoon fork, which consisted of one or two prongs that pierced a hay load and transported it to a designated spot (Figure 3.20), and the grapple fork, a set of claw-shaped prongs that grasped a hay load and carried it to a specific location (Figure 3.21). The grapple fork, which could handle loose or baled hay, replaced the harpoon as the hay fork of choice during the early 1900s.[34] Hay forks required a power source, usually horses, to raise and lower them as well as to move them back and forth along the roof of the barn. Although they still required multiple farmhands to operate them, hay forks and other nineteenth-century innovations, as the agricultural press put it, "substituted mechanical and animal powers for human muscles at times when the demand for the latter is often far greater than the supply."[35]

The hay press, though slower to be adopted than the hay fork, was another invention that changed the way hay was stored (Figure 3.22). Hay presses, which were available as early as the mid-nineteenth century, were usually portable, moved from

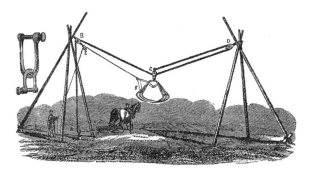

Figure 3.21. Grapple-style hay fork. ("Raymond's Hay and Straw Elevator," Broadside Collection, New York State Historical Association Research Library, Cooperstown.)

DEDERICK'S PORTABLE HAY PRESS.

Figure 3.22. Hay press, 1855. Although baling hay did not immediately become a common practice, hay presses, for compacting loose hay, were available before the Civil War. ("Dederick's Portable Hay Press," *Moore's Rural New-Yorker* 6, no. 20 [May 19, 1855]: 157.)

farm to farm, and used to create compressed bundles of hay.[36] In the early twentieth century, the term "hay press" was gradually replaced by "hay baler." The small bales these machines produced could be stacked on top of one another in open fields, sheds, or haymows. Baled hay was highly transportable, more readily sold, and easier to store in large quantities, causing farmers to turn away from loading loose hay into barns to baling and stacking it instead (Figure 3.23).[37]

New balers introduced in the late twentieth century can bind hay into massive cylindrical bales, which farmers usually leave in the fields like old-fashioned haystacks. Although it is not as distinctive as one of New York's Dutch hay barracks, the same ultimate function is accomplished today by the white plastic wrap that is often used to protect the large bales from moisture (Figure 3.24).

Figure 3.23. *Hay Wagons on Main Street,* 1910, by Arthur J. Telfer (1859–1954), dry collodion plate, C-5–08332. Hay formed into small bales was much easier to transport on a wagon and sell than loose hay. (Fenimore Art Museum, Cooperstown.)

Silos

The term "silo" brings to mind the towering structures located adjacent to barns. In practice, the word can be applied to a number of different storage options for silage, a moist, fermented fodder fed to cows and sheep. Silage, unlike the grains and grasses discussed earlier, is stored moist. Its high moisture content leads to fermentation in an oxygen-deprived environment, a process known as ensilage. Silage can be made from a variety of plant materials, especially corn, which is harvested and processed with the stalk, cob, and husk. Silage made from alfalfa may be referred to as haylage; that from oats is known as oatlage.

Silos for storing silage come in four principal forms: pits, towers, bunkers, and bags. In all forms, silos are a relatively recent introduction to the farm landscape. The earliest silos were storage pits located within the barn itself. In 1875 the *American Agriculturalist* published what may be the first account of an American example on a large dairy farm owned by the Brady family in Katonah, in Westchester County (Figure 3.25). The article explained:

> The pit in which the grains are stored, is a deep cellar, walled with stone and cement, and covered with a roof. A door from the bottom of the pit

Figure 3.24. Hay bales in white plastic wrap, near Schenevus, Otsego County. Large, cylindrical hay bales wrapped in plastic dot farmers' fields like giant marshmallows. (Photograph by Cynthia Falk, June 2010.)

Figure 3.25. Pit silo, 1877, Brady Farm, Katonah, Westchester County. In the earliest silos, most of the storage was below grade. (*American Agriculturalist* 36, no. 9 [September 1877]: 336.)

opens into the stable, and permits the removal of the grains as may be needed. In this pit several thousand bushels of grains may be stored, and being packed down closely, and kept from access of air, may be preserved in good order for months. It is upon a similar plan to this, that French farmers are now preserving their corn-fodder in a green state, until the new crop comes in.[38]

More than two years later authors were still commenting on the novelty of the arrangement—now using the term "silo"—and promoting its adoption for corn in the United States.[39]

Over the last two decades of the nineteenth century, farmers in New York and elsewhere experimented with silo forms. One of the chief concerns was how to fill the silo after the crop was harvested and then empty it as the silage was needed for feed. Pit silos could be easily loaded from the top but were often difficult and danger-ous to empty, owing to a buildup of toxic gases at the base. Tower silos, by contrast, required some sort of mechanical means to fill. When questioned in 1899 about fill-ing a twenty-four-foot-tall tower silo, the New York Bureau of Farmers' Institutes noted that horse power was not enough; an engine, at that time most likely powered by steam, was needed to elevate the crop material to the top of a tower silo.[40]

Tower silos were built either within or immediately outside the barn so that feed was convenient to where animals were housed. The first tower silos, originating in the

Figure 3.26. Stone silo, ca. 1890, Town of Williamson, Wayne County. Once attached to the side of a basement barn, this stone silo now stands divorced from the rest of the building of which it was a part. It is a rare example from the earliest days of tower silo usage when silos were built above ground with a square cross-section. (Photograph by Cynthia Falk, June 2010.)

1880s, were rectangular in form and consisted of a wood frame covered with vertical or horizontal boards. Sometimes the interior was lined with vertical tongue-and-groove boards, and the inside corners could be rounded off to create a polygonal shape.[41]

Progressive farmers understood that there were certain characteristics required for a good silo: strong walls that would allow the silage to be firmly packed, smooth walls that silage could slide down without leaving air pockets, and tight walls that

Figure 3.27. Wood stave (left) and concrete stave (far right) silos, Town of Warren, Herkimer County. The two round tower silos in the foreground were constructed with vertical tongue-and-groove wooden staves held in place by iron bands and turnbuckles. The third silo is composed of concrete staves. (Photograph by Cynthia Falk, November 2009.)

prevented air and moisture from getting inside. Because of New York's climate, silos were also expected to keep silage freezing to a minimum. And for economic reasons, the longevity of a silo was a concern.[42] The rectangular wooden silo was therefore not a good choice: it had corners in which silage could get trapped; it was not well insulated; and the wooden siding was subject to rot. Even more durable stone silos that were square in cross-section proved problematic as silage remained caught in the corners (Figure 3.26).

Farmers abandoned the rectangular silo for round tower silos in the 1890s. Although wood remained the chief building material, vertical tongue-and-groove staves, held in place with iron bands and turnbuckles, became the standard after 1894 (Figure 3.27). As a turn-of-the-century barn builders' guide noted: "The cheapest form of a silo is the round stave construction. . . . Probably the average life of a stave silo is somewhere between five and ten years. But a farmer can tear down and rebuild because the material is comparatively cheap and there is not much of it." An alternative to the cylindrical form was a wooden silo that was polygonal in cross-section. In either case, farmers usually ordered silos from a silo company, which in New York included the Harder Manufacturing Company in Cobleskill and the Unadilla Silo Company. The life of the wooden members could be extended to some extent by coating them in creosote.[43]

Figure 3.28. Harvestore silos and concrete stave silo, Roedale Farm, Town of Springfield, Otsego County. Blue Harvestore silos made of fiberglass bonded to sheets of metal often dwarf older wood or concrete silos. (Photograph by Cynthia Falk, November 2009.)

For those who wanted a material other than wood, fieldstone, brick, and clay tile were other options, although they all required the skills of a mason. Galvanized metal also provided an alternative.[44] It was concrete, however, that revolutionized tower silo building in the twentieth century. Round silos could be built out of curved concrete block, poured in place to create a monolithic concrete structure, or composed of precast vertical concrete staves held in place by metal hoops similar to those used on wooden stave silos. The last technique, which would become especially common, was developed in the first decade of the twentieth century. As one book on the topic predicted as early as 1883, "probably the larger number of silos built in this country will be of concrete," though of course at that date the author was thinking about pit silos rather than the towering variety that would largely replace them.[45]

After World War II, yet another material was added to the arsenal for silo construction. The A. O. Smith Company introduced a silo constructed from fiberglass bonded to sheets of metal. Known by the trade name Harvestore, these blue silos provided enough insulation to prevent silage from freezing, and they could be unloaded from the bottom, saving on the human labor required to feed stock (Figure 3.28). Harvestore silos were often larger than other types of tower silos, and they were also more expensive, which limited their use to large, prospering farms.[46]

Figure 3.29. Bunker silo, Town of Warren, Herkimer County. Old tires hold white plastic wrap on top of haylage. (Photograph by Cynthia Falk, November 2009.)

Figure 3.30. Haylage in white plastic "ag-bags," Town of Exeter, Otsego County. (Photograph by Cynthia Falk, January 2010.)

Today farmers continue to use tower silos, usually of concrete or fiberglass and metal panels, as well as two other silo types. Bunker silos recall the pits used to store silage in the late nineteenth century, although they are located outside rather than inside the barn (Figure 3.29). Often dug into the side of a hill, they are usually enclosed with concrete walls on three sides. Access for modern farm equipment is on the fourth, downhill side. Silage is protected by plastic tarps on top, often secured with automobile tires. Farmers use bunker silos, which can hold a large capacity, to store haylage. They became common after World War II in areas of large-scale dairying.[47]

Bag silos are the newest type of silage storage. White plastic bags, up to eight feet in diameter, can be filled with grass silage, such as hay. They provide maximum flexibility, as varying quantities of haylage can be stored, and the location of storage can be changed from year to year. Round or loaf shaped, bag silos are often found in fields, especially on dairy farms (Figure 3.30). They are an economical way to store grass silage on the modern farm.

The need to store grain and hay on the farm has resulted in some of New York State's most iconic agricultural buildings. In the colonial period, Dutch immigrants introduced the hay barrack, and its use for years after testifies to the persistence of Dutch culture even after the English crown assumed control of New York. Hay barracks, like Dutch barns, are distinctive forms that can be traced to a particular area with a specific cultural pedigree. While these impermanent structures do not survive intact today, their documentation in paintings, in written records, and through museum reconstructions attests to the long history of agriculture in the Empire State.

At the other end of the spectrum, the eye-catching tower silos that dot New York's rural landscape today were never unique to one area or group, and they do not have as long a history. They do, however, tangibly represent changes in agricultural practices in the late nineteenth and twentieth centuries. Often found on dairy farms, tower silos allowed for grass and grain crops to be stored moist and fermented, thus providing nutritious fodder. Like the granaries and corncribs that came before them, these storage structures give evidence of new ideas for solving old problems. Through their forms, they attest to the continual evolution of the traditional New York farmstead.

Chapter Four

A Farm Building for
Every Purpose

Monday [Oct.] 10—My birth day—Oh how the years roll! God give
me an increase of heavenly wisdom with an increase of years—Lewis
picked apples . . . [I] drew apples to R-ville—in evening self & wife
attended Clark's concert at Wilson—had about 150 in attendance.

Reuben L. Lamb, Town of Wilson, Niagara County, 1881

While Reuben Lamb's prayer in 1881 on his fifth-sixth was for heavenly wisdom, he did his best to ensure that he possessed worldly knowledge as well, especially when that knowledge could help him improve his Niagara County farm. Lamb cut out and saved newspaper articles on killing potato beetles, ants, and worms and making black ink, cement for repairs, and white sugar candy. But most of the clippings he pasted in the front and back of his diary were about fruit farming. He collected advice on using salt to keep worms away from apple trees and peach tree borers away from peach trees, as well as how to stop "peach yellows," caused, according to D. P. Penhallow, a professor in the Experimental Department at Houghton Farm in Mountainville, New York, by "improper nutrition, involving an excess of lime and a want of potash in the wood and fruit."[1]

Lamb and fellow farmers in Niagara County had a lot to gain by learning all they could about cultivating fruit. In the Town of Wilson alone, there were over 100,000 apple trees in 1875; the county as a whole boasted over a million apple trees in the same year.[2] But fruit farming was just part of the agricultural economy in the area. On Lamb's farm, the day after his birthday, he harvested corn and picked grapes while his children dug sweet potatoes. Although much of the work done by the Lambs occurred in a structure described simply as "the barn," certain crops required more specialized spaces for processing or storage. The Lambs' apples, for instance, went into a cellar, where they would keep longer on account of the cool temperatures. It is likely that the family's potatoes, beets, carrots, turnips, parsnips, and cabbage were stored in a similar manner. Lamb also transported apples from his farm to that of George Moote, since Moote had a "dryer," a building that allowed for the preservation of apples by reducing their moisture content.[3]

As Reuben Lamb's experience suggests, distinct crops often required specialized knowledge and skills to cultivate and process, as well as specialized buildings for storage or handling. Throughout the state's history, New York farmers have been leading producers of foods such as apples, grapes, cabbage, and maple products. In specific periods, other agricultural goods have served as staple crops. Hops, used in brewing beer, is one example of a comparatively short-lived but extremely important crop for the central New York farmers who grew it in the second half of the nineteenth century. Even tobacco, not generally thought of as a New York product, provided an important stream of revenue for farmers in Onondaga County in the decade following the Civil War.

Some of the most distinctive features on New York State farms are specialized structures that provided spaces to grow, store, dry, press, collect, and process various crops ranging from potatoes to honey. Farmers and inventors found ways to craft buildings that would efficiently protect delicate fruits and vegetables from freezing temperatures, provide perishable goods such as grapes in the off-season, shelter activities like maple syrup making that traditionally occurred outdoors, and reduce the moisture content in harvested plants such as hops and tobacco so they could be made into beer and cigars. In some cases, these buildings continue to be used much as they were in the past; in other cases, new technologies or competition from other regions has made once active farm buildings obsolete. In certain instances, growers have found ways to reuse such buildings in new endeavors, for example, housing winepresses in former potato barns.

Hop Houses

In the nineteenth and early twentieth centuries, hop houses were a common feature in the central New York State landscape. Inside these buildings farmers processed the seed cone, also known as the strobile, of the hop plant. The green hop cones contain lupulin, which provides the aroma, bitters, and distinctive taste of ales and beer. The prevalence of the hops industry prompted James Fenimore Cooper, grandson of the famous novelist, to label the nineteenth century a time when "hops were king" in New York.[4]

Imported hop plants from England were first introduced to the Massachusetts colony as early as 1629.[5] In 1633 the Dutch established a brewery in New Amsterdam.[6] It was not until 1808, however, that James D. Cooledge established the first commercial New York State hop yard, in Madison County, near Waterville. Cooledge migrated to New York State from Massachusetts, which had been the center of North American hops production since colonial times. From Waterville, hop growing spread throughout Madison and into neighboring Otsego and Oneida counties through the 1820s. In 1840 the census recorded 447,000 pounds of hops grown in New York. By 1855 New York State had eclipsed Massachusetts as the national leader, producing over 7 million pounds.[7]

The seed cones of hop plants must be harvested from the vine and dried before they are useful in brewing. While hops can be dried with the aid of only the wind and sun, a specialized building with a heat source made the process more efficient.[8] As an 1852 article explained, "hops as gathered, are damp and clammy, and are liable to mould. It will be necessary to dry them artificially, as soon as practicable. For this purpose, cheap, convenient dry houses, with kilns all prepared, are constructed by every hop grower."[9] When hops are initially picked, they contain approximately 70 to 75 percent water. In the hop house, the water content is reduced to 7 to 10 percent.[10] Throughout the nineteenth century, several building types provided farmers with the distinct spaces they needed to facilitate the process.

Common Hop Houses

The most typical, though certainly not the most distinctive, type of hop house in nineteenth-century New York State was a rectangular building, built from wood, with a gable roof (Figure 4.1). Now referred to as a common hop house, it was constructed according to a four-room plan, with two rooms on each of its two floors (Figure 4.2).[11] On the ground floor, one of the rooms was the kiln or stove room, which supplied the heat to dry the hops. The green hops were loaded through an exterior door into the second-floor drying room, located directly above the kiln room. Slatted wood floors in the drying room allowed hot air to circulate upwards from the kiln room (Figure 4.3). Burlap or another loosely woven cloth was laid on the floor to prevent hops from falling through and to protect the shape of the hops.[12] The drying room walls were plastered or covered with wooden boards to hold heat in. A cupola, located above the drying room, provided ventilation and encouraged the continued upward circulation of the stove-heated air.[13] In a building without one of these rooftop devices, windows for air circulation could be located on the gable ends or below the eaves of the roof in the drying room.

One or two doors provided access from the drying room to an adjoining second-floor storage room. The storage room was located a few feet lower than the drying room to make it easier to move the dried hops from one room to the next. Steep stairs afforded access between the two rooms. When hops were not being processed, the drying room was used for other storage.

Figure 4.1. Hop house, 1855–1860, originally in Burlington Flats, Otsego County, now at The Farmers' Museum, Cooperstown, Otsego County. This type of hop house, with a gable roof and cupola, is known as a common hop house. It is tightly clad with board and batten siding to help keep the hot air inside the building during the drying process. (Photograph by Cynthia Falk, March 2008.)

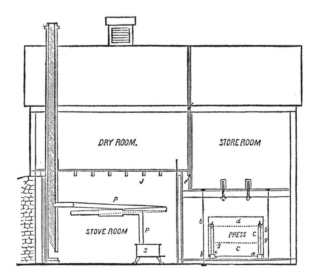

Figure 4.2. Section of a hop house, 1914. The stove in the stove room on the bottom floor provided the heat to dry the hops. Hop growers brought the hops into the "dry room" above, which had a slatted floor to allow the heat to rise. After drying, the hops were transferred to the storeroom, which was slightly lower than the dry room and directly above the press room. Before leaving the hop house, the dry hops were pressed for more economical shipping. (Herbert Myrick, *The Hop: Its Culture and Cure, Marketing and Manufacture* [Springfield, Mass.: Orange Judd, 1914], 195.)

Figure 4.3. Stove room ceiling at a common hop house located at the Parshall farm, Middlefield, Otsego County. A slatted ceiling allowed hot air from the stove to rise to the second floor, where the hops were dried. (1958 photograph from Florence P. Ward file, "Hops," folder 1, Special Collections, New York State Historical Association Research Library, Cooperstown.)

The fourth room, located underneath the storage room on the ground floor, was the press room (Figure 4.4). A chute, often created from burlap or another type of cloth, led from the storage room to the space below. Farmers used a press to consolidate the dried hops. The press compacted the dried hops into dense bales weighing about 180 pounds each, which would be shipped to commercial markets.[14] To ease in transporting the heavy bales of processed hops, hop houses were usually situated by main roads or rivers, and sometimes banked into a hill.[15]

Common hop houses built after the 1860s were typically larger with higher ceilings. From the exterior, what continued to differentiate the common hop house from newer types was its gable roof. Whereas new types of hop kilns often had circular or square floor plans and more complex roof shapes to assist with the drying process, common hop houses had rectangular forms and simple roof lines.

Draft-Kiln Hop Houses

In the late nineteenth century, hops gained increasing prominence in New York State. By the end of the century, American-grown hops were being exported to Great Britain and Continental Europe, Central and South America, the Caribbean, India, and even Australia.[16] An 1868 report proclaimed, "A hop fever rages in some portions of the land, and we are inclined to think it will go hard with many who have a full course of it."[17] The emergence of a "hop belt" in the middle of New York State primarily

Figure 4.4. Hop press, 1870–1900, located in the Pope Hop House, The Farmers' Museum, Cooperstown, Otsego County. The opening in the ceiling above the press allowed hops to be easily transferred from the storeroom above. (Photograph by Cynthia Falk, July 2010.)

Figure 4.5. Draft-kiln hop house, ca. 1878, Peter Parshal farm, Elmdale, near Whig Corners, Otsego County. A story about the hop harvest in the popular press featured this illustration of a hop house with the kiln and drying rooms in the tall pyramidal roofed section and the storage and press areas in the longer rectangular wing attached to it. (*Frank Leslie's Illustrated Newspaper* 47, no. 1201 [October 5, 1878]: 72.)

contributed to the high rates of production. The principal growing area stretched from Cooperstown and Middlefield in Otsego County to Waterville in Madison County and branched out to both the east and west to include portions of Oneida, Montgomery, and Herkimer counties.[18] The broader region of hops cultivation roughly corresponds with the path of today's Route 20 running west from Sharon Springs seventy miles east to Cazenovia, and stretching north and south about twenty miles.[19]

With hop fever in the second half of the nineteenth century came the second type of hop house, featuring a draft-kiln with either a pyramidal or conical roof (Figure 4.5). The draft-kiln type followed the same basic four-room plan as the common hop house, with kiln, drying, storage, and press rooms. The kiln and drying rooms, however, housed in a taller portion of the building with a distinctive roofline, were clearly differentiated from the storage and press rooms, located in a more typical rectangular gable-roofed wing. A cowl on the top of the roof above the kiln room replaced the stationary cupola of common hop houses on at least some draft kiln models (Figure 4.6). Made of sheet metal, it rotated with the wind to draw hot air upward from draft holes at the base of the structure. While wood—either of post and beam or lighter frame construction—was the primary building material, some pyramidal-roof hop houses had brick nogging within the interior to help maintain the drying temperatures required, and some were built at least in part of stone.

Figure 4.6. Metal cowls on pyramidal-roof hop kilns. Swinging sheet metal cowls rotated to capture the prevailing winds. (Illustration by J. P. Morgan, Waterville, N.Y., ca. 1880, in Ezra Meeker, *Hop Culture in the U.S.* [Puyallup, Washington Territory: E. Meeker & Co., 1883], following 94.)

For hop producers with economic means and a desire to experiment, round, conical-roof draft-kiln hop houses were sometimes built of fieldstone or cobblestone (Figure 4.7). This design had its architectural predecessor with the English oast house. The two-story stone building housed the kiln room on the first floor and the drying room above. An enclosed, elevated bridge provided access to a separate building, which contained the storage and press rooms.[20]

More common on farms that specialized in hops production were multiple hop houses, generally draft-kiln models, but sometimes common hop houses as well. More storage space could be achieved by building a separate, usually rectangular farm building to the side of a draft-kiln. Increased drying space could be created by erecting a hop house with twin draft kilns (Figure 4.8). The two kilns were located either along the width of the storage area or at opposite ends, spaced far enough apart to allow for adequate air circulation.[21] The twin draft-kilns were intended to increase the efficiency of drying and processing hops by sharing common storage and press areas. Also, the second kiln could continue production if one kiln malfunctioned.

Twentieth-Century Hop Houses

At the end of the nineteenth century, fierce domestic and international competition coupled with several poor harvests prompted New York farmers to lobby for legislation to place higher taxes on imported hops. An unsympathetic *New York Times* article that reported on the petitions from growers specifically informed readers of

Figure 4.7. Hop kiln, Wrobel Farms, near Bridgewater, Oneida County. This rare circular conical-roofed hop house was built of cobblestones. A bridge connected it to the adjoining hop barn. (Photograph by Cynthia Falk, September 2010.)

Figure 4.8. Twin draft-kiln hop house, 1893, Frank Parshall farm, Middlefield, Otsego County. A draft kiln with a pyramidal barn roof was located at either end of the central storage area of this late-nineteenth-century hop house. (Photograph from Florence P. Ward file, "Hops," folder 1, Special Collections, New York State Historical Association Research Library, Cooperstown.)

the considerable profits made by James F. Clark, the largest New York State hops producer in the 1880s.[22] Yet even Clark's "Hop City" in Otsego County, which included seven hop houses and living quarters for hundreds of seasonal hop pickers who traveled to Cooperstown by train (Figure 4.9), would not be able to survive the coming decades.[23]

By the late nineteenth century, New York faced competition in hops production not only from abroad but also from the West Coast. This area, especially surrounding Washington State's Yakima County, pioneered a new type of hop house, industrial in scale. Much larger than any previous hop house type, these buildings modified the four-room plan, utilizing innovations such as fan blasts, movable drying floors, and conveyor belts. The rapid West Coast development of this model in part caused New York to be eclipsed as the national leader in hops production by the early twentieth century.

Yet at the conclusion of the Prohibition Era at least one New York State farm invested in industrial-scale hop houses. The structures at Oneida Chief Farms, located near Bridgewater, serve as an example of the type (Figure 4.10).[24] Even the new

Figure 4.9. James F. Clark's "Hop City," near Cooperstown, Otsego County, ca. 1880. Twin-kiln hop houses line both sides of the road. (Photograph, Florence P. Ward file, "Hops," folder 1, Special Collections, New York State Historical Association Research Library, Cooperstown.)

Figure 4.10. Hop kilns and cooling and baling barn, Oneida Chief Farms, ca. 1940, near Bridgewater, Oneida County. (Photograph by Cynthia Falk, September 2010.)

buildings, however, could not combat West Coast competition, damaged crops from blight, mold, and pests, and the loss of momentum due to Prohibition legislation. New, larger complexes soon joined the majority of earlier hop houses as obsolete landmarks of a bygone era of hops production in New York. Today only a few New York farmers grow hops, and those who do operate on a small scale, filling the needs of local producers and microbrewers.

Vineyards and Wineries

New York State is currently the nation's third-largest producer of grapes by weight, trailing only California and Washington, and the country's largest producer of grape juice. The state's growers harvest an average of 175,000 tons of grapes, and New York has over one thousand vineyards, 255 wineries, five major juice manufacturers, and twenty-five table grape marketers.[25] Settlers had been trying to grow grapes in eastern New York since the late 1600s, but had little success growing European varieties and little taste for native New York grapes. Some farmers began to specialize in grapes in the early nineteenth century after more favorable grape varieties were introduced from other states.[26] The earliest documented evidence of large-scale growing was along the southern shore of Lake Erie by 1818, and shortly after in the Hudson Valley and the Finger Lakes region.[27] Many early vineyards produced table grapes that were sent to eastern cities through networks of turnpikes, railroads, and steamships.[28]

Brotherhood Winery, the first in New York, was established in 1839 in Washingtonville, near the Hudson River, and is the nation's oldest continuously operating winery. Most other early wineries were established near the Finger Lakes, especially at the base of Keuka Lake. The Pleasant Valley Wine Company was founded there in 1860, and by 1893 the Finger Lakes region was producing fourteen thousand tons of table grapes and six thousand tons of grapes for wine production.[29]

Prohibition, in effect from 1920 to 1933, was a major blow to most local grape growers and wine producers. Only a few wineries survived by producing grape juice, sacramental wine, and medicinal alcohol. Even after the Eighteenth Amendment was repealed, there was little resurgence in vineyard production until the 1970s. Some of the recovery was due to the work of Charles Fournier and Konstantin Frank, who pioneered the grafting of European *Vitis vinifera* varieties, such as chardonnay, Riesling, pinot noir, and cabernet sauvignon, onto hardier native grape rootstock.[30]

Another boost to the state's wine industry was the 1976 Farm Winery Act, which allowed direct sales from small wineries. In 2008, of the 255 wineries in New York State, 235 had been established after 1976.[31] Today, the major grape-growing areas of the state include the Finger Lakes, the Chautauqua region on the southeastern shore of Lake Erie, the Hudson Valley, the Niagara Escarpment, and Long Island. Sixty percent of grapes grown in New York are used for juice production, 35 percent for wine, and 5 percent for table consumption. Grape varieties commonly grown in the

Figure 4.11. Grape trellises and pickers, Silver Creek, Chautauqua County. (Postcard Collection, "Silver Creek," Special Collections, New York State Historical Association Research Library, Cooperstown.)

state have included Concord, Catawba, Delaware, Isabella, Clinton, Diana, Niagara, and Dutchess, and now include European varieties as well.[32]

Acres of trellis rows, rather than any distinct building, serve best to identify vineyards (Figure 4.11). Table grapes are sent off almost immediately, and grapes made into wine can be pressed in any building. The few building types that can historically be linked to wine and grape production include glass houses, wine cellars, and packing houses. Nearly all of the glass houses used to shelter and grow plants no longer exist, and a variety of buildings can be used to house the harvesting and pressing equipment. Many newer wineries are located on old chicken, fruit, potato, or dairy farms.

Glass Houses

Many nineteenth-century American wine drinkers preferred European grape varieties for their flavor and familiarity, but those same varieties had trouble surviving New York winters and native pests, specifically the insect phylloxera. Although the cultivation of European varieties would increase exponentially in the late twentieth century with the successful grafting of the vines onto hardier American rootstock, earlier grape growers who wanted to cater to the market had to experiment with ways to shelter their European grape plants.[33] Glass houses, with ceilings and walls constructed of glass panes, provided the right environment. Plants could be grown in raised beds, pots, or borders along the walls.[34] Glass houses had different architectural

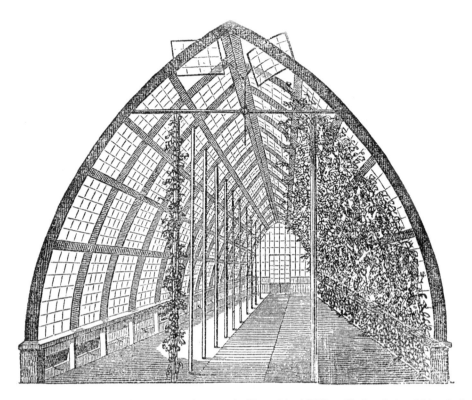

Figure 4.12. J.C. Green's cold grapery, ca. 1850, Borough of Staten Island. William Chorlton designed this arched-roof grapery. Windows near the ridge are open for ventilation. (William Chorlton, *The American Grape Grower's Guide* [New York: C.M. Saxton & Co., 1856], 23.)

elements depending on whether they were designed to start, speed up, or slow down plant growth, but they all served to protect the crop from the elements and from pests.

The term "grapery" could be used to describe nearly any glass house in which grapevines were grown, but it most often referred to buildings that sheltered plants but lacked artificial heating. The history of such cold graperies in New York can be traced to about 1840, when the first was erected in Hudson.[35] Graperies varied in appearance because of the shape of their roof, which could be gabled, arched, or a straight or curved lean-to (Figure 4.12). Various authors recommended different roof shapes for different reasons. A lean-to was the cheapest and simplest to construct, while an arch shape was considered "most agreeable to the eye," and a spanroof, a gable roof with glass on both sides, was judged "the best for a cold grapery" because it received sunlight from morning to evening. Experts suggested that cold graperies be placed on well-drained land, facing south or southeast to get maximum exposure to the sun's rays, and that they include a tank and pump to water the vines. Guides for growers generally recommended that grapes be planted in a border spanning either side of the exterior wall and prepared to a depth of two feet with loam, compost, and manure. Upper windows could sometimes be opened to help ventilate the space and ensure the vines, which were trained within the glass house, did not get too hot.[36]

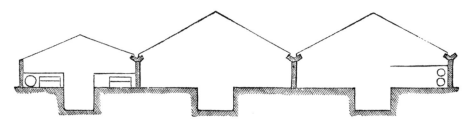

Figure 4.13. Succession houses. Instead of building a very long grapery, growers could build succession, or ridge and furrow, houses. The houses insulated one another, and plants could be easily moved between houses with different functions. In this diagram, a propagation house starts the chain of buildings on the left. (W. C. Strong, *Culture of the Grape* [Boston: J. E. Tilton and Co., 1866], 57.)

Instead of making glass houses very long, the grape grower could build multiple houses next to one another so that plants and equipment could be transferred more easily. These series of buildings were called succession, or ridge and furrow, houses (Figure 4.13). Plank gutters between the houses could be cleared of snow in the winter.[37] Commercial growers, such as Messrs. Parson & Co. of Flushing, were most likely to make the considerable investment necessary to build succession houses.[38] In 1854 the firm displayed fifteen varieties of hothouse grapes at the Queens County Agricultural Society, taking first premium.[39]

Other glass structures used to grow grapes had more specialized functions and were less common than graperies. To propagate means to increase, and propagation houses were glass buildings in which eyes of vines were cut and planted to start new grapevines (Figure 4.14). They typically had a glass gable, or span, roof and were low to the ground. Hot air flues or water pipes were used to raise the temperature of the planting beds gradually to promote rooting and growth. Water tanks and channels running beneath the beds could be made of brick, slate, iron, or wood. A central propagation pit, or walk, was cut into the ground to create more headroom for the people who tended the plants, as well as easy access to the heating system.[40] An inexpensive alternative to the propagation house was a hotbed, a low wooden structure with a glass sash roof that sheltered the plants and was heated by decomposing material and sunlight (Figure 4.15). Hotbeds could be any size but were generally about four to six feet on each side.[41]

In addition to simply sheltering plants, glass houses could also be used to supply ripe grapes in the off-season, when they were in greatest demand. Forcing houses, or early graperies, were glass structures used to produce a spring grape harvest. Plants would be put in the house in November, and by replicating spring and summer temperatures, growers could have grapes ripened by April. Forcing houses were usually south-facing lean-to structures with three glass walls and a brick or wooden wall on the north side (Figure 4.16).[42]

Retarding houses served the opposite function from forcing houses. By keeping the house cool, the grower could keep grapes dormant longer and make them ripen more slowly, ensuring a crop in late fall or early spring. Several greenhouse architects

Figure 4.14. Propagation house, 1876. Glass houses with gable roofs were known as "span"-roof houses. In this model propagation house, the raised planting beds have heating pipes running below. (Andrew S. Fuller, *The Grape Culturist* [New York: Orange Judd, 1867], 42.)

Figure 4.15. Hotbed with four sashes, 1876. Rather than build an expensive grapery, grape growers used hotbeds like this one as a cheaper way to start and protect young plants. Sunlight, fermenting plant matter, and manure would heat the bed. (Andrew S. Fuller, *The Grape Culturist* [New York: Orange Judd, 1867], 32.)

Figure 4.16. Plan for a grapery, 1859. Lean-to houses were often used to force or retard plant growth so grapes would ripen in the off-season. The narrow room on the north wall could be used as a storage and furnace room. (J. Fisk Allen, *A Practical Treatise on the Culture and Treatment of the Grape Vine* [New York: A. O. Moore, 1859], 31.)

and grape experts suggested that a west-facing lean-to house be used, though span-roof houses were also built. Heating equipment was needed only to protect the plants from fall frosts.[43]

Several greenhouse architects and grape experts wrote about glass buildings, but few were built in New York. Whether for viniculture, horticulture, or floriculture, glass houses were generally feasible only for large-scale growers or wealthy enthusiasts. After the introduction of better-tasting grape varieties, including hybrids of native American and European species, which could be grown outdoors, many of the old gable-roof glass graperies fell into decay.[44] Greenhouse architects working in the second half of the nineteenth century imagined their being replaced by elaborate curved-roof houses, but many growers simply never rebuilt.

Wineries and Cellars

Since grapes can be pressed in nearly any building, there is not necessarily a particular architectural style for wineries. Some wineries replicate buildings from the wine-growing regions of Europe, and some are located in reused farm buildings. The oldest wineries in New York State, however, did tend to have similar features. Storage and production areas were often multistory and made of local stone. Built into hillsides, they had double doors leading into cellars below. The stone and hillside location acted as insulation, keeping temperatures cool and steady for fermentation

SCIENTIFIC AMERICAN

[Entered at the Post Office of New York. N. Y., as Second Class Matter.]

A WEEKLY JOURNAL OF PRACTICAL INFORMATION, ART, SCIENCE, MECHANICS, CHEMISTRY AND MANUFACTURES.

Vol. XLIII.—No. 6
[NEW SERIES.]

NEW YORK, AUGUST 7, 1880.

[$3.20 per Annum.
[POSTAGE PREPAID.]

WINE MAKING.—THE URBANA WINE COMPANY, HAMMONDSPORT, N. Y.—[See page 84.]

Figure 4.17. Wine making at the Urbana Wine Company, Hammondsport, Steuben County. In 1880 *Scientific American* highlighted the accomplishments of Urbana Wine Company on Keuka Lake. The illustrations begin with exterior views of the main buildings on the property. Other pictures show the press room, wine and champagne cellars, and finishing room of this Finger Lakes winery. (*Scientific American* 43, no. 6 [August 7, 1880]: 79.)

Figure 4.18. Packing and shipping house, South Hector, Schuyler County. Painted on the front were the words "Cherries, Peaches and Grapes." This enclosed structure allowed sorting of fruit and packing on multiple levels, each of which was accessible to wagons or trucks. (Photograph by Amy Gundrum Greene, 2006.)

and storage. Grapes could be loaded into upper floors and transferred to presses below, and the juice stored in casks on the lower floors.[45]

Cool, dry, and well-ventilated cellars could be used to store grapes but were more important in the production of wine (Figure 4.17). Fermentation, or the conversion of sugar into alcohol, is dependent on temperature and has to be carefully regulated.[46] The oldest cellars in New York have stone walls and barrel-vaulted ceilings. Later examples may be built of brick. Today, fermentation and storage can be done in any facility with modern cooling technology.

Packing Houses

Besides sheds for equipment, packing houses were the only buildings directly related to grape harvesting. If a grower made wine on-site, grapes usually went directly from the vine to the winepress, meaning there was little need for storage. If grapes were to be kept for any length of time, they could be stored in any cool and ventilated space.[47] Grapes meant for the table or to be pressed at an off-site winery or juice plant had to be packed and shipped to market, which was often done by steamship or railroad.

Although any shelter would work, it was common for grape growers to build packing houses near cool lake locations or rail stations (Figure 4.18). Houses for packing and storing grapes usually had a ventilated cellar built into a hillside, a first floor used for packing and shipping, and second-floor storage. Packing houses not used for storage often lacked a cellar and had an overhang covering the driveway where fruit was loaded, a front packing room, and a rear short-term storage room. A half-story above was used to keep baskets or trays, crates, sorting tables, and barrel presses.[48] Many packing houses in New York packed a variety of produce, including grapes, peaches, apples, and cherries.

Orchards and Fruit Facilities

Fruit crops have been an important product for New York farmers since the colonial period. Apple trees were first planted on Long Island and in the Hudson Valley after 1700 and the first apple trees in western New York around 1750.[49] By the early nineteenth century, orchards were established from Grand Island near Buffalo to Long Island on the coast.[50] In the lower Genesee Valley in 1838, farmers grew apples, pears, plums, quinces, cherries, peaches, apricots, and nectarines.[51] During the mid-nineteenth century, New York dominated the cultivation of orchard products, leading the other states in crop value in 1850, 1860, and 1870.[52] In 1880 New York produced $8.4 million in orchard products, once again leading U.S. production. According to the 1880 census, all counties in New York, including New York County, grew some type of fruit.[53]

Historically, the largest-volume crops were peaches, pears, and apples. Similar buildings can be used for all of these fruits, but the processing of apples, the most abundant of the three crops, led to the greatest variety of building types. During the nineteenth century, it was not always easy to preserve fresh fruit throughout the year. Reuben Lamb in Niagara County sold many of his apples fresh right after they were picked. On October 24, 1885, for example, he reported the sale of his early crop, Rhode Island Greenings, for $1.25 per barrel. Six days later he sold 160 to 165 barrels of Baldwins, seven barrels of a type he called "Wispy," six barrels of Roxbury Russets, and two barrels of Spitzenbergs, all for $1.62 1/2 per barrel. On November 13, another 171 barrels brought in $277.[54]

Apples that were not sold immediately could be dried, canned, or converted to cider or vinegar. The Lambs, for example, took apples they harvested and did not sell fresh to be dried in an apple evaporator at the farm of George L. Moote.[55] Larger-scale, off-farm operations provided other options for processing apples by the second half of the nineteenth century. According to the 1870 federal census, New York could boast 274 cider mills, 49 vinegar manufactories, and 10 plants for canning or preserving fruit.[56] In 1874, over half a million barrels of cider were produced in the state, with the largest quantities coming from Erie, Monroe, and Onondaga counties—the counties where the cities of Buffalo, Rochester, and Syracuse are located. Of the more than 23 million bushels of apples harvested that year, Niagara, Wayne, and Westchester counties had the highest totals, more than a million each.[57]

Figure 4.19. Storage shed, near Lyons, Wayne County. Filled with empty crates that will be packed with apples in the fall, this simple pole barn–type building—constructed of metal trusses supported by metal posts—attests to the continued vitality of fruit farming in upstate New York. The apples trees, another important landscape feature, are visible in the background. (Photograph by Cynthia Falk, June 2010.)

In recent years New York has ranked second behind Washington State in apple production. Three major geographic areas of apple cultivation are, as they were in the nineteenth century, the southern shore of Lake Ontario, the Hudson Valley, and the Lake Champlain Valley.[58] A variety of building types, including those designed for packing, storage, cider making, and drying, facilitate the storing and processing of fruit (Figure 4.19).

Packing Houses

The harvesting of apples, peaches, pears, and other fruit crops was labor intensive. On Election Day in 1885 Reuben Lamb reported, "attendance light—people engaged very busily upon apples." On the Lamb farm that year, Augustus Newman and Henry Logan joined Lamb, Lamb's fifteen-year-old son Walton, and his eleven-year-old son Willie picking and packing. As with most fruit farmers of their era, their work did not involve a specialized structure. Once picked, fruits, especially apples, could be processed right in the field by packing them into boxes or barrels (Figure 4.20). At the Lambs', some protection from the weather was offered in the wagon house, where sorting occurred. And when the family could not obtain barrels for packing, the apples were temporarily stored in the barn.[59]

Figure 4.20. Apple harvesting, Clark Allis's apple orchards, Medina, Orleans County. Workers in the orchard, with bags worn over the shoulder, pack apples into barrels for shipment or storage. (Postcard collection, "Medina," Special Collections, New York State Historical Association Research Library, Cooperstown.)

In the twentieth century, some large-scale growers began to look to more specialized structures, such as packing sheds or packing houses, which allowed more thorough handling of fruit crops. According to an agricultural guidebook, there were many advantages to having a packing shed: it centralized the operation, the process could continue despite bad weather, labor-saving devices could be installed, and fruit packages could be kept cleaner.[60] Packing houses may also have helped to segregate seasonal laborers who harvested fruit from the farm family. Reuben Lamb's diary contained a news clipping from 1885 about a new law allowing for the arrest of tramps and vagrants, suggesting that even in the late nineteenth century, itinerant workers were met with suspicion. The feelings were likely heightened in later decades as seasonal workers traveled from farther afield to find employment.[61]

Packing facilities ranged in complexity and degree of permanence. Some were simple shelters over a workspace, while others incorporated mechanical devices such as machines to sort fruit by size. In the early twentieth century, the largest and most advanced had a capacity of 300 to 1,200 barrels and made use of conveyor belts and other features to increase efficiency. The optimum packing house, regardless of the size and level of mechanization, had ample floor space, a receiving platform, and a hillside location so that two floors could be easily accessed from the exterior.[62] Nevertheless, even with the advent of new building types and technologies, many fruit farmers continued packing their crops outdoors or in a portion of the barn. One Wayne County farmer reports that it was not until the 1950s that packing sheds came into use there.[63]

Figure 4.21. Charles Downing fruit house, before 1885, Newburgh, Orange County. Charles Downing, brother of Andrew Jackson Downing, was an accomplished New York fruit grower in the nineteenth century. A fruit house provided storage for the many varieties of apples and pears that he grew. (L. H. Bailey, *The Principles of Fruit Growing* [New York: Macmillan, 1918], 418.)

Storage Buildings

Apples and other fruits continue to ripen after they have been picked from the tree. Cold storage helps keep them from spoiling. According to a 1912 guide for apple growers, there were three methods of keeping stored fruit cool: ventilation, ice, and mechanical refrigeration.[64] For most of the nineteenth century, ventilation and ice were the only options available to farmers. By 1941, refrigerated storage was recommended as the best choice, with the temperature kept at 32 degrees Fahrenheit, just above the freezing point for apples, and the relative humidity at 85 percent.[65] Refrigeration, including refrigerated train cars to carry fresh fruit, allowed apples to be shipped greater distances and made it easier to store fruit.[66]

Prior to the widespread availability of mechanical refrigeration, farmers with small crops of apples stored them in cellars, using the insulative properties of the underground location to keep them cool.[67] Growers involved in commercial production might utilize specialty buildings that relied on ice to keep their fruit crops from spoiling (Figure 4.21). In the mid-nineteenth century, a series of inventors developed and patented various models for use and then sold rights to individual growers or

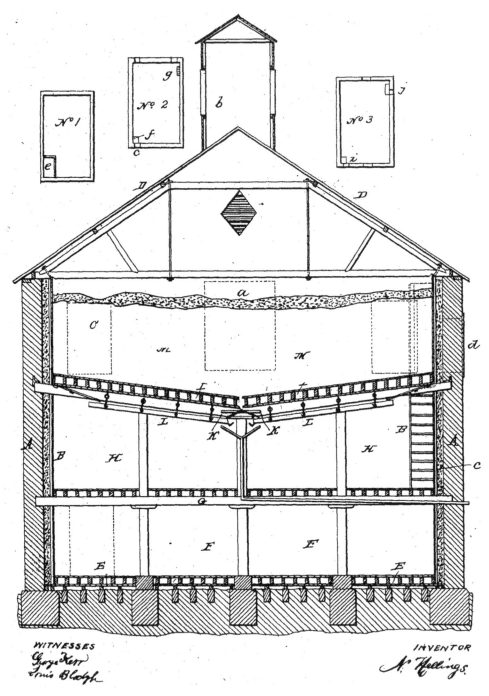

Figure 4.22. Section of a fruit house, 1867. Nathan Hellings's patent provided for a building with two levels of storerooms at the bottom. The space above was the ice chamber, which had a slanted watertight sheet iron floor and a drainage system to keep any water from reaching the fruit stored below. In the storage rooms, Hellings reported, the air temperature stayed at 33–37° Fahrenheit. (N. Hellings, "House for Preserving Fruit and Other Articles," U.S. Patent 69,806, issued October 15, 1867).

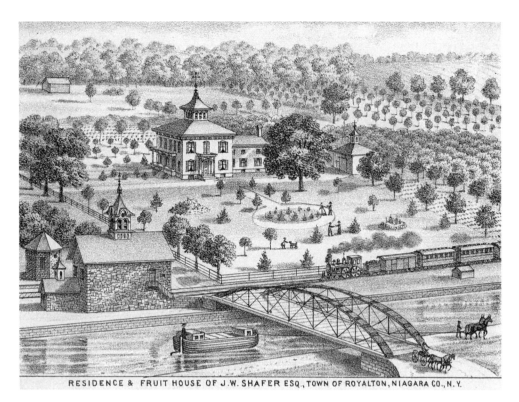

RESIDENCE & FRUIT HOUSE OF J.W. SHAFER ESQ., TOWN OF ROYALTON, NIAGARA CO., N.Y.

Figure 4.23. Residence, fruit house, and orchard of J. W. Shafer, Esq., 1878, Town of Royalton, Niagara County. Shafer's stone ice-cooled apple storage building was conveniently located adjacent to the Erie Canal and the train tracks to facilitate transportation of his crops. (*History of Niagara County, N.Y., with Illustrations Descriptive of Its Scenery, Private Residences, Public Buildings, Fine Blocks, and Important Manufactories* [New York: Sanford & Co., 1878], preceding 359.)

cooperative ventures, the latter often located in cities such as Rochester and Buffalo with ready access to transportation.[68] "Shephart's Patent Fruit and Vegetable Preserver" is one example of the type. It was described in 1849 as "a cellar for fruit, surrounded with a wall, inside of which are two boardings 6 or 12 inches apart, filled between with charcoal dust, tan, or sawdust. Over this is an ice-house . . . and as the ice melts it descends inside the boarding, runs to the centre of a tight floor, and then runs off."[69] In the ensuing years, "improved" models offered different variations on the concept. Inventor Nathan Hellings emphasized the importance of dry conditions in "preserving fruits, vegetables, meats, and all like articles of a perishable nature" (Figure 4.22). As he explained in his patent application for his fruit house in 1867, "the great purpose and the end actually attained is to preserve the air of the storage chamber pure, to maintain a temperature from 33° to 37° Fahrenheit, whatever quantity of fruits may be in store, and to prevent the deposit of moisture on any surfaces or walls, and also to prevent any dripping from the ceilings or ice-floor, or parts in contact with ice."[70] The Hellings model was embraced by fruit farmers like John W. Shafer of Gasport in Niagara County, whose sizable orchard was advantageously located on the Erie Canal (Figure 4.23).[71]

Figure 4.24. Kimlin Cider Mill, mid-1800s barn converted to cider mill, ca. 1925–1935, Poughkeepsie, Dutchess County. Part processing plant, part entertainment venue, cider mills like Ralph Kimlin's provided a place for locals to sample farm products. (Photograph by Neil Larson, Larson Fisher Associates, 2009.)

Although there were clear differences between the various models, all ice-cooled fruit houses needed to be of ample size and frost-proof. They could be built partially underground in a hillside or bank to take advantage of the natural insulating qualities of the earth around them. The flooring on the lower level, where the fruit was stored, could be simply dirt or later cement. Walls were of interlocking tile, thick stone, or wood-frame construction.[72] An 1859 source suggested that a fruit storage building could be made of anything as long as the structure kept out moisture, excluded light, and maintained a uniform temperature.[73]

Cider Mills

Although a press for making cider can be housed in an agricultural building designed for some other purpose, by the mid-nineteenth century, specific structures were being created for producing cider on a larger scale with the use of mechanical innovations. In 1874 *The Cider Makers' Manual* described the "Model Cider Mill" as "a large and commodious building in a suitable location" near the orchards and waterpower. Building the mill into the side of a hill would make each of the three floors accessible to wagons and would protect the building from the extremes of frost and heat. The lowest floor of the "Model Cider Mill" consisted of storage; the middle, the press room; and the top floor, the fruit room. Mechanical equipment helped growers unload apples, transfer fruit between levels, and press apples for cider and apple cider vinegar. The estimated expense of building and equipping the "Model Cider Mill" was $3,000 to $5,000 in 1874.[74]

Figure 4.25. Shaker Church family apple-drying kiln, Mount Lebanon, Columbia County. This stone dry house was built in the nineteenth century and demolished sometime after 1931. (Photograph by William F. Winter Jr., August 1931, Historic American Buildings Survey NY, 11-NELEB.V, 14-.)

In addition to offering dedicated space, multiple presses, and mechanical equipment, cider mills also provided commercial outlets. Between 1925 and 1935, Ralph Kimlin developed his cider mill in Poughkeepsie into a "Public Park and Game Conservancy" with a museum wing added to the back of the mill (Figure 4.24). Customers, including Vassar College students, would come to the mill for an outing.[75] Today some cider mills continue to serve this function, providing space not only to make cider but also to sell farm products and local crafts.

Evaporators

Before the widespread adoption of canning and freezing, a popular method of preserving fruit, particularly apples, was to dry them, a process that was also called evaporating. Its use peaked with World War I.[76] A room for drying could be provided within an existing structure simply by constructing a slatted floor over a coal fire.[77] The fruit rested on the slats and was dried by the heat. In apple-growing regions, dedicated buildings designed specifically for drying were also constructed.

Shaker communities in eastern New York, because of their communal nature, were one place where apple evaporators could be put to good use. Photographs

Figure 4.26. Fruit-drying kiln, Shaker North family, Mount Lebanon, Columbia County. Located within the washhouse, this drying area took advantage of heat from the water boilers below. (Photograph by N. E. Baldwin, February 1940, Historic American Buildings Survey, NY, 11-NELEB.V, 27–9.)

from the Historic American Buildings Survey document an apple-drying house on the Shaker Church family site in Mount Lebanon (Figure 4.25). At the nearby North family property, interior photographs of the washhouse from the 1930s show a fruit-drying area that made use of the heat from boilers for preparing hot water for laundry (Figure 4.26). Given the Shakers' income from selling seeds and the use of the upper floors of the washhouse for seed processing, it is likely that fruit-drying facilities were used for collecting seeds as well as preserving food.[78]

Farther west, evaporator buildings were an even more prominent part of the agricultural landscape in the fruit-growing regions of Wayne County (Figure 4.27). In 1904, in Sodus Township alone, there were 450 family-size evaporators.[79] Also known as dry houses, evaporators functioned much like hop houses, although the final product did not need to be pressed for shipment. A model apple evaporator described in 1906 consisted of two rooms in its upper story, one above a deep basement containing a coal furnace. Each room was sixteen feet square. One room was for preparing apples—paring, bleaching, and slicing—and the other, above the basement, was for drying (Figure 4.28). As in a hop house, the floor in the drying room

Figure 4.27. Apple-drying house, Rose Valley Farm, near Rose, Wayne County. Later used as a chicken house, this large dry house had a kiln and drying room on the left, a passageway at the center of the building, and preparation and packing room to the right. Here sulfur, burned at the far end of the building, was used to keep the apples white through the drying process, and mechanical equipment helped raise and lower apples between floors. (Photograph by Cynthia Falk, June 2010.)

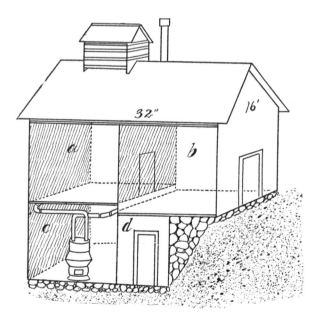

Figure 4.28. Apple evaporator, based on examples in Wayne County, New York. Built into a hillside, this model evaporator included a receiving room (labeled b), where the apples were cored, peeled, sliced, and bleached with sulfur; the drying room (labeled a); and the furnace room (labeled c), in which a coal-fired heater produced hot, dry conditions. (Byron David Halsted, *Barn Plans and Outbuildings*, rev. ed. [New York: Orange Judd, 1906], 367.)

was made of wooden slats with space left between them so that heat would rise more effectively to dry the produce.[80]

Vegetable Storage

New York has been a leader in vegetable cultivation since the mid-nineteenth century, currently ranking fifth in the nation in the value of fresh market vegetables. Crops produced in the rich farmland of the state feed local consumers, people in urban areas such as New York City, and in some cases international buyers. Vegetables such as cabbage, onions, snap beans, squash, cauliflower, and cucumbers are especially important to the state's agricultural economy. In 2009, for example, New York ranked third behind California and Florida in acreage planted with cabbage to be consumed fresh; the resulting 3 million pounds of cabbage had a value of more than $54 million.[81]

Structures for storing vegetables have been part of New York's agricultural landscape for over two centuries. While not all vegetable crops require specialized buildings for storage or processing, and many market vegetables are shipped away from the farm for sale almost immediately, farmers have constructed a few types of buildings to help keep their produce fresh. Although changes in technology, particularly mechanical refrigeration and faster forms of transportation, have decreased the need for such buildings on modern farm complexes, many that survive have been adapted for other useful functions.

Root Cellars

Until well into the twentieth century, farmers commonly stored their potatoes and other root vegetables such as turnips, beets, and carrots in root cellars, or root houses. In the winter, if these vegetables got too cold, they froze; in the summer, too much heat also caused spoilage. Root cellars were designed to provide a relatively constant temperature so the harvest could be stored until sold, used for family consumption, or even fed to animals. The author of one mid-nineteenth-century guide to raising hogs, for example, reported, "Almost all our common roots are well adapted for feeding pigs; carrots, turnips, parsnips, beet-root, and last, but not least, the potato, are all exceedingly nutritive, even when given in raw state."[82]

In the eighteenth century, root cellars were commonly constructed of native stone and sometimes plastered on the inside. They were built into a bank or hillside to take advantage of the natural insulation of the earth (Figure 4.29). The entrance was on the downhill side of the structure with a door large enough for a person to access the interior. During this time and into the nineteenth century, a small building was sometimes constructed on top of the cellar to hold storage baskets, rooting tools, and other agricultural implements.

Figure 4.29. Root cellar, before 1777, Herkimer Home State Historic Site, Little Falls vicinity, Herkimer County. The barrel-vaulted shape of the Herkimer root cellar, banked into a hill not far from the main house, provided ample storage for provisions and took advantage of the natural insulating properties of the earth. (Photograph by Lesley Poling, 2006.)

Farmers during the mid-nineteenth century recognized the necessity of root-raising to the farm economy and often built root cellars near livestock barns or, more conveniently, under the stock barn floor (Figure 4.30). Guides for farmers provided instructions for constructing a root cellar as part of the main barn or even beneath the farmhouse, where it could be used for vegetable storage as well for preserving dairy products.[83] Although by the second half of the nineteenth century the invention of mechanical refrigeration provided the potential to store roots and other vegetables in cool places other than root cellars, the use of the subterranean spaces did not die out. On November 1, 1900, Frank B. Ingraham, a farmer in South Bristol, Ontario County, reported in his dairy, "We dug potatoes & put them in the cellar a very nice day."[84]

Cabbage Houses

For over one hundred years New York has been a leading producer of cabbage. At present the counties south of Lake Ontario, including Genesee, Monroe, Ontario, and Orleans, are the largest producers of fresh market and processed cabbage. During the first half of the twentieth century, the counties of Onondaga and Cortland in central New York were also producing and storing large quantities of the vegetable.[85]

Figure 4.30. Basement barn plan, 1861, Ira Armstrong farm, Wheatland, Monroe County. Armstrong's barn, which won second place in a *Moore's Rural New-Yorker* competition, included a sizable root cellar (labeled B), where root crops for animal feed were stored. According to the accompanying description, "there is a large *Root Cellar* opening into the main hall or carriage floor [unlabeled but running through the center of the building], fifteen by twenty-three feet, convenient to both horse [labeled E] and cow [labeled F] stables" (*Moore's Rural New-Yorker* 12, no. 22 [June 1, 1861]: 173.)

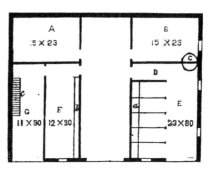

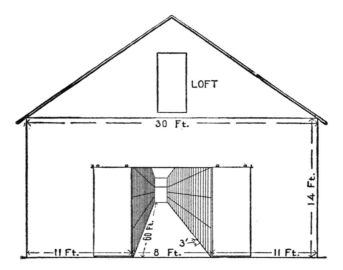

Figure 4.31. New York cabbage house, ca. 1900, based on an example near Rochester, Monroe County. A cabbage house such as this one could hold up to two hundred tons of cabbage. The loft above provided additional storage for barrels and crates. (Ralph L. Watts, *Vegetable Gardening* (New York: Orange Judd, 1912), 276; University of California Internet Archive.)

After cabbage was harvested, the crop needed to be stored until it could be consumed, taken to market, or shipped to a sauerkraut factory. One method for preserving cabbage heads was to bury them underground. In the fall of 1860, for example, Orville Slosson of Onondaga County reported that he had finished harvesting all the garden vegetables except the cabbage. These he had buried, but he felt that his crop would "need additional covering for cold weather."[86] For later New York farmers who raised large quantities of cabbage, especially for market, well-insulated cabbage houses offered an alterative to burying and covering or using a root cellar. These building were often constructed alongside railroad tracks to facilitate shipment, but smaller versions could be built on family farms. By the twentieth century, guides for vegetable growing recognized the distinct building type, which was referred to as a "New York Cabbage House" (Figure 4.31).[87]

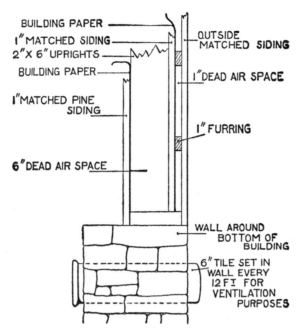

BUILDING PAPER

1" MATCHED SIDING

2" X 6" UPRIGHTS

BUILDING PAPER

OUTSIDE
MATCHED SIDING

1" DEAD AIR SPACE

1" MATCHED PINE
SIDING

1" FURRING

6" DEAD AIR SPACE

WALL AROUND
BOTTOM OF
BUILDING

6" TILE SET IN
WALL EVERY
12 FT FOR
VENTILATION
PURPOSES

Figure 4.32. Detail of wall construction, New York cabbage house. Storing cabbage required a careful balance between keeping the heads cool and controlling moisture that caused wilting while at the same time preventing freezing and allowing for adequate ventilation. Walls were constructed with a series of dead air spaces, and foundations contained ventilation holes to create the right conditions. (Ralph L. Watts, *Vegetable Gardening* [New York: Orange Judd, 1912], 277; University of California Internet Archive.).

Cabbage houses required ventilation as well as insulation. The walls of these wood-frame buildings were constructed in multiple layers with air pockets created to help protect the cabbage heads from the cold (Figure 4.32). Sometimes a layer of tarpaper was added between the first and second layer of framing. Some cabbage houses were even equipped with a boiler room. During frigid conditions, hot water would flow through the building via a pipe system to keep the cabbage from freezing.[88]

Generally, cabbage houses are more easily distinguished by their interior structure than their outside appearance. In fact, in the first half of the twentieth century, some were converted from tobacco sheds or other farm buildings. Inside, on either side of a central aisle, was a row of slatted bins which ran the length of the building (Figure 4.33). The bins measured as high as the structure itself, typically eight to fourteen feet, and could be as much as five feet wide. These bins were separated by approximately a foot of space, which, along with the slats, aided ventilation. At the peak of use, some large storage houses could hold at least three hundred tons of cabbage.[89]

Figure 4.33. Interior of a cabbage house, Tully, Onondaga County. On either side of the center aisle are floor-to-ceiling slatted bins that held the cabbage. (Photograph by Lesley Poling, 2006.)

Potato Houses

Although there is no specific potato barn building style exclusive to New York, census information clearly shows how integral potato farming has been to the state's economy: in 1855 the state's farmers produced about 15 million bushels of potatoes; by 1874 the figure had more than doubled to 36,639,601. Three regions have made up the heart of New York's potato production: west-central New York, eastern Long Island, and northern New York around the north rim of the Adirondack Mountains.[90] Potato houses, designed specifically for storing potatoes, were most common in New York from the last quarter of the nineteenth century into the twentieth century, and are often associated with Long Island farming (Figure 4.34). Owing to changes in New York's agricultural economy, many of these structures have been abandoned or remodeled to serve new purposes; hay and wine storage are two practical examples.

In early New York, potatoes were frequently stored in outdoor pits, root cellars, or the basements of barns or houses to prevent them from freezing. During the late nineteenth century, in response to the nation's rapid population growth and more efficient transportation networks, farmers needed larger, crop-specific buildings in which to store their harvest until it could be shipped to market. The lower level of potato houses, also known as potato barns, was built partially underground to keep

Figure 4.34. Potato barn, ca. 1950, Sagaponack, Suffolk County. At this concrete block Long Island potato barn, dirt was mounded on the outside to provide additional insulation for the root crop. (Photograph by Elizabeth Callahan, September 2010.)

potatoes cool and garden fresh without freezing before shipping. A typical potato house was two stories tall and built into a hillside with earth heaped around walls made of stone, concrete block, or poured concrete (Figure 4.35). This provided adequate insulation and protection against the weather.

Typically, potato houses had a gable, arched, or gambrel roof that could extend almost to the ground. Large double doors were located on the gable end. Ideally, the doors would have been lined to keep out frost in extreme cold weather. Inside the structure, the main level was divided by a center aisle. Slatted wooden bins on either side of this aisle held potatoes, which were often first packed in barrels. Potatoes stored loose in bins were ideally piled no higher than three feet to allow for ample ventilation. Sometimes a lower level also contained wooden bins, which were filled with potatoes via trapdoors in the upper level.[91]

Tobacco Barns

While tobacco has never been a major crop in New York, the Empire State saw a dramatic increase in tobacco farming immediately after the Civil War. Tobacco cultivation was centered in Onondaga County, particularly in the towns of Lysander, Van Buren, and Clay.[92] During the nineteenth and early twentieth centuries, Onondaga

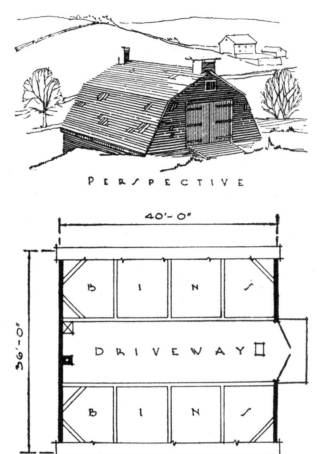

PERSPECTIVE

Figure 4.35. Potato house floor plan and perspective view, 1944. When large potato crops were harvested, a well-insulated building provided the most effective means of storage. This plan features "deep-bin storage," a technique recommended by the U.S. Department of Agriculture. (Deane G. Carter and W. A. Foster, *Farm Buildings* [Washington, D.C.: John Wiley & Sons for the United States Armed Forces Institute, 1944], 291.)

County consistently harvested roughly one third to one half of the total weight of tobacco grown in the state. In 1865, for example, New York State farmers produced 13 million pounds of tobacco, of which 4 million pounds came from Onondaga County. As more and more farmers began growing tobacco, an overabundance of the crop led to a plunge in prices.[93] Within ten years, many farmers had abandoned tobacco farming. By 1875 the numbers had decreased: Onondaga County produced 1.5 million pounds of New York State's total of 3.1 million.

It is important to look at New York's tobacco production in a national context. Compared with that of other states, New York's contribution was negligible—only 1.3 percent of the nation's total in 1859.[94] Other states known for their tobacco production such as Virginia and Kentucky accounted for one quarter each of the total tobacco crop grown in the United States. Because of the arduous cultivation process, weather, and market unpredictability, tobacco was considered a risky crop and one best grown as "a sideline for those engaged in diversified farming."[95]

Tobacco was not easy to grow in New York's variable climate. Diligent care, laborious cultivation, and the right kinds of buildings were imperative to the successful production of the crop. Generally, New York tobacco growers sowed seed imported

Figure 4.36. Onondaga County tobacco barn, 1897. Hinged vertical boards provide ventilation to aid in the curing of the tobacco leaves. (J. B. Killebrew and Herbert Myrick, *Tobacco Leaf: Its Culture and Cure, Marketing, and Manufacture* [New York: Orange Judd, 1897], 191.)

from Havana that produced a large, broad, silky leaf suitable for cigar wrappers.[96] In New York, tobacco farmers first sowed seeds in hotbeds in early April.[97] The farmers kept the hotbeds in a warm, sheltered dry spot. Careful weeding was crucial, and farmers monitored the seeds' early growth. As tobacco requires very rich land, *Moore's Rural New-Yorker* and other sources encouraged farmers to use "well-rotted" manure (preferably hog manure) in abundance and to prepare the ground by plowing.[98]

In early to mid-June, when tobacco plants were about three inches high, farmers set them out in the fields, planting them approximately every two feet in rows that were three feet apart. Farmers broke the tops of the plants off when flower buds appeared; the plants were ready for cutting about two weeks after topping, in early to mid-September. After the plants had been cut, farmers transported them to barns to dry. A suitable building, one erected specifically for the purpose of drying tobacco, was vital to the proper curing process.

Tobacco barns, which on average provided space for an acre of the crop, were frequently longer than they were wide, with a recommended size of thirty, thirty-six, or thirty-nine feet in width by forty-five feet in length.[99] They had a gable roof with a door at one or both gable ends. What further distinguished them from other type of barns were features that provided the necessary ventilation for the tobacco crop to air-cure. Tobacco barns in New York typically had vertical board siding; every four or five feet, one vertical board would be hinged to open and act as a ventilator (Figure 4.36).[100] Some barns also had horizontal roof ventilators along the ridge to aid

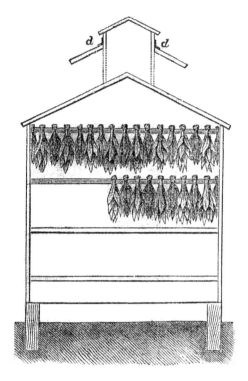

Figure 4.37. Tobacco hanging in a barn with a ridge ventilator. Based on a Connecticut example, this illustration includes a rooftop ventilator, considered "a great improvement on the old method, which consisted wholly of lateral ventilation." ("Tobacco Culture in Connecticut," *Moore's Rural New-Yorker* 25, no. 5 [February 10, 1872]: 98.)

the curing process, as was common in the Connecticut River Valley (Figure 4.37). Farmers could open and close ventilators at will, permitting dry breezes to enter or blocking strong winds and rain.

Inside, farmers hung tobacco from horizontal tiers of poles supported by framing on the side of the building and a row of posts through the middle. The poles were approximately four feet apart laterally and four and a half feet apart vertically. The first tier of poles was usually seven feet from the ground, which allowed for ventilation below the plants, lessening the likelihood of rot because of moisture. Farm workers used twine to fasten about three dozen plants to each pole. Another option was to spear the plants with a wooden rod immediately after they had been cut. The rod, holding eight to ten plants, would then be hung across the poles (Figure 4.38).[101]

As soon as the tobacco was sufficiently cured and the stem had hardened (usually in early December), farmers took the plants down, stripped the leaves from the stalks, and sorted them into different grades. This was usually done on a damp day to protect the leaves from injury. Many barns had attached stripping sheds. The largest, best-colored whole leaves were saved for cigar wrappers. Narrow, torn, or light-colored leaves were second class, often used as filler for cheap cigars.

In the years after the Civil War, there was a gradual improvement in the style, convenience, and character of tobacco barns. It was unusual to see a structure spe-

Figure 4.38. Tobacco leaves suspended on lath, Hamlin farm, Clay area, Onondaga County. (Published in the *Syracuse Post-Standard Pictorial,* December 1, 1957, collection of the Onondaga Historical Association Museum & Research Center, Syracuse.)

cifically for hanging and curing tobacco before the 1860s. Tobacco farming in New York experienced a dramatic growth immediately after the Civil War, and haphazard arrangements were supplanted by substantial buildings constructed for the sole purpose of hanging and curing tobacco.[102] As tobacco cultivation decreased, these structures were abandoned or repurposed; as cabbage became the dominant crop in the area, some found a new use as cabbage houses.

Sugar Bushes and Sap Houses

New York produced 17 percent of all maple syrup in the United States in 2005, making it the fourth-largest producer of maple syrup in the world.[103] Among the most prolific maple-producing counties are St. Lawrence County and Lewis County in the northern Adirondacks as well as Chautauqua and Cattaraugus counties in the southwestern corner of the state. Maple production also occurred throughout the Catskills, in northern New York, and in much of central New York.

Maple sap has traditionally been converted into two different products, maple sugar and maple syrup, the latter sometimes referred to historically as molasses. Through the late nineteenth century, maple sugar was used as an alternative to cane sugar. One French traveler who became acquainted with maple sugar while visiting the new United States in the late eighteenth century raved about its beneficial qualities, including the fact that it was produced without slave labor, unlike cane sugar from the Caribbean. He noted: "The maple is produced by nature; the sap to be extracted, requires no preparatory labour; it runs in February and March, a season unsuitable for other rural operations. Each tree, without injury to itself, gives twelve to fifteen gallons, which will produce at least five pounds of sugar. A man aided by four children, may easily, during four weeks running of the sap, make fifteen hundred pounds of sugar." According to this observer, American farmers could not only supply domestic needs but also "fill the markets of Europe with a sugar, the low price of which will ruin the sale of that of the islands."[104]

By the mid-nineteenth century, however, maple sugar had lost its status to refined white cane sugar. Susan Fenimore Cooper, daughter of the novelist, reported in 1850 that maple sugar was made "chiefly for home consumption on the farms" rather than to be sold internationally. She pointed to the future of maple products in New York when she further noted that some people preferred maple syrup to molasses from sugar cane because of its "peculiar flavor which is liked with puddings, or buckwheat cakes."[105] Indeed, the United States census shows a sharp growth in maple syrup production after 1850 and a corresponding decline in the production of maple sugar.[106]

Whether ultimately converted to sugar or syrup, maple sap has to be reduced, usually by boiling. Equipment used for this processing ranges from wooden troughs and iron cauldrons to sophisticated sap evaporation units. Regardless of the scale and technology employed, the production facility will be located in or near a sugar bush, a grove of sugar maple or black maple trees from which sap is drawn. The process is a simple one: appropriate trees are tapped and their sap is collected. The sap is boiled, allowing water to escape and the natural maple sugar to remain. The evaporation of the water leads to a thickening of the sap. As an alternative to boiling, maple sap can also be frozen in order to reduce the water content.[107]

Traditional collection techniques require buckets or other vessels to be hung directly underneath a tap penetrating the trunk of certain species of maple trees. Eighteenth-century reports of American Indian practices refer to quills or wood

SCENE IN A SUGAR BUSH, OTSEGO COUNTY, NEW YORK.—PHOTOGRAPHED BY A. S. AVERY, MORRIS, NEW YORK.—[SEE PAGE 286.]

Figure 4.39. *Scene in a Sugar Bush, Otsego County, New York,* ca. 1867, by A. S. Avery for *Harper's Weekly* (May 4, 1867), paper and ink, 8 11/16" x 11". This early spring outdoor scene illustrates buckets hanging on maple trees to collect sap and the open fire where the sap will be reduced in an iron kettle. (New York State Historical Association, Cooperstown, N0872.1963[02]. Photograph by Richard Walker.)

being used as taps.[108] Maple sugar makers collected the sap from each tree for processing. By the twentieth century, rather than hanging a bucket at each tree, producers used metal pipes and wooden troughs to transport sap from individual trees to a common collection area. Modern producers use plastic tubing, which is more elastic and sterile, to carry sap from trees to collecting tanks and the sugarhouse.

As a nineteenth-century print demonstrates, sap was often boiled down outdoors in a large cast iron pot suspended from a wooden frame over a fire (Figure 4.39). Evaporators, composed of an enclosed firebox and boiling pan, could also be used without the protection of any additional shelter (Figure 4.40). The desire for comfort, sanitation, and commercial-scale production, however, has led to the creation of larger evaporators usually located in a building alternately called a sap house or sugarhouse. The size and shape of the sap house is dictated by the evaporator within its walls. Additional concerns regarding production and fuel affect the building's design.

Figure 4.40. Maple evaporator, The Farmers' Museum, Cooperstown, Otsego County. Although sap could be boiled in a large iron pot, a shallow rectangular evaporator pan spread the sap out in a thin layer, allowing it to be reduced more quickly, therefore using less fuel and producing a lighter colored syrup. (Photograph by Cynthia Falk, March 2008.)

A sap house is most often situated at the foot of a hill, with the long side of the rectangular building parallel to the crest. It is usually a one-story structure with a low-pitched gable roof.[109] The low height of the building promotes quick release of the water evaporated in the sap-boiling process. A sap storage tank is attached to the building's exterior on the hillside, allowing for the gravitational flow of sap into the evaporator (Figure 4.41).

A ventilation system, designed to prevent unsanitary production and unsafe working conditions, is a key identifying hallmark of the sap house. When syrup production occurs inside a building, the steam that is generated from the evaporation process must have a way to escape. Traditionally a cupola, located directly over the evaporator and fitted with hinged vents, served this purpose. In modern facilities the evaporator is often hooded, and the cupola is replaced with a metal steam pipe rising at least one foot above the roof ridge.[110]

A sap house, generally rectangular in floor plan, may have an adjoining processing room, situated perpendicular to the room in which the evaporator is located, usually forming a T or L shape. The use of wood fuel requires a covered area adjacent to the sap house to store a standard cord for every sixty to seventy trees tapped.[111]

Bee Hives and Apiaries

Successful beekeeping, or apiculture, is contingent on the proper housing of its producer, the honeybee. Honey is a product made from plant nectar gathered by honeybees, naturally processed within the bee, and stored in the hive for consumption by the bee colony. A colony of bees can vary in size, and a single colony resides in a hive. Each colony is composed of a single queen bee, female worker bees, and male drone bees. The worker bees, the largest group in a colony, are responsible for gathering nectar, producing honey, and storing honey within the hive.

Beekeepers traditionally used straw skeps, wooden boxes, or natural containers such as hollowed logs to house bee colonies. Among the first hives in America were straw skeps, which are woven much like straw baskets into spherical containers (Figure 4.42). Americans soon turned to wooden boxes, however, because of the large quantity of available lumber and the lack of skilled skep weavers.[112] All of these different types of containers had the same disadvantage: the honeycomb was not removable. This meant that the hive and the colony were destroyed each time honey was collected.

Lorenzo Langstroth of Pennsylvania is credited as the father of modern beekeeping. In 1852 he patented a wooden box hive with removable frames on which bees would produce honeycomb (Figure 4.43). The practice of placing vertical frames into a box had been used for hundreds of years, but Langstroth discovered that setting the frames three eighths of an inch apart allowed bees to move freely without instinctively building the honeycomb into the next frame. This meant that the frames

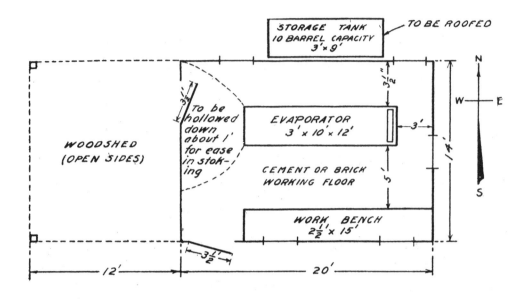

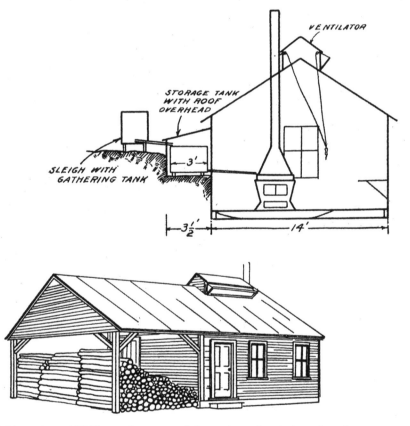

Figure 4.41. Model sugar house, 1935. The exterior storage tank for sap, the ventilator in the roof over the evaporator, and the covered wood storage area were key features of a sugar or sap house. (G. H. Collingwood, J. A. Cope, and M. P. Rasmussen, *The Production of Maple Sirup and Sugar in New York State,* Cornell Extension Bulletin 167 [Ithaca: New York State College of Agriculture at Cornell University, 1935], 37.)

Figure 4.42. Beehive, ca. 1829, maker unknown; straw, wood, string, and leather, 17 1/8" x 21 3/8". Before hives with removable frames, beekeepers housed their colonies in a variety of containers, including woven straw skeps. (Fenimore Art Museum, Cooperstown, F0036.1950. Photograph by Richard Walker.)

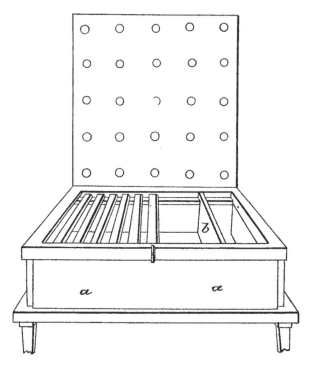

Figure 4.43. Langstroth hive, 1852. In previous styles of hives such as straw skeps, honeycombs had to be destroyed in order for the honey to be collected. As Langstroth noted in his patent application, "this often seriously annoys the bees and wastes the time of both the apiarian and the bees." Movable frames, installed 3/8" apart, made it possible to remove a section and collect honey without damage to the honeycomb. (Lorenzo L. Langstroth, "Bee Hive," sheet 2, United States Patent 9,300, issued October 5, 1852.)

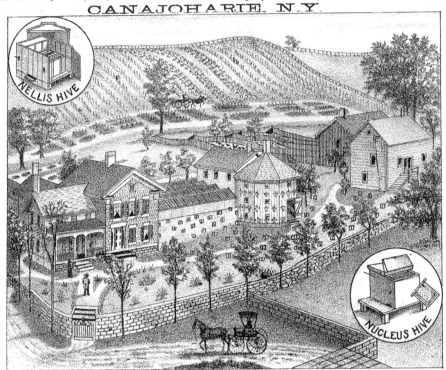

HODGE & STAFFORD,
Wholesale and Retail Dealers in
DRUGS, MEDICINES, PAINTS, OILS, BOOKS, STATIONERY, Etc.
CANAJOHARIE, N.Y.

STICHT & SHUBERT'S
BOOT and SHOE STORE.

SUBURBAN RESIDENCE OF
HORATIO NELLIS, CANAJOHARIE, N. Y.
Also the House, Apiary, and Work-Shop of J. H. NELLIS; and the Greenhouses, Seed and Flower Gardens, Poultry
House and Yards of A. C. NELLIS.

Figure 4.44. Residence of Horatio Nellis with the house, apiary, and workshop of J.H. Nellis and the greenhouses, seed and flower gardens, and poultry house of A. C. Nellis, 1878, Canajoharie, Montgomery County. The Nellis family engaged in a variety of different agricultural pursuits, but the artist responsible for this print decided to focus on beekeeping, highlighting hives in inset images. (*History of Montgomery and Fulton Counties, N.Y., with Illustrations Descriptive of Scenery, Private Residences, Public Buildings, Fine Blocks, and Important Manufactories* [New York: F. W. Beers & Co., 1878], plate following 96.)

would not be connected to one another by the bees, so each could be removed, the honey extracted, and the frames replaced without destroying the hive.[113]

In New York, Moses Quinby, of Coxsackie and then St. Johnsville, became one of the leading figures in beekeeping. In 1853, calling himself a "practical beekeeper," he published *Mysteries of Beekeeping Explained,* in which he described the advantages and disadvantages of the new changeable hives. Four years later, he and "a few neighbors" in Montgomery County produced over twenty thousand pounds of honey for market.[114] One of these neighbors may have been J. H. Nellis. In a county history produced in 1878, Nellis advertised himself as a "dealer in Italian bees." An illustration of the Nellis property includes an apiary surrounded by hives and two details of hive construction (Figure 4.44).[115]

Figure 4.45. Beehives, East Worcester area, Otsego County. Modern beekeepers continue to use hives based on principles developed in the nineteenth century. (Photograph by Cynthia Falk, June 2010.)

In 2005 New York State beekeepers produced a staggering 4.38 million pounds of honey, making New York the tenth-largest honey-producing state.[116] Today's beekeepers still use Langstroth hives, though slight adjustments have been made. The hive system begins at the boxes, called supers, which contain the bees and removeable frames (Figure 4.45). The bees build off the frames and form honeycombs, which are easily extracted from the hive. The bottom super is the brood super, essentially the living quarters of the hive. It sits on a bottom board, often placed on a foundation, commonly of cinderblock, to keep the hive safe from weather and invasion. A small gap or hole is provided at the base of the brood super to allow the bees access into and out of the hive.

Above the brood super is a combination of dadant and shallow supers, from which the honey is collected. The size of the hive and the equipment available to move the supers determines how many are stacked. Managing tall, multi-super hives necessitates mechanized equipment such as forklifts, and is nearly exclusive to commercial beekeepers. Most casual beekeepers maintain two-, three-, or four-level supers.

From honey to potatoes to apples to wine, New York farmers have specialized in a variety of agricultural products. While some crops are cultivated as part of a diversified growing strategy, in many cases fruit, vegetables, or similar cash crops have become the mainstay of individual farms or whole farming regions. Because of New

York's diverse topography, climate, and soil conditions, crops associated with specific areas, such as Long Island or the Niagara Escarpment, may not be profitable, or desirable, in other locations. Furthermore, consumer preferences, economic conditions, and technological innovations have made agricultural products like hops, tobacco, or dried apples popular among New York farmers at specific times.

Because many of the structures discussed in this chapter were designed to meet specific requirements for drying, pressing, preserving, propagating, or packing products as diverse as grapes, cabbage, and maple syrup, they convey the history of farming in New York State. Charting the location of certain building types, such as hop houses or tobacco barns, makes the range of production of these crops—in both time and space—a physically visible part of the landscape.

Chapter Five

POWERING THE FARM

On the day in question when we were about seven years old,
he persuaded me into Grandpa's barn, pointed to an empty bulb
socket overhead and handed me a pitch fork. I would see pretty
sparks, "like fireworks!" he promised, if I just touched the tine
of the pitchfork into the light socket. I believed him, as usual, and
next thing I knew I was on my back on the other side of the barn
floor and indeed, seeing all sorts of sparks.

JANE LAWLISS MURPHY, West Chazy, Clinton County

A memoir written by Jane Lawliss Murphy, filled with anecdotes about growing up on a farm in northern New York in the World War II era, attests to the transformation of agriculture and rural life in the twentieth century. When she was a child, her father physically transformed their West Chazy farmstead by enlarging the barn, building a silo, and adding a milk house. Family members milked the purebred Holstein cows with a milking machine and hauled full milk cans to the roadside, where they were picked up by a truck to be taken away to the cooperative dairy. Much of the work on the Lawliss farm was influenced by new tools, some of them in the form of machines, like those for milking and transporting milk, and some in the form of new procedures such as artificial insemination and sanitation inspections, less tangible but nonetheless central to changing patterns in agricultural production.[1]

Murphy's reflections on her childhood suggest her family's relationship with new technologies. Despite her near electrocution in her grandfather's barn, the arrival of electric lights and motors on the farm certainly made other activities, like milking before dawn or after dusk, less cumbersome. As Murphy remembered, "the lines looping from pole to pole along the road as far as the eye could follow were the threads that connected us to everything Out There."[2] Although her thoughts were focused on telephone rather than electrical lines, many of the innovations that farm families have adopted throughout the years have had a similar effect. Farmers like the Lawlisses have long incorporated the latest advances to make farm tasks more manageable and efficient, and often this involved lessening the metaphorical distance between the farm and the world "out there."

The rural landscape attests to the agricultural role of new technologies, especially those systems and pieces of equipment that provided power to help perform farm work. In the nineteenth century, inventors began to devise ways to mechanize the chopping, cutting, threshing, and transport of corn, wheat, and animal fodder, the distribution of water, and the transfer and reuse of animal waste. Power was provided for these tasks by horses, wind, steam and gasoline engines, and, as on the Lawliss farm in the mid-twentieth century, electricity.

Generally speaking, horse-powered devices and steam engines began to appear by the middle of the nineteenth century, with horse-powered machines remaining prevalent until the turn of the twentieth century. Gasoline-powered internal combustion engines emerged in the 1890s, and by the first decade of the twentieth century were considered practical alternatives to steam engines on the farm. Electric motors as a source of farm power were not common until the widespread electrification of rural areas in the 1930s and 1940s.

Windmills became a viable source of energy in some parts of New York State beginning in the 1850s, when technological developments allowed them to make the most of available winds. With the advent of more reliable sources of energy, such as the gasoline engine in the late nineteenth century and electricity in the twentieth, the use of windmills dwindled. Only today, with the high cost of energy produced from fossil fuels, are farmers beginning to explore anew the possibility of wind as a source of power.

Regardless of the type of power used, the barn's traditional threshing floor and its adjacent storage bins and haymows remained the focus of much of a day's work. Tall silos used to store animal feed were the most visible alteration to the farmstead as a result of access to power machinery, for without animal or machine power, it would have been impossible to load most silos in an efficient manner (Figure 5.1). Smaller ancillary buildings, such as pump houses, garages, and machine sheds, which protected new equipment, were also added to some farm complexes. Other new portable devices, including horse-powered treadmills, steam engines, and electric motors, allowed the farmer to bring the power source to the task rather than vice versa. As a result, some farm work could be done farther away from the main barn.

Not all farmers implemented new technologies immediately. Wealthy gentleman farmers and progressive farmers who strove to create model farms were more likely to utilize new energy sources when they first became available. Other farmers accepted or rejected tools like steam, gasoline, electric, and wind power as their needs

Figure 5.1. Heart's Delight Farm, ca. 1915, Chazy, Clinton County. Tall silos require a power source to be effectively filled. On the Heart's Delight Farm, a steam tractor is used to elevate feed corn. (William Henry Miner, *Heart's Delight Farm, Chazy, New York, U.S.A.* [Chicago: Lammers Shilling Company for W. H. Miner, ca. 1915], 86.)

dictated and finances allowed. What is important to remember, however, is that farming and technological innovation were never diametrically opposed and often went hand in hand. If a new device, such as a hay fork or mechanical water pump or even the telephone, could make work easier, it became part of the arsenal of tools that farmers put to use.

When Jane Lawliss Murphy's Irish ancestors first arrived in northern New York State in the mid-nineteenth century, they used animals and sheer muscle to clear the fields of stone. As Murphy described it: "A team of horses was driven up, down and across the acreage, dragging behind them a broad wooden platform called a stoneboat. As it scraped over the ground, the stones were tossed onto it one by one until the load reached the limit of the horses' strength. Hauled to the edge of the field, each stone then had to be lifted off." Murphy called the technique "onerous, backbreaking work."[3] Today, gasoline-powered tractors and other heavy equipment do similar jobs. Though clearing a field is still tedious, much of the physical labor has been transferred to machines. The transition is most apparent not in the field itself but in the silos where its crops are deposited for future use, and in the redesigned barn bays or new support buildings that have been constructed to house not animals but machines.

Horse Wheels and Treadmills

As on the Lawliss farm in generations past, animals once facilitated much of the work done in New York State's barns, barnyards, and fields. Although oxen and horses are called upon less frequently today, it is important to understand everything that animals were expected to do in order to appreciate fully the workings of the farmstead and older farm buildings. By the mid-nineteenth century, some farmers began to utilize equipment that allowed animal power, especially horsepower, to be used not only for tasks such as plowing and hauling but also for threshing, cutting, lifting, and grinding. References to horse wheels and treadmills appeared in New York's agricultural press by the 1840s and 1850s. These pieces of equipment allowed horses' walking motion to be translated into mechanical energy.

The horse wheel was a device that converted the movement of horses into power that could be used to perform other farm tasks (Figure 5.2). As the name suggests, horse wheels were circular in configuration: as horses walked around a ring-shaped track they turned gears that in turn powered equipment. Horse wheels could be permanent installations in a barn or other enclosed space, or they could be portable. By the 1840s, wealthy farmers in New York were increasingly incorporating this new technology, and the agricultural press praised and publicized their innovative installations (Figure 5.3).

The barn on the William D. Cook farm, as described in the *Transactions of the New-York State Agricultural Society* for 1846, housed the horse wheel in an attached shed "30 feet square" to accommodate "an inclosed [*sic*] tread wheel 28 feet in diameter."[4] The sheds used to house horse wheels typically extended from the front of the barn, with a set of doors opening toward the main doors of the barn. Cook's horse wheel powered a thresher and an elevator that carried straw "ten feet higher than the machine," presumably to a storage area.[5]

Horse wheels designed to be permanently installed in one place could also be located inside a barn, eliminating the need for an attached shed. John Delafield's stationary horse wheel, installed in the barn on his farm near Seneca Lake, is described in detail in the August 1847 issue of *The Cultivator:*

> A stationary horse-power, on which six horses, if needed, can be worked, is placed in the barn. By this power he [Delafield] threshes and winnows his grain, cuts all his hay, straw, and corn-stalks, and other fodder, cuts wood, cuts boards and timber into various shapes and sizes, and grinds corn, (cob and all,) or other grain.

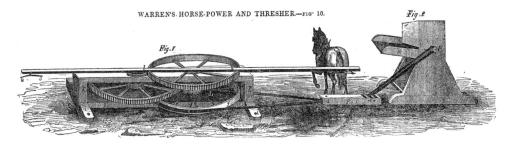

WARREN'S HORSE-POWER AND THRESHER.—FIG. 10.

Figure 5.2. Horse wheel and thresher, 1845. Using a "horse-power," a horse or horses walking in a circle could power a variety of mechanized agricultural equipment. The author of the accompanying article cautioned: "It is important to use steady horses. . . . Let the horses walk briskly, and go their circle about 4 times a minute." ("Warren's Horse-Power and Thresher," *American Agriculturist* 4, no. 2 [February 1845]: 60–61.)

LEWIS F. ALLEN'S BARN.

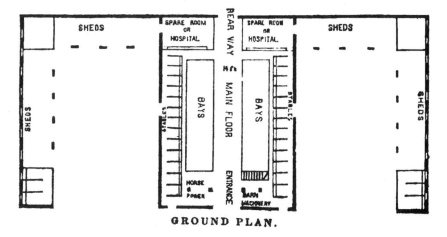

GROUND PLAN.

Figure 5.3. Lewis F. Allen barn, ca.1855, Grand Island, Erie County. Allen's barn featured a built-in horse wheel, marked "horse power" in the lower center section of the floor plan. ("Lewis F. Allen's Barn," *The Illustrated Annual Register of Rural Affairs and Cultivator Almanac for the Year 1855* [Albany: Luther Tucker, 1855], 180; original at Princeton University Library.)

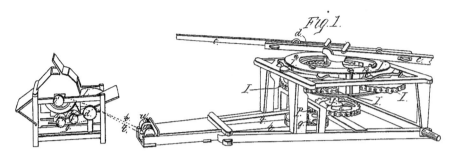

Figure 5.4. Horse power patent, 1847. David Anthony of Sharon, Schoharie County, submitted this drawing of his combination horse wheel and thresher with his patent application. (David Anthony, "Horse-Power," U.S. Patent 5,215, issued August 7, 1847.)

> The grain is threshed on the second floor. It is at once separated from
> the straw by an apparatus used for the purpose, and passes into the fan-
> ning-mill, which is in the basement, and is worked at the same time and
> by the same power which carries the thresher.

Delafield exemplifies the type of farmer who had the resources and inclination to incorporate a stationary horse wheel in his barn. Described in *The Cultivator* as "John
Delafield, Esq.," he had recently relocated from New York City. The article praised
him for his model farm, which provided "everything for the performance of the
various operations in the best manner."[6]

The grain is threshed on the second floor. It is at once separated from
Portable horse wheels, popularly known as sweep powers, were also available to
farmers by the 1840s, providing a means to move the horse wheel out of the barn
to wherever it was needed on the farm. The Sharon, New York, inventor and me-
chanic David Anthony patented a horse wheel and thresher in 1847 that displayed
the advances being made in animal-powered machines in the mid-nineteenth
century. Anthony's design for a "horse-power" required two horses harnessed to
levers—or sweeps—to walk in a circle around a central shaft that was connected to
a metal gearbox. A pulley attached to the gearbox drove a belt that was attached to a
thresher. After the threshing was completed, the horse wheel could be disassembled
and mounted on wheels to be pulled to a new location (Figure 5.4). Anthony sold his
patent rights and foundry for $5,500 to Reuben and Minard Harder, who manufac-
tured the apparatus as the "Harder thresher" at the Empire Agricultural Works of
Cobleskill.[7]

In addition to portable horse wheels, horse treadmills could also be used for powering threshers and other machines; in contrast to many horse wheels, they could be
moved easily by wagon from place to place and stored out of the way when not in
use (Figure 5.5). The Badger Machine Shop in Fly Creek, Otsego County, began the
manufacture of patented horse treadmills around 1840. Orestes Badger's design was
not the first for a horse treadmill (the novelty of his patent was found in a particular
aspect of treadmill design), but it was typical of devices produced by many similar

Figure 5.5. Portable treadmill, 1880–1910. The two horses on the treadmill provide power for a thresher. (New York State Archives. New York [State], Education Dept., Division of Visual Instruction, instructional glass lantern slides, ca. 1856–1939, ser. A3045–78, no. D47_Z4.)

agricultural implement factories in New York at the time. Looking much like a modern exercise treadmill, Badger's "endless chain horse power" used the walking motion of a horse to move an "endless floor," which in turn conveyed power to a flywheel on the side of the machine. The flywheel would then impart its motion to a belt that could be attached to a thresher, saw, crusher, or churn. Horse treadmills were used at least until the turn of the twentieth century; a reference to the utility in filling "small silos" with "a two-or three-horse tread" appeared in *A Book on Silage,* published in 1900.[8]

Windmills

Windmills became a viable source of energy starting in the 1850s, when innovations in design allowed them to turn automatically toward the wind and govern their own speed.[9] They could be used for numerous activities on farms including pumping

Figure 5.6. Farmstead, near Ithaca, Tompkins County. Farm Security Administration photographer Paul Carter explained that this portable windmill provided power to grind grain. He also noted during his 1936 visit: "Twenty years ago the farmer backed into his wife with their Model T Ford. This was fatal to their conjugal bliss. She made him move into the workshop." The workshop is pictured to the left of the windmill. (Photograph by Paul Carter, April 1936, Library of Congress, Prints & Photographs Division, FSA-OWI Collection, LC-USF341- 011052-B.)

water, grinding feed, sawing wood, chopping fodder, operating churns and washing machines, running shop machinery, draining swampland, irrigating fields, and distributing liquid manure (Figure 5.6). But windmills were never fully adopted in New York for most of these chores because of the unreliability of the wind. The one consistent use of windmills was for pumping water into a storage tower, tank, or cistern. This enabled water to be available even when the air was calm.[10]

The first patented windmill to self-regulate, or turn toward the wind and control its own speed, was exhibited at the New York State Fair in 1854. Invented by Daniel Halladay, it was "elevated on a single oak post a foot square" and consisted of five-foot-long wings composed of narrow boards secured to iron rods. In normal conditions, the boards were "thrown up edge to the wind" to capture its energy; when strong gusts threatened to damage the windmill, it would rotate and stand still with "the edge of the wings to the wind." A reporter for the *American Agriculturalist* noted soon after its invention, "Wind is undoubtedly the cheapest power that a farmer can use, and notwithstanding its inconstancy, if this improvement operates as well as it bids fair to in the single mills erected, it will be applied to many valuable uses."[11]

The following decades would usher in windmills designed with a circular arrangement of shutters or sails, first in wood and then, by the 1880s, in metal (Figure 5.7). Locally based companies such as the Empire Wind Mill Manufacturing Company of Syracuse, the Tornado Windmill Company of Elba (Genesee County), and the Automatic Wind Motor Company of Blasdell (Erie County), as well as firms from farther afield, made "American-style" windmills available to farmers in New York.[12]

While American-style windmills were most common, other windmill types have been used on New York State farms, including "Dutch" windmills, one distinct vertical wind turbine, and modern industrial horizontal-axis turbines. Four-sail European-style windmills, sometimes called "Dutch" because of their iconic association with Holland, were mounted on either a post or a tower-like building known as a smock. Built in New York in the seventeenth, eighteenth, and early nineteenth centuries, they required the operator to pivot the blades in order to catch the wind

Figure 5.7. Windmill, Stone Acre Farms, Phelps vicinity, Ontario County. Tall metal "American-style" windmills, often connected to a pump like this one, used wind energy to draw water for home and agricultural use. (Photograph by Cynthia Falk, June 2010.)

(Figure 5.8). European-style windmills often functioned as grain mills but could also be used to power sawmills or to pump water around the grounds of a farm. Although no known post mills survive, a group of smock mills are found on Long Island, where New England migrants built them to take advantage of flat land and the steady winds from the ocean.[13]

Likely the singular example of a vertical wind turbine on a New York State farm was built near Napoli in Cattaraugus County by George Gladden in 1890–91 (Figure 5.9). Gladden designed his four-story turbine to use wind power to elevate and grind grain, grate and press apples, and turn a wood lathe.[14] Gladden built his turbine at the end of the period of most intensive windmill usage. With the increased use of electricity in the twentieth century, windmills became less popular. Only today, in light of the high costs and environmental degradation associated with other fuels, are New York farmers beginning to utilize wind power again—usually renting land to power companies for the erection of multiple horizontal-axis wind turbines (Figure 5.10). Today's wind farms are generally constructed to supply electricity on an industrial scale to the larger power grid rather than to the farm itself.

Figure 5.8. Hook windmill, 1806, East Hampton, Suffolk County. This windmill utilized wind power to turn two sets of millstones within the "smock" that supported the rotating cap and sails. The center post at the Hook windmill is all that remains of a post mill built on the same site in 1736. (Photograph by Jet Lowe, 1978, Historic American Engineering Record, NY, 52-HAMTE, 2–36.)

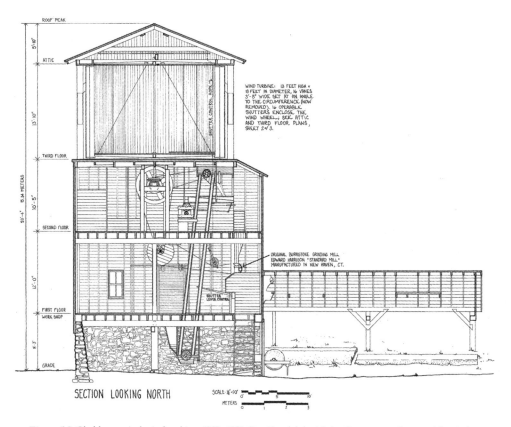

ROOF PEAK

ATTIC

WIND TURBINE: 13 FEET HIGH × 13 FEET IN DIAMETER, 16 VANES 3'-8" WIDE SET AT AN ANGLE TO THE CIRCUMFERENCE (NOW REMOVED), 16 OPERABLE SHUTTERS ENCLOSE THE WIND WHEEL; SEE ATTIC AND THIRD FLOOR PLANS, SHEET 2 & 3.

THIRD FLOOR

SECOND FLOOR

ORIGINAL BURRSTONE GRINDING MILL EDWARD HARRISON "STANDARD MILL" MANUFACTURED IN NEW HAVEN, CT.

FIRST FLOOR WORK SHOP

SHUTTER LEVER CONTROL

GRADE

SECTION LOOKING NORTH

SCALE: ⅛"=1'-0"   METERS

Figure 5.9. Gladden vertical wind turbine, 1890–1891, East Randolph vicinity, Cattaraugus County. After seeing an example in Lincoln, Nebraska, George Gladden decided to build a wind turbine on his farm. The resulting structure is the only known nineteenth-century vertical wind turbine in New York State. In a vertical wind turbine, the enclosed blades rotate parallel to the ground rather than perpendicular to it. (Drawing by Allen Lubow, 1975, Historic American Engineering Record, NY, 5-NAP, 1-.)

Steam and Gasoline Engines

By the 1850s, agricultural publications in New York were beginning to acknowledge the use of steam engines for threshing and "any kind of work to which stationary power is applied." In 1855 Gurdon Evans, writing for *The Cultivator,* noted the use of a "portable steam engine for farm purposes" in Madison County (Figure 5.11). Mounted on skids, the four-horsepower engine was used on multiple farms to operate "a threshing machine and cleaner." Evans recommended replacing horse power with steam power, pointing out that "the high prices of feed for teams as well as men, has this year especially impressed all with the necessity of curtailing as much as possible team labor."[15]

On estate farms and other large-scale operations, a steam engine could be permanently installed in an engine house and provide power for a variety of equipment. The William Crozier farm, located on Eatons Neck on the north shore of Long

Figure 5.10. Wind turbines, Madison area, Madison County. Located high on the ridgeline, today's wind turbines often sit on land leased by local farmers to power companies. (Photograph by Cynthia Falk, June 2010.)

Island, for example, had a brick and iron boiler and engine house that transmitted power to the main barn using a one-hundred-foot-long "endless wire rope." The wire rope entered the barn on the ground floor and turned a line shaft that powered a thresher, corn sheller, root cutter, hay cutter, and stalk cutter on the second floor and a gristmill, saw, and grindstone on the ground floor (Figure 5.12).[16] An engine house like that on the Crozier farm would be located in close proximity to the main barn or other building for which it provided power and could be readily identified by its smokestack or chimney (Figure 5.13).

While steam engines could be used to power farm machines inside the barn, they also had implications for work done away from the barn in the barnyard or adjoining fields. The steam traction engine, or steam tractor, which evolved between the 1870s and the 1890s, featured large iron wheels mounted at the rear of the engine and powered through a series of gears. A set of smaller wheels mounted under the front of the boiler made the steam engine mobile. Belts could connect the flywheel of the traction engine to a threshing machine in the barn or to an elevator used to fill silos with silage (see figure 5.1).[17]

An outgrowth of the steam traction engine was the gasoline tractor, which replaced the firebox, boiler, and steam-powered cylinders of the steam tractor with an internal combustion engine. Appearing by the 1890s and continuously improved into the first decades of the twentieth century, the gasoline tractor performed the same plowing, threshing, and silo-filling duties as the earlier steam tractor with-

PORTABLE STEAM ENGINE FOR FARM PURPOSES.

Figure 5.11. "Portable Steam Engine for Farm Purposes," 1855. An article in *The Cultivator* extolled the virtues of this engine, exhibited by A. M. Wood & Co. at the Madison County Fair in 1852. The steam engine sold for between $275 and $510, depending on the horsepower. ("Steam Power for Threshing and Other Farm Work," *The Cultivator,* 3rd ser., 3, no. 9 [September 1855]: 283.)

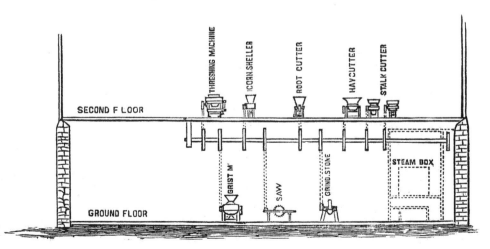

Figure 5.12. Crozier barn, ca. 1875, Eatons Neck, Suffolk County. The horizontal line shaft, just below the ceiling of the first floor, was used to power a threshing machine, corn sheller, root cutter, hay cutter, stalk cutter, gristmill, saw, and grindstone. A steam engine, located in a brick engine house about a hundred feet from the barn, provided the power to turn the shaft. (J. J. Thomas, "Steaming Food and Farm Management by William Crozier," in *Rural Affairs: A Practical and Copiously Illustrated Register of Rural Economy and Rural Taste,* vol. 7 [Albany: Luther Tucker, 1875], 133.)

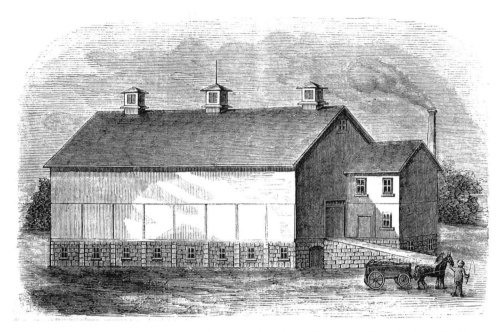

Figure 5.13. "Large Stock Barn" with engine house (on right), 1871. On the exterior of the engine house, the chimney stack provides evidence of the steam engine inside. (*Moore's Rural New-Yorker* 23, no. 15 [April 15, 1871]: 233.)

out the need for a nearby supply of wood, coal, or water for a boiler (Figures 5.14 and 5.15). By 1915 agricultural writers could extol the advantages of gasoline tractors over steam or animal power, citing their simplicity of operation and the gasoline tractor's ability to "be housed cheaper than the number of horses needed to do the same work . . . and it requires no care and does not eat or consume energy when not in use as animals do."[18]

The number of farms with tractors and other gas-powered equipment increased significantly in the ensuing decades. According to the 1920 federal census, fewer than eight thousand New York farms had a tractor. By 1930 that number had increased more than fivefold, with over forty thousand farms, or approximately one quarter of all New York farms, making use of the machine. That same year, census officials began recording the prevalence of stationary gas engines on farms: 40 percent of New York farms had one.[19]

The housing of tractors, and the increasing variety of other machines used on farms, required new buildings. Before the gasoline engine, farm equipment had been stored in a variety of places, including the main barn, sheds attached to the main barn, detached sheds, and wagon houses (Figure 5.16). Unlike horse-drawn implements, however, gasoline tractors carried with them the risk of fire, which made their storage in or near the main barn less desirable, since a fire would destroy not only the machinery but also the stored provisions and the animals. By the 1920s,

Figure 5.14. (left) Gasoline tractor, farm of Alfred Shaffner, Sugar Hill area, Schuyler County. The tractor provided power for other farm equipment through the flywheel and belt located on its side. (Photograph by Jack Delano, September 1940, Library of Congress, Prints & Photographs Division, FSA-OWI Collection, LC-USF34–041470-D.)

Figure 5.15. (right) Threshing at the farm of Alfred Shaffner. The threshing machine in this barn was powered by a gasoline tractor. (Photograph by Jack Delano, September 1940, Library of Congress, Prints & Photographs Division, FSA-OWI Collection, LC-USF34–041499-D.)

Figure 5.16. Wagon shed, ca. 1845, formerly located in Nassau, Rensselaer County, now at The Farmers' Museum, Cooperstown, Otsego County. Wagon, or drive, sheds provided covered space for farmers to store equipment long before the advent of the gasoline engine. This one is currently used at The Farmers' Museum to protect materials and tools used by the blacksmith. (Photograph by Cynthia Falk, October 2010.)

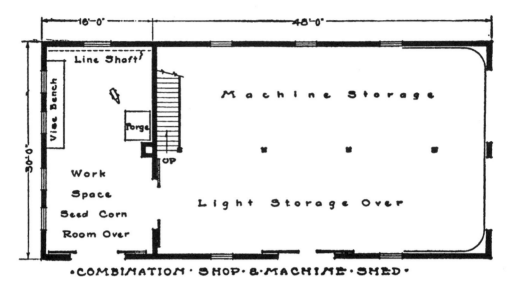

Figure 5.17. Plans for a shop and machine shed, 1922. Tractors and other equipment would be stored in the first-floor "machine storage" area, while other parts of this multiuse building provided work space and room for seed corn and other light storage. (W. A. Foster and Deane G. Carter, *Farm Buildings* [New York: John Wiley & Sons, 1922], 175.)

writers recommended inexpensive wood-frame buildings—constructed only well enough to exclude dust and rain—built for $400 to $500 to plans available from the United States Department of Agriculture. Published plans for machine sheds or machine houses typically depict a long rectangular building with a series of open bays or wide doors along one side (Figure 5.17).[20] Similarly, as farmers adopted the automobile, garages designed for cars and trucks replaced carriage houses and wagon houses on the farmstead.

The use of steam and gasoline engines additionally led to the need for pump houses to protect the equipment used to convey water for farm purposes. Many different devices, including simple bucket and pulley mechanisms, well sweeps, and most notably pumps, have been used to retrieve water from wells on New York State farms. The advantage of using a mechanical pump is that the well does not need to be open to the air, and therefore contamination can be curtailed. With the advent of steam-operated pumps in the mid-nineteenth century, gasoline pumps by the late 1800s, and electric pumps after the turn of the twentieth century, pump houses became necessary to protect the pump from the elements (Figure 5.18). Pump houses were generally wood-frame structures of simple construction. A door or hatchway, depending on the size of the structure, afforded access to the interior. Windows or latticework were useful for allowing light to enter but became less necessary as electricity was adopted.

Figure 5.18. Pump house, Mt. Vision, Otsego County. Pump houses protected the mechanical equipment required to draw water from harsh weather conditions. (Photograph by Cynthia Falk, 2009.)

Electricity on the Farm

Although the electric motor as a power source was available to some New York farmers in the first two decades of the twentieth century, its broad use depended on the electric grid, which had yet to reach most New York farms. Agricultural how-to books, including *Electricity for the Farm and Home* and *Farm Motors,* were by 1913 explaining the practicality of electric motors for supplying power for tasks including threshing, running gristmills, pumping water, and operating refrigerators. When electricity was not available from a central power plant, farmers were instructed on the costs of constructing an independent farm-based electrical plant. In New York, by 1913 hydroelectric facilities had been erected on several farms, including those of E. B. Miner near Oriskany Falls in Oneida County, J. Van Wagenen in Lawyersville in Schoharie County, J. T. McDonald near Delhi in Delaware County, and Heart's Delight Farm in Chazy, Clinton County. Nevertheless, in the early years of the twentieth century, as in later years, the independent generation of electricity for farm use was the exception rather than the rule.[21]

Figure 5.19. Road from Cooperstown to Fly Creek (now County Route 28), Otsego County. Utility poles brought twentieth-century farmers in rural New York electricity to power both agricultural and domestic equipment. (Photograph of "Road to Fly Creek" from the Florence Peaslee Ward Collection, New York State Historical Association Research Library, Cooperstown.)

The more widespread adoption of electricity and electric motors was dependent on both the willingness of private power companies to extend their wires into rural areas and the distribution of power at low rates where service already existed. According to the 1930 census, about a third of New York farm households reported a dwelling lighted by electricity. An even smaller number, about 15 percent, owned an electric motor for farm work.[22] Federal rural electrification programs in the 1930s and 1940s would be required before electricity—evidenced in historical photographs by the presence of utility poles and power lines—became more widely available to power machinery on the farm (Figure 5.19).[23]

While the term "barn" is likely to summon images of imposing structures with gable-roofed haylofts, basement cattle stanchions, and adjoining tall silos, New York farmers have made use of a much greater diversity of structures to house animals and machinery, store or process crops, and perform other important farm functions such as drawing water or powering equipment. These elements of the built environment provide a tangible chronology of the changes in agricultural practices and products over time. Perhaps nowhere is this more evident than in structures related to power, which have varied from horse stables, wheels, and treadmills to windmills, engine houses, and utility poles.

Farm buildings, however—through their location, construction, form, and use—convey more than just a simple timeline related to new technologies. They communicate information about the varying scale of operations by providing evidence of how many cows could be housed, bushels of corn or potatoes stored, or maple trees tapped. As a group, they chart agricultural strategies geared toward subsistence, diversified farming, and market-oriented cash crops. Their location attests to the relationship between the farm, transportation networks, and the broader community; their use to the regional dominance of certain crops within the Empire State. Additions or adaptations to increase square footage, incorporate new equipment, or shift to new products speak to transformations in the practice of agriculture.

Throughout the history of New York State, farmers have always been faced with choices. Traditional approaches have been balanced with the latest innovations, and change has been inevitable. Looking to the future of New York's rural landscape, we need to recognize that farming has always been a dynamic, as opposed to a static, practice. New types of buildings, such as freestall barns, address the needs of farmers today. Hay bales and silage stored in white plastic bags present an economical alternative to haylofts or tower silos and offer maximum flexibility in term of placement from year to year.

Yet many older farm buildings also have benefits and can be important resources for their owners and the local community. Constructed durably with materials and methods often unobtainable today, historic structures represent a storehouse of energy as well as knowledge. Their continued utilization is a sustainable alternative to new construction since it makes use of existing building materials and the power that put them in place. As farmers and consumers renew a commitment to organic and local products, historic farm buildings often provide the appropriate scale and spaces for farming regional crops in both traditional and innovative ways. Not only are these agricultural buildings appreciated for their architectural, aesthetic, and historic qualities, but rural communities looking to their past and the bucolic landscape as a way to foster economic growth in the form of tourism can benefit from their preservation as well.

Observing the New York countryside, it is easy to focus on abandoned barns and other farm buildings, which stand as evidence of no longer practical or profitable crops or practices. In the mid-nineteenth century, changes in viniculture made glass houses for sheltering European grape plants unnecessary, and it did not take long for the fragile structures to vanish from the landscape. In today's culture, however, adaptive reuse allows some types of seemingly obsolete structures to remain viable. With mechanical refrigeration, ice-cooled apple storage buildings, apple-drying houses, root cellars, and cabbage houses—all formerly essential for the storage and preservation of New York farm products—became vestiges of the past. Those that have survived into the twenty-first century were often converted for other purposes. In various parts of the state, hop houses and apple evaporators became chicken coops or machine sheds; dairy farms and potato barns became wineries.

New York barns serve as tangible reminders of the state's rich farming legacy. They speak to the history of certain locations, of specific periods, and of creative and tenacious individuals. In the museum setting, restored agricultural buildings help visitors understand the past, both its people and its practices. On working farms, historic barns also force us to consider the future—of farming, of food, and of the rural countryside. Through a better understanding of the construction, function, and appearance of agricultural buildings throughout New York State's history, we get a better sense of what comes next and what role continued use, and creative reuse, of farm buildings can play in the years ahead.

PLACES TO VISIT

Various museums and historic sites throughout New York State provide an opportunity to see old farm buildings and learn more about past agriculture and rural life. The properties listed here were identified while I was conducting research for this book.[1] At some sites, farming is the primary focus. At others, barns or outbuildings are interpreted only as they relate to a larger theme or mission. Museumgoers are encouraged to contact the institutions before visiting. Many of the buildings are open only seasonally and may have limited hours even during the summer months.

Albany County

ALTAMONT FAIR MUSEUMS
P.O. Box 506
129 Grand Street
Altamont, NY 12009
(518) 861-6671
http://altamontfair.com/about/museums

In 1994 a New World Dutch barn was moved from near Fort Plain in Montgomery County to the Altamont Fairgrounds. The barn is used by Old Songs, Inc., a group dedicated to preserving traditional music and dance, for its annual festival. Fairgoers can also visit the Antique Farm Machinery Museum to see demonstrations of historic farm equipment.

SHAKER HERITAGE SOCIETY
25 Meeting House Road
Albany, NY 12211
(518) 456-7890
www.shakerheritage.org

The Shaker Heritage Society preserves and interprets the Church family site, one of four areas within the larger Watervliet Shaker community. The property includes a 1916 Shaker-designed barn, which visitors can enjoy from the exterior. One of its distinctive features is an intact manure shed connected to the barn by a track to transport a manure cart.

Cayuga County

RURAL LIFE MUSEUM
Genoa Historical Association
P.O. Box 316
920 State Road 34B
King Ferry, NY 13081
(315) 364-8202
www.genoahistorical.org

The museum holds the Annual Wheat Harvest Festival on the first Saturday in August. Its property includes an English barn, which was originally constructed in the Town of Venice in 1810 and moved to the museum in 1991.

Columbia County

CLERMONT STATE HISTORIC SITE
One Clermont Avenue
Germantown, NY 12526
(518) 537-4240
http://nysparks.state.ny.us/historic-sites/16/details.aspx
www.friendsofclermont.org

Clermont was the Hudson River country seat of New York's prominent Livingston family. Although no agricultural buildings survive from the time of gentleman farmer Robert Livingston (1746–1813), who bred merino sheep and experimented with new crops and fertilizers, the visitor center is housed within a circa 1860 carriage barn.

HUDSON VALLEY OLD TIME POWER ASSOCIATION, INC.
190 Fingar Road
Hudson, NY 12534
(518) 822-1511
www.northerndutchess.com/hv-oldtimepower.htm

The Hudson Valley Old Time Power Association promotes interest in and preservation of the tools and equipment of yesterday's rural America. It hosts "Old Time

Days," featuring demonstrations of traditional agricultural power sources, the first weekend in October.

MOUNT LEBANON SHAKER VILLAGE
202 Shaker Road
New Lebanon, NY 12125
(518) 794-9100
www.shakermuseumandlibrary.org/mtlebanon.html

The former home of Mount Lebanon's North family group is owned by the Shaker Museum and Library and is currently being preserved with the goal of increasing public access. Until 1972, when a fire gutted the building, the centerpiece of the site was the two hundred–foot-long Great Stone Barn, constructed from 1857 to 1859. Today only the exterior stone walls of the barn remain, but a large 1838 granary speaks to the agricultural vitality of this community. A garden house and hothouse, the latter converted from a henhouse, demonstrate the Shakers' role in the garden seed industry.

OLANA STATE HISTORIC SITE
5720 Route 9G
Hudson, NY 12534
(518) 828-0135
www.olana.org

Olana, the estate of painter Frederic Edwin Church, is best known today for its castle-like Persian-style house. During Church family ownership, however, the property also included numerous agricultural buildings that were skillfully incorporated into the picturesque landscape. Today the main barn, stable, tool shed, pump house, and reconstructed wagon house serve as reminders that Olana was both a showplace and a working farm.

Delaware County

HANFORD MILLS MUSEUM
P.O. Box 99
73 County Highway 12
East Meredith, NY 13757
(607) 278-5744
www.hanfordmills.org

A mill site since 1846, for most of its commercial life Hanford Mills was owned and operated by the family of David Josiah Hanford, who purchased the mill in

1860. Under the Hanfords, the mill grew into a "rural industrial complex" that included a sawmill, gristmill, feed mill, woodworking shop, and hardware store. Over time the Hanfords used water, steam, and gasoline engines to power the mill and its electric dynamo. The mission of Hanford Mills Museum is to be a leading interpreter of the evolution of power generation and technology.

Dutchess County

MOUNT GULIAN HISTORIC SITE
145 Sterling Street
Beacon, NY 12508
(845) 831-8172
www.mountgulian.org

The Mount Gulian Historic Site is the colonial-period homestead of the Verplanck family. An early-eighteenth-century New World Dutch barn associated with the Verplancks was relocated from Hopewell Junction in Dutchess County to the Mount Gulian site in 1975. On the gable end of the barn, above the main doors, the upper level projects beyond the plane of the building, providing a novel way to shield the doors from bad weather and to increase ventilation.

STAATSBURGH STATE HISTORIC SITE
P.O. Box 308
Old Post Road
Staatsburg, NY 12580
(845) 889-8851
http://nysparks.state.ny.us/historic-sites/25/details.aspx
www.staatsburgh.org

Staatsburg is the former country estate of Ruth Livingston and Ogden Mills. The main house was extensively enlarged and remodeled by Stanford White in 1895, and the estate contains several large brick barns, most of which are contemporary with the main house. All of the barns are currently used for maintenance and storage, so only the exteriors can be accessed by visitors. Located nearby are three brick barns associated with Hoyt House, a mid-nineteenth-century estate designed by Calvert Vaux, which can also be viewed from the exterior.

Erie County

KNOX FARM STATE PARK
437 Buffalo Road
East Aurora, NY 14052

(716) 655-7200

http://nysparks.state.ny.us/parks/163/details.aspx

Ess Kay Farm, the estate farm of Buffalo's Knox family, was acquired by the state in 2000 for use as a public park. The agricultural buildings on the property were geared toward breeding and training horses, and the site is currently host to the East Aurora Carriage Drive and Competition.

Essex County

FORT TICONDEROGA

30 Fort Ti Road

Ticonderoga, NY 12883

(518) 585-2821

www.fortticonderoga.org

Fort Ticonderoga is best known for the pivotal role it played in the international conflicts of the eighteenth century. By the early twentieth century, the site was already being interpreted and preserved. The King's Garden at Fort Ticonderoga contains a Lord & Burnham greenhouse, built in the 1920s as part of the Colonial Revival movement and restored in 2004.

JOHN BROWN FARM STATE HISTORIC SITE

115 John Brown Road

Lake Placid, NY 12946

(518) 523-3900

http://nysparks.state.ny.us/historic-sites/29/details.aspx

This National Historic Landmark was the home and farm of abolitionist John Brown. Agricultural buildings on the property include a barn that was moved and rebuilt on the site.

SANTANONI PRESERVE

P.O. Box 113

North of Route 28N

Newcomb, NY 12852

(518) 582-3916

www.aarch.org/santanoni/santanoni.html

The preserve includes Great Camp Santanoni, the former estate of Robert C. Pruyn. Designed with the help of Edward Burnett, a prominent agriculturalist and farm designer, Santanoni had a sophisticated farm operation that consisted of more than twenty buildings and two hundred acres of cleared land. Many of the original farm buildings have been lost, but the herdsman's cottage, gardener's cottage, farm manager's cottage, smokehouse, creamery, and cold frames and hotbeds remain, as well as ruins of the barn and other smaller outbuildings.

Franklin County

WILDER HOMESTEAD
Almanzo and Laura Ingalls Wilder Association
P.O. Box 283
177 Stacy Road
Malone, NY 12953
(518) 483-1207
www.almanzowilderfarm.com

The Wilder Homestead, located in Burke, was the boyhood home of Almanzo Wilder, who later married Laura Ingalls. Her book *Farmer Boy* describes a year in Almanzo's life on this rural New York farm. The site includes the Wilder family house and reconstructed barns used to interpret the period from 1857 to 1875, when the Wilders moved to Minnesota.

Greene County

GREENE COUNTY HISTORICAL SOCIETY/BRONCK MUSEUM
P.O. Box 44
Coxsackie, NY 12051
(518) 731-6490
www.gchistory.org

The Greene County Historical Society and Bronck Museum includes a New World Dutch barn, an unusual thirteen-sided barn, a Victorian horse barn, and three supporting agricultural buildings, including a pigsty and chicken coop. The original farm, which dates to 1653, was a grain farm by the early 1700s, a milling complex in the 1720s, and later transitioned to dairying. The New World Dutch barn, built in the Revolutionary War era, now houses farm equipment and vehicles. The thirteen-sided barn is a three-story structure built in 1832 for hay storage. The horse barn has been turned into exhibit space for the historical society.

Herkimer County

HERKIMER HOME STATE HISTORIC SITE
200 State Route 169
Little Falls, NY 13365
(315) 823-0398
www.littlefallsny.com/HerkimerHome/Page1.htm

This site, which interprets the life of Revolutionary War general Nicholas Herkimer, includes an eighteenth-century root cellar and a reproduction hay barrack.

Although no eighteenth-century barns survive, a nineteenth-century barn on the property has been remodeled to serve as a visitors' center.

Jefferson County

STONE MILLS MUSEUM/NORTHERN NEW YORK AGRICULTURAL HISTORICAL SOCIETY
P.O. Box 108
34312 Route 180
La Fargeville, NY 13656
(315) 658-2353
www.stonemillsmuseum.org

The Stone Mills Museum tells the story of the development of agriculture in northern New York State, including Jefferson, St. Lawrence, Lewis, and Oswego counties. The site includes a carriage house, a relocated icehouse, and a late-twentieth-century storage barn, which is now used for exhibits. Across the street, visitors can tour a cheese factory, built in 1896 for a dairy cooperative and later donated to the historical society.

Lewis County

ADIRONDACK MENNONITE HERITAGE FARM
Adirondack Mennonite Heritage Association & Historical Society
P.O. Box 368
8778 Erie Canal Road
Croghan, NY 13327
(315) 346-1122
www.mennoniteheritagefarm.com

Located in Kirschnerville, near Croghan, the Adirondack Mennonite Heritage Farm preserves the homestead of John and Joseph Moser, who emigrated from Europe in the 1830s. The Moser farm served three generations of this Mennonite family. The site is used to interpret the Mennonite faith and local history. It features the homestead, which was used as a religious meeting place into the twentieth century, two barns, a granary, and a garage.

AMERICAN MAPLE MUSEUM
9753 State Route 812
Croghan, NY 13327
(315) 346-1107
www.americanmaplemuseum.org

The American Maple Museum interprets and preserves the history of maple syrup production in North America. Displays include maple sugar evaporators, wooden storage tanks, and other equipment used in sap collection and processing. A replica sugarhouse is located within the museum.

Madison County

LORENZO STATE HISTORIC SITE
17 Rippleton Road
Cazenovia, NY 13035
(315) 655-3200
http://nysparks.state.ny.us/historic-sites/15/details.aspx
www.lorenzony.org

Lorenzo, situated on Cazenovia Lake, was established in 1807 by land agent John Lincklaen. The property, featuring Lincklaen's neoclassical house, stayed in the family for five generations. The outbuildings, which date from the last years of the nineteenth century, include a carriage barn that has been adapted for use as a visitor center, an icehouse, and a brick smokehouse.

Monroe County

GENESEE COUNTRY VILLAGE AND MUSEUM
1410 Flint Hill Road
Mumford, NY 14511
(585) 538-6822
www.gcv.org

The Genesee Country Village interprets farm and village life in the Genesee Valley and surrounding region. The village consists of sixty-eight buildings moved to the property or re-created on the site. Agricultural buildings include barns, corncribs, smokehouses, and icehouses, as well as a hop house, brewery, carriage house, chicken coop, and windmill. The buildings tell the story of early settlement, the antebellum period, and the late nineteenth century, and therefore provide evidence of how life in rural New York changed throughout the 1800s.

STONE-TOLAN HOUSE
2370 East Avenue
Rochester, NY 14610
(585) 546-7029
www.landmarksociety.org

This Landmark Society museum interprets household and rural tavern life on the frontier in Brighton between 1790 and 1820. A barn dating to the 1880s has been adapted to serve as the education center for the site. The property also includes a smokehouse and a privy, the latter of which was relocated to the museum.

Montgomery County

FORT KLOCK HISTORIC RESTORATION
P.O. Box 42
Route 5
St. Johnsville, NY 13452
(518) 568-7779
www.fortklock.org
To replace the original barn that was destroyed in a fire in the 1930s, a nearby New World Dutch barn was moved to the site of Fort Klock, the mid-eighteenth-century property of the Palatine German Klock family. In addition to the barn, a cheese house, currently being used as the caretaker's residence, attests to the agricultural richness of the Mohawk Valley.

KATERI SHRINE
P.O. Box 627
3628 State Highway 5
Fonda, NY 12068
(518) 853-3646
www.katerishrine.com
This shrine venerates the Mohawk woman Kateri Tekakwitha, who was baptized into the Catholic faith here in 1676. A New World Dutch barn, built for Simon Veeder in 1782, serves as the museum and chapel. Although the building has been altered to create a more church-like appearance, the framing is still visible on the interior.

WINDFALL DUTCH BARN
Salt Springville Community Restoration, Inc.
County Route 31
Salt Springville, NY
www.cherryvalley.com/windfall
The Windfall New World Dutch barn is one of the few publicly accessible New World Dutch barns that has not been moved from its original site. It is currently open for special events and is used as a venue for concerts, dances, exhibitions, and other community activities.

Nassau County

Cow Neck Peninsula Historical Society
336 Port Washington Boulevard
Port Washington, NY 11050
(516) 365-9074
www.cowneck.org

The Cow Neck Peninsula Historical Society interprets the Sands-Willets house, a Long Island farmhouse that is named for the two prominent families that resided there from the eighteenth through the mid-twentieth centuries. In 1978 a New World Dutch barn, originally located on a nearby Sands Point farm, was added to the site. Despite reinforcement of the frame and the replacement of some materials, the barn contributes to the once rural setting of this part of Nassau County.

Old Bethpage Village Restoration
1303 Round Swamp Road
Old Bethpage, NY 11804
(516) 572-8400
www.nassaucountyny.gov/agencies/Parks/WhereToGo/museums/central_nass_museum/old_bethpage_rest.html

Old Bethpage Village is a living history museum comprising more than fifty buildings relocated to the site and several buildings that have been reconstructed. The museum includes several "farms": the Hewlett farm with a bank barn and corncrib, the Schenk farm with a New World Dutch barn and hay barracks, the Lawrence farm with an English barn and granary, the Williams farm with an English barn, the Powell farm with an English barn and corncrib, and the Noon Inn with an English barn. Other supporting agricultural buildings are also included on the more than two hundred–acre property, which is run by Nassau County.

Planting Fields Arboretum State Historic Park
P.O. Box 58
1395 Planting Fields Road
Oyster Bay, NY 11771
(516) 922-8600
http://nysparks.state.ny.us/historic-sites/24/details.aspx
www.plantingfields.org

Planting Fields is the former country estate of William Robertson Coe. The estate includes several buildings associated with the estate's agricultural operation. Most prominent of these is the hay barn, a very large brick structure constructed in 1916. Designed by Walker & Gillette with a central area for hay storage, wings with stalls for horses and cows, a semidetached dairy, and bedrooms for farm laborers, the building has been adapted for use as park offices, a research and reference library, and the park's visitor center. Other buildings on the estate include early-twentieth-century greenhouses by the William Lutton Company and Lord and Burnham.

SAGAMORE HILL NATIONAL HISTORIC SITE
20 Sagamore Hill Road
Oyster Bay, NY 11771
(516) 922-4788
www.nps.gov/sahi/index.htm

Sagamore Hill was the home of Theodore Roosevelt, and during his time as president of the United States it served as the summer White House. The property includes a 1907 dairy barn, known as the "New Barn." Other agricultural buildings, including a chicken house, icehouse, gardener's shed, farm shed, and pump house, are late-nineteenth-century structures. A reproduction American-style windmill was added to the site in 2009 to replicate a no longer extant example known from historic photographs. Although the interiors of most of the buildings are not accessible to visitors, the exteriors communicate the role of agriculture on this presidential estate.

New York County

DYCKMAN FARMHOUSE MUSEUM
4881 Broadway at 204th Street
New York, NY 10034
(212) 304-9422
www.dyckmanfarmhouse.org

The Dyckman site centers on the house that William Dyckman built immediately after the Revolutionary War. Now located in an urban setting, the house was once part of a farm of more than 250 acres. A stone smokehouse, reconstructed in 1916, makes visitors aware of the former agricultural nature of the area.

Niagara County

SANBORN AREA HISTORICAL SOCIETY FARM MUSEUM
2660 Saunders Settlement Road
Sanborn, NY 14132
(716) 946-6811
www.sanbornhistory.org/farm.htm

The Sanborn Area Historical Society, which was founded in 1996, acquired the Nancy and Leonard Wienke farm property in 2002. Now the Farm Museum, this fifty-six-acre site is an open-air museum with early farm equipment on display around the property. Buildings include a historic barn with hayloft, granary, and space for a few cows and horses; a cold storage shed; and a more recently constructed pole barn that is used to display artifacts.

Oneida County

ERIE CANAL VILLAGE
5789 Rome New London Road
Rome, NY 13440
(315) 337-3999
www.eriecanalvillage.net

The Erie Canal Village is home to the New York State Museum of Cheese, housed in the Merry and Weeks Cheese Factory, moved to the site from nearby Verona. The Erie Canal Village also includes an icehouse and the Harden barn.

Ontario County

NEW YORK STEAM ENGINE ASSOCIATION
3349 Gehan Road
Canandaigua, NY 14424
(315) 331-4022
www.pageantofsteam.org

This organization presents the Annual Pageant of Steam, an event designed to promote and encourage interest in the operation, ownership, and preservation of antique vehicles, many of them agricultural, which are powered by steam or other means.

Orange County

THE BULL STONE HOUSE
183 County Route 51
Campbell Hall, NY 10916
(845) 496-2855
www.bullstonehouse.org

This historic site is the location of the eighteenth-century house of William Bull and Sarah Wells. The property also includes a New World Dutch barn, believed to be the only building of this type still standing in Orange County. Interestingly, Bull, a stonemason and English immigrant, chose to have a wood-frame Dutch barn erected on his property, a decision that attests to the creole nature of vernacular architecture in the colony of New York.

Otsego County

THE FARMERS' MUSEUM
P.O. Box 30
5775 State Highway 80 (Lake Road)
Cooperstown, NY 13326
(607) 547-1450
www.farmersmuseum.org

Created on the site of the Clark family's Fenimore Farm, The Farmers' Museum now includes relocated buildings from throughout central New York, which are used to interpret farming and rural life in the nineteenth century. Buildings include three English barns, a granary, hop house, smokehouse, and poultry house, as well as the twentieth-century dairy barn, creamery, and stone silos from the Fenimore Farm.

HYDE HALL STATE HISTORIC SITE
P.O. Box 721
1527 County Highway 31
Cooperstown, NY 13326
(607) 547-5098
http://nysparks.state.ny.us/historic-sites/11/details.aspx
www.hydehall.org

Designed by Philip Hooker for George Clarke (1768–1835), the expansive residence known as Hyde Hall is the centerpiece of this historic site. Situated within Glimmerglass State Park on the edge of Otsego Lake, the property also includes "Tin Top," an unusual circa 1820 gatehouse with a hemispherical domed roof, which remains as evidence of the formal nature of this early country estate. The carriage barn has been adapted for use as a visitor center and office for Hyde Hall, Inc., which operates the site. A one-story stone combination laundry and smokehouse is located between the visitor center and the mansion.

Putnam County

BOSCOBEL HOUSE AND GARDENS
1601 Route 9D
Garrison, NY 10524
(845) 265-3638
www.boscobel.org

The property, focused on the relocated federal-style mansion of States and Elizabeth Dyckman, also includes a stone and brick springhouse. An orangery, based on the greenhouse at Thomas Jefferson's Monticello, and a carriage house were added to the grounds in the 1960s. Old barn timbers were used in the construction of the carriage house, which currently contains the administrative offices, museum store, and an exhibit on the rescue and preservation of the site.

Queens County

QUEENS COUNTY FARM MUSEUM
73-50 Little Neck Parkway
Floral Park, NY 11004-1129
(718) 347-3276
www.queensfarm.org

The Queens County Farm Museum, the only working historical farm in New York City, has two barns on its site, both built in the 1930s. The first has a historic exterior appearance, but the interior has been converted for modern offices. The second, a smaller structure, was formerly a dairy barn and has been restored to its original condition, with four cow stalls. It is used for the storage of hay in the hayloft and for vegetable storage, and it can be seen by visitors by special arrangement. The barn was designed for use by the Creedmoor State Hospital, which pioneered agriculture-based therapy for patients. The museum also includes a chicken coop, cowshed, beehives, and a greenhouse, the last of which is operated by the Martin Van Buren High School Vocational Horticulture Program and is not accessible to visitors.

Rensselaer County

BENNINGTON BATTLEFIELD STATE HISTORIC SITE
Route 67
Walloomsac, NY 12090
(518) 686-7109
http://nysparks.state.ny.us/historic-sites/12/details.aspx

The Bennington Battlefield State Historic Site marks the location of the August 1777 Revolutionary War engagement. The property includes an early-nineteenth-century farmstead with a timber-frame barn and a wood corncrib. Because the farm is currently operated by a local organization, the interiors of the buildings may not be accessible to the public.

Richmond County

DECKER FARM
Staten Island Historical Society

441 Clarke Avenue
Staten Island, NY 10306
(718) 351-1611
www.historicrichmondtown.org

The Decker farm is located in the New Springville section of Staten Island and is owned and operated by the Staten Island Historical Society. Members of the Decker and Alston families worked the site from the early 1800s to the 1950s, and the farm is still actively cultivated by local community members. In addition to the circa 1810 farmhouse, the site includes a barn, an animal barn, and a drive shed, all of which likely date to the late nineteenth or early twentieth century. The exteriors of the buildings are accessible during group visits, special events, and seasonal programs.

Schenectady County

MABEE FARM HISTORIC SITE
1080 Main Street
Rotterdam Junction, NY 12150
(518) 887-5073
www.schist.org/mabee.htm

The Mabee farm, a property of the Schenectady County Historical Society, includes the relocated eighteenth-century Nilsen New World Dutch barn, originally built in nearby Johnstown. A smaller barn, reconstructed carriage shed, and reconstructed corncrib are among the other agricultural buildings on the property. A residential structure, thought to have been slave quarters, attests to the use of enslaved laborers on colonial-era farms in New York. The Mabee farm is also home to the Dutch Barn Preservation Society, a nonprofit group dedicated to the study and preservation of New World Dutch barns.

Schoharie County

BLENHEIM-GILBOA VISITORS CENTER
P.O. Box 898
1378 State Route 30
North Blenheim, NY 12131
800-724-0309
www.nypa.gov/vc/blengil.htm

Lansing Manor, initially developed in the early nineteenth century by John Lansing Jr., a prominent New York politician, is now owned by the New York Power Authority, which operates a nearby hydroelectric facility. The Blenheim-Gilboa

Visitors Center, which features exhibits on energy, electricity, and natural history, is housed in a late-nineteenth-century dairy barn on the property. The dairy complex includes the barn, silo, milk house, and icehouse.

OLD STONE FORT MUSEUM
145 Fort Road
Schoharie, NY 12157
(518) 295-7192
www.schohariehistory.net/index.htm

Headquartered at the Old Stone Fort, a building constructed as a Reformed church in 1772 and fortified during the Revolutionary War, the Schoharie County Historical Society has added a number of other area buildings to its museum complex. One of these is a local New World Dutch barn known as the Schaeffer-Ingold barn.

Seneca County

INTERLAKEN HISTORICAL SOCIETY
8389 Main Street
Interlaken, NY 14847
(607) 532-8899
www.interlakenhistory.org

The Nivison Grain Cradle Factory is home of the Interlaken Historical Society's Farmers' Museum. Before being moved to its current site to serve as a museum, the building was used to manufacture grain cradles and then apple crates. The historical society additionally holds programs in the Brook farm barn. Built in 1908–1909, this dairy barn has patented truss roof framing.

Steuben County

BENJAMIN PATTERSON INN MUSEUM
59 West Pulteney Street
Corning, NY 14830
(607) 937-5281
www.pattersoninnmuseum.org

The Benjamin Patterson Inn Museum is a living history museum comprising a 1796 inn and tavern, an 1878 one-room schoolhouse, an 1850s log cabin, a blacksmith shop from circa 1870, and the Starr barn and implement shed. The barn was constructed in the 1980s to house a collection of farm implements and tools. The post-and-beam timber frame of the Starr barn came from a dismantled barn in Canandaigua.

Suffolk County

Bellport-Brookhaven Historical Society
31 Bellport Lane
Bellport, NY 11713
(631) 776-7640
www.bbhsmuseum.org

The museum complex includes a number of buildings and structures, some original and some moved to the site. The Post-Crowell house, built in 1833, is the main attraction. A springhouse, built in conjunction with the house, and the Post-Crowell horse barn are also on the property. The Historical Society's Barn Museum is housed in a building that was erected nearby in the late 1800s as a livery stable. It was converted to a carpenter's workshop in the 1920s and in 1962 was moved to its current location. The Barn Museum opened as an exhibit building in the early 1970s.

Caumsett State Historic Park
25 Lloyd Harbor Road
Huntington, NY 11743
(631) 423-1770
http://nysparks.state.ny.us/parks/23/details.aspx
www.caumsettfoundation.org

The park is the site of Marshall Field III's country estate. The "Farm Group," which includes a calf barn, dry-stock barn, milking barn, hay barn, horse and machinery barn, dairy, and several equipment sheds, was co-designed by Alfred Hopkins. The property also includes a polo stable and associated horse stables. Caumsett State Historic Park is also the site of the Henry Lloyd Manor House, dating to 1711. A nineteenth-century Long Island timber-frame barn recently moved to the manor house site is used for educational programs.

East Hampton Historical Society
101 Main Street
East Hampton, NY 11937
(631) 324-6850
www.easthamptonhistory.org

The Mulford farm on James Lane is one of the properties of the East Hampton Historical Society. The English-style Mulford barn is original to the site and was constructed in 1721. A wooden smokehouse and a wooden corncrib, the latter recently relocated to the complex, help interpret farm life around 1790. Other out-buildings date to the late nineteenth or early twentieth century.

Greenlawn-Centerport Historical Association

P.O. Box 354
31 Broadway
Greenlawn, NY 11740
(631) 754-1180
www.gcha.info

The Greenlawn-Centerport Historical Association preserves the local history of Greenlawn and Centerport, Long Island. One of its historic properties, the John Gardiner farm, dates back to circa 1750 and has been in continuous agricultural use for over 250 years. It includes a smokehouse, outhouse, carriage barn, chicken coop, garage, and hay barn. The hay barn, built in 1908, has historically been associated with the farm but had to be moved from across the street to its current site in 2002. While tours are not offered regularly, the Gardiner farm is the site of the historical association's Annual Pickle Festival.

Hallockville Museum Farm

6038 Sound Avenue
Riverhead, NY 11901
(631) 298-5292
www.hallockville.com

The Hallockville Museum Farm is a twenty-eight-acre site located on the North Fork of Long Island. It includes nineteen historic buildings representing farm life over three centuries. The Hallock Homestead barn is an English-style barn, portions of which date to 1765; a shed used in packing brussels sprouts is located on the portion of the property used to interpret the nineteenth century; the 1937 Naugles barn helps tell the story of twentieth-century immigrant farmers. Other agricultural buildings include a corncrib, hog house, garage, cowshed, wood shop, smokehouse, and chicken coop.

Huntington Historical Society

209 Main Street
Huntington, NY 11743
(631) 427-7045
www.huntingtonhistoricalsociety.org

The Huntington Historical Society interprets multiple historic sites including the 1795 Dr. Daniel Kissam House Museum on Park Avenue and the circa 1750 David Conklin Farmhouse on High Street. Both properties include vestiges of the area's agricultural past. A barn stands on the Conklin property, and the Kissam house site includes a barn relocated from Lloyd Harbor, a smokehouse, and other outbuildings.

The Long Island Museum of American Art, History & Carriages

1200 Route 25A

Stony Brook, NY 11790

(631) 751-0066

www.longislandmuseum.org

The Long Island Museum includes an art museum, a carriage museum, and a number of historic buildings that have been relocated to the site. Among the historic buildings is the late-eighteenth-century Williamson barn, which was constructed as a two-bay barn but later expanded to include a third bay. Other buildings moved to the museum from area farms include a nineteenth-century carriage shed and an early-twentieth-century privy.

Mattituck-Laurel Historical Society and Museums

P.O. Box 766

Main Road (Route 25) at Cardinal Drive

Mattituck, NY 11952

(631) 298-5248

www.mlhistoricalsociety.org

The museum site on Main Road includes a wood-frame milk house, which was relocated from the nearby Bergen farm. It is currently used to display implements for processing milk, cream, butter, and cheese. Another agricultural outbuilding, original to the site, demonstrates the multipurpose nature of many farm structures. Sometimes referred to today as a barn, it had a well and cistern in the basement, large doors allowing for the storage of vehicles or equipment on part of the first floor, and sash windows providing light and ventilation to the other side of the first floor and garret above.

Oysterponds Historical Society

P.O. Box 70

1555 Village Lane

Orient, NY 11957

(631) 323-2480

www.oysterpondshistoricalsociety.org

The Red Barn at the Oysterponds Historical Society was originally a grain storage shed located on the Orient wharf. In 1890 Thomas Young, a dock agent, moved it to the rear of his property on Village Lane and used it as a seine house for repairing and storing fishnets. It was later moved to the museum grounds, where the building is used to store horse-drawn carriages and house a small general store display.

Smithtown Historical Society

239 Middle Country Road (Route 25)

Smithtown, NY 11787

(631) 265-6768

www.smithtownhistorical.org

The Smithtown Historical Society is responsible for the Franklin O. Arthur farm, which includes a main barn, carriage house, and corncribs. The main barn was built in two parts, the first likely dating to the 1860s and the second to 1881. The farm was donated to the society by Charles Embree Rockwell, Arthur's great-great-grandson. Today the main barn houses the society's live animals as well as its vehicle collection.

SOUTHOLD HISTORICAL SOCIETY

54325 Main Road

Southold, NY 11971

(631) 765-5500

www.southoldhistoricalsociety.org

The historical society's complex at the intersection of Maple Lane and Main Road includes a number of agricultural buildings, as well as houses, workshops, and a school. Relocated to the site in 1961 and 2005, respectively, the Pineneck barn and the L'Hommedieu barn both date to the eighteenth century. The Downs carriage barn, built circa 1840, now houses the society's working print shop. A corncrib and unusual cylindrical brick icehouse were both constructed on local farms around 1875. The milk house on the property is original to the site and shows the continued importance of agriculture in this area into the twentieth century.

Tioga County

NEWARK VALLEY HISTORICAL SOCIETY

P.O. Box 222

9142 Route 38

Newark Valley, NY 13811

(607) 642-9516

www.nvhistory.org

The Newark Valley Historical Society operates the Bement-Billings farmstead. Although the original English threshing barn on the property was destroyed by a fire, the Herrick barn from Candor, New York, was moved to the site in the late 1990s. Other relocated agricultural buildings include a small granary, a corncrib, and two buildings with a history of use in maple syrup production.

Ulster County

LOCUST LAWN

400 Route 32 South

New Paltz, NY 12561

(845) 255-6070

www.locustlawn.org

Locust Lawn is best known for the 1814 Federal-style mansion from which it takes its name. Originally built for Josiah Hasbrouck, the house is part of a complex that also includes the 1738 house of the Dutch Terwilliger family and numerous agricultural outbuildings from the period of Hasbrouck ownership. The latter include two carriage barns, a tool shed, slaughterhouse, smokehouse, and two privies.

Washington County

SLATE VALLEY MUSEUM

17 Water Street

Granville, NY 12832

(518) 642-1417

www.slatevalleymuseum.org

The Slate Valley Museum is housed in a New World Dutch barn relocated from the Ravena area in Albany County. In 1996 the museum won a preservation award from the Washington County Advisory Board on Historic Preservation for the reconstruction of the barn, which provides exhibition space for the institution.

WASHINGTON COUNTY FAIR FARM MUSEUM

392 Old Schuylerville Road

Greenwich, NY 12834

(518) 692-2464

www.washingtoncountyfair.com/farmmuseum.asp

The Washington County Fair Farm Museum has a milk house and corncrib, which are accessible during the fair in August. The early-twentieth-century milk house was formerly located on a farm about a mile from the fairgrounds and was moved to the museum in 2006. The corncrib was built in the early 1900s and was moved about two miles from its original location to the museum in 1999. The interior is divided so both corn and other grains can be stored and also includes an area where family members remember shelling corn.

Wayne County

CRACKER BOX PALACE AT ALASA FARMS

P.O. Box 174

6450 Shaker Road

Alton, NY 14413

(315) 483-2493

www.crackerboxpalace.org

Now a large animal shelter, this site was occupied by a Shaker community from 1826 to 1838. Alvah Griffin Strong, grandson of the first president of Eastman Kodak, acquired the tract in 1924 and developed it into a model farm. Agricultural buildings include a dairy barn, large horse barn, pony barn, and granary. A banked structure, known as the Shaker barn, provides animal housing on its lower level and hay and corn storage above. A chimney and cooking area on the front of the building may have been used for butchering hogs or heating feed grain.

Westchester County

JOHN JAY HOMESTEAD STATE HISTORIC SITE

P.O. Box 832

400 Jay Street

Katonah, NY 10536

(914) 232-5651

http://nysparks.state.ny.us/historic-sites/4/details.aspx

www.johnjayhomestead.org

Best known as the country seat and farm of founding father John Jay, this National Historic Landmark property was the site of farming until the World War II period. The main barn, which is currently used to interpret farming on the property, has an intriguing mix of elements, including a stone lower level and wood-frame second story, main doors on the gable ends, and a hay track projecting to the exterior of the building. A carriage barn (being developed as a visitors' center), draft horse barn, the foundations of a cow barn, and several smaller supporting structures provide further evidence of the agricultural landscape.

LYNDHURST

635 South Broadway

Tarrytown, NY 10591

(914) 631-4481

www.lyndhurst.org

Lyndhurst, a National Trust Historic Site, is best known for the Gothic Revival mansion designed by A. J. Davis. The carriage house complex, believed to have been designed by A. J. Davis as well, achieved its present appearance about 1865, when a circa 1838 stable area was enlarged. Also of interest is the 376-foot greenhouse, built in 1881 for Jay Gould. Only the wood and steel framework of the building remains, but it is fully interpreted with signage explaining its history and use.

MUSCOOT FARM
51 Route 100
Katonah, NY 10536
(914) 864-7282
www.muscootfarm.org

Muscoot Farm is a 777-acre Westchester County Park. A gentleman's dairy farm from the late nineteenth through the mid-twentieth centuries, it is now a historic working farm that includes a large concentration of agricultural buildings. Some structures, including an 1840s barn, 1890s barn, carriage house, and corncrib, were moved to the site in 1901 to accommodate the Muscoot Reservoir, which supplies water to New York City. Other buildings, such as the Upper and Lower Dairy barns and milk house, were constructed on-site in 1911, reflecting up-to-date dairy practices. In the 1920s–1940s a brooder house, chicken house, carpenter's shop and wagon shed, and new milk house were added to the farm complex.

PHILIPSBURG MANOR
Route 9
Sleepy Hollow, NY 10591
(914) 631-3992
www.hudsonvalley.org/content/view/14/44/

Eighteenth-century agriculture, milling, and trade are all interpreted at the Philipsburg Manor site, which includes a manor house and gristmill as well as buildings related to farming. The New World Dutch barn at Philipsburg Manor was relocated to the site from Guilderland Center, New York, to replace a barn that burned in 1981. A reconstructed combination sheepcote and chicken coop houses some of the farm animals on the property.

STONE BARNS CENTER FOR FOOD AND AGRICULTURE
630 Bedford Road
Pocantico Hills, NY 10591
(914) 366-6200
www.stonebarnscenter.org

In the 1920s John D. Rockefeller Jr., seeking to modernize his family's farming operations in Pocantico Hills, hired the Olmsted Brothers landscape design firm to advise him. In the early 1930s he commissioned noted architect Grosvenor Atterbury to design a complex of stone farm buildings to house a dairy operation. The barns and eighty surrounding acres were later donated by David Rockefeller to form Stone Barns Center, a nonprofit farm and education center that works to increase public awareness of food and farming issues, educate children about the sources of their food, and train the next generation of sustainable farmers. Visitors can see the original hay barn and draft horse stables, which are now used for a variety of public programs, as well as the original dairy barn, which is now home to Blue Hill at Stone Barns restaurant.

Out of State

THE BARNS AT WOLF TRAP
Wolf Trap Foundation for the Performing Arts
1635 Trap Road
Vienna, VA 22182
(703) 255-1900
www.wolf-trap.org

The Wolf Trap Foundation relocated a barn from Blenheim in Schoharie County and a barn from the Town of Jackson in Washington County to be part of its performing arts complex known as "The Barns."

NOTES

Preface

1. In 1964 the *American Agriculturalist* and the *Rural New Yorker* merged. Subsequent volumes were published in Ithaca, where the *American Agriculturist*'s editorial offices had already been relocated. For further information on the publication history of these and other farm journals, see "Core Historical Agricultural Literature Project, Mann Library, Cornell University, August 1999," http://neh-usain.mannlib.cornell.edu/biblio/us_core_ag_journals.html (accessed January 16, 2011).

2. Ulysses Prentiss Hedrick, *A History of Agriculture in the State of New York* ([Albany]: New York Agricultural Society, 1933), 439–40.

3. United States Department of Agriculture, Economic Research Service, "State Fact Sheets," http://www.ers.usda.gov/statefacts (accessed January 20, 2011); United States Department of Agriculture, "2009 State Agriculture Overview: New York," http://www.nass.usda.gov/Statistics_by_State/Ag_Overview/AgOverview_NY.pdf (accessed January 20, 2011). Statistics are based on 2007 Census of Agriculture data.

4. This definition is based on that provided in the Farm Security and Rural Investment Act, 7 U.S.C. §2008o (a)(1) (2003).

5. Peter Henderson, "Combined Cellar and Greenhouse," *American Agriculturalist* 33, no. 4 (April 1874): 141–42.

6. "A Barn Cellar," *Moore's Rural New-Yorker* 3, no. 38 (September 16, 1852): 298.

7. Douglas Harper, *Changing Works: Visions of a Lost Agriculture* (Chicago: University of Chicago Press, 2001), esp. 252.

8. "Historical Highlights: 1992 and Earlier Census Years," http://www.agcensus.usda.gov/Publications/1992/Volume_1/New_York/ny1_01.pdf (accessed January 10, 2011); United States Department of Agriculture, "2009 State Agriculture Overview: New York"; U.S. Bureau of the Census, *United States Census of Agriculture: 1959,* vol. 1, *Counties,* pt. 7, *New York* (Washington, D.C.: Government Printing Office, 1961), xxiv, http://www.archive.org/stream/uscensusofagricu179unit#page/

n31/mode/2up (accessed January 20, 2011). In 1959, the agricultural census divided commercial farms into six categories based on sales values, ranging from under $2,500 to over $40,000. There were roughly equal numbers of farms in the lowest range (under $2,500) and the combined total of the top three groupings ($10,000 to $19,999, $20,000 to $39,000, and over $40,000). In 2007, farms were grouped into ranges from under $1,000 to over $500,000. A total of 1,750 New York farms fit the highest category, while 9,847 farms, the largest number of any grouping, fell into the lowest.

9. Mary Humstone, *Barn Again! A Guide to Rehabilitation of Older Farm Buildings* (Meredith Corporation, 1997).

10. Michael Woodford, "New York Annual Barn Preservation Activities Report—2004," www.barnalliance.org/2004NY.pdf (accessed January 8, 2008); "Governor, Sen. Hoffman Announce Awards for Historic Barns," June 25, 2001, Press Release 1202, New York State Department of Agriculture and Markets News (accessed January 8, 2008).

11. New York State Department of Taxation and Finance, Form IT-212-ATT: 2010.

12. "Barns in the United States Built Prior to 1960," Preservation Nation, http://www.preservationnation.org/issues/rural-heritage/barn-again/additional-resources/Barns-in-US-by-state-PDF.pdf (accessed January 20, 2011). The results are based on the 2007 USDA Census of Agriculture and are limited to farms with more than $1,000 in sales.

Introduction

1. Diary of George S. Buckmaster, 1854–55, New York State Historical Association Research Library, Diary B857.

2. Ibid.; New York State Census, 1855, Orange County, New Windsor, entry 98 for Thomas O. Buckmaster, New York State Historical Association Research Library, microfilm, New York Census, 1855, Orange County, Roll 2.

3. Allen G. Noble and Richard K. Cleek, *The Old Barn Book: A Field Guide to North American Barns and Other Farm Structures* (New Brunswick: Rutgers University Press, 1995), 31.

4. W. A. Foster and Deane G. Carter, *Farm Buildings* (New York: John Wiley and Sons, 1922), 310.

5. Byron David Halsted, *Barn Plans and Outbuildings,* rev. ed. (New York: Orange Judd, 1906), 9. This same advice was not found in the original 1881 edition of the book.

6. Ibid., 9–14; Herbert A. Shearer, *Farm Buildings with Plans and Descriptions* (Chicago: Frederick J. Drake & Co., 1917), 10–15; Henry D. Dewell, *Timber Framing* (San Francisco: Dewey Publishing Company, 1917), 147–55.

7. Halsted, *Barn Plans and Outbuildings,* 18–20.

8. Foster and Carter, *Farm Buildings* (1922), 299–302, 306–10.

9. Ibid., 287–89.

10. Ibid., 102.

11. Isaac Phillips Roberts, *The Farmstead: The Making of the Rural Home and the Lay-out of the Farm* (New York: Macmillan, 1900), 296–97.

12. Henry Glassie, "The Variation of Concepts within Tradition: Barn Building in Otsego County, New York," *Geoscience and Man* 5 (June 10, 1974): 220.

13. H. P. Holman, "Painting on the Farm," United States Department of Agriculture Farmers' Bulletin no. 1452 (April 1925), 1, 2, 8.

14. Jules David Prown, "Style as Evidence," *Winterthur Portfolio* 15, no. 3 (Autumn 1980): 209.

15. Daniel Fink, *Barns of the Genesee Country, 1790–1915* (New York: James Brunner, 1987), 216–21.

16. L. John Lovell, "Decorative Barn Painting in Schoharie County: The Documentation of a Folk Aesthetic" (master's thesis, Cooperstown Graduate Program, SUNY Oneonta, 1979).

17. John Fitchen, *The New World Dutch Barn: The Evolution, Forms, and Structure of a Disappearing Icon,* 2nd ed., ed. Gregory D. Huber (Syracuse: Syracuse University Press, 2001), 23, 116; Vincent J. Schaefer, *Dutch Barns of New York: An Introduction* (Fleischmanns, N.Y.: Purple Mountain Press, 1994), 46.

18. William G. Simmonds, *Advertising Barns: Vanishing American Landmarks* (St. Paul: MBI Publishing, 2004).

19. "Signs of a Prosperous Farm," *Moore's Rural New-Yorker* 1, no. 43 (October 24, 1850): 338.

20. Alfred Hopkins, *Modern Farm Buildings* (New York: McBride, Nast, and Co., 1913), 15.

21. Rodric Coslet, John Crippen, and Eric Paige, "From Cooper to Cow Palace: The Tradition of Gentleman Farmers and Fenimore Farm," *Heritage: The Magazine of the New York State Historical Association* 9, no. 1 (Spring 1993): 32–36.

1. Diversity, Dairying, and Designing the Main Barn

1. "Rural First Premium Barn," *Moore's Rural New-Yorker* 10, no. 5 (February 3, 1859): 45.

2. Diary of Orville M. Slosson (b. 1829), 1860–1862, New York State Historical Association Research Library, Diary Sl55, entries for July 20, August 15, September 26 and 27, and November 14, 1860; "Agricultural Societies," *Cultivator* 8, no. 5 (May 1860): 165.

3. "A Barn Cellar," *Moore's Rural New-Yorker* 3, no. 38 (September 16, 1852): 298.

4. John Fitchen, *The New World Dutch Barn: The Evolution, Forms, and Structure of a Disappearing Icon,* 2nd ed., ed. Gregory D. Huber (Syracuse: Syracuse University Press, 2001), 20.

5. Ibid., 15–16, 207.

6. Peter Kalm, *Peter Kalm's Travels in North America: The English Version of 1770,* ed. Adolph B. Benson (New York: Dover Publications, 1987), 118.

7. Gregory D. Huber, "The Dutch Barn in America," *De Halve Maen* 73, no. 2 (2000): 43.

8. Fitchen, *New World Dutch Barn,* xxv–xxxii, xlx.

9. Huber, "The Dutch Barn in America," 39. Huber, in an appendix to the second edition of Fitchen's *New World Dutch Barn,* does note that some Dutch barns in New York originally had vertical rather than, or in addition to, horizontal siding, and some had siding made of shakes rather than clapboard (207).

10. Vincent J. Schaefer, *Dutch Barns of New York: An Introduction* (Fleischmanns, N.Y.: Purple Mountain Press, 1994), 34–37; Fitchen, *New World Dutch Barn,* 24, 121, 122, 127.

11. Schaefer, *Dutch Barns of New York,* 19, 46.

12. Fitchen, *New World Dutch Barn,* lv–lvi, 15, 159, 206.

13. Ibid., xxvi, 14; Huber, "The Dutch Barn in America," 35.

14. Although the three-part configuration was the standard, Gregory Huber has documented some Dutch barns without aisles built prior to 1815, perhaps as accessory structures to a larger Dutch barn. Fitchen, *New World Dutch Barn,* xxx, 26.

15. Kalm, *Travels in North America,* 118.

16. Fitchen, *New World Dutch Barn,* 46–48.

17. Ibid., xxvi–xxx, xxxii, lii.

18. Henry Glassie, "The Variation of Concepts within Tradition: Barn Building in Otsego County, New York," *Geoscience and Man* 5 (June 10, 1974): 182.

19. Daniel Fink, *Barns of the Genesee Country, 1790–1915* (New York: James Brunner, 1987), 95; Glassie, "The Variation of Concepts within Tradition," 217–19; Allen G. Noble and Richard K. Cleek, *The Old Barn Book: A Field Guide to North American Barns and Other Farm Structures* (New Brunswick: Rutgers University Press, 1995), 77.

20. Fink, *Barns of the Genesee Country,* 95.

21. Ibid., 99–101, 188.

22. Fink, *Barns of the Genesee Country,* 188; Glassie, "The Variation of Concepts within Tradition," 184.

23. Robert Blair St. George, *Conversing in Signs: Poetics of Implication in Colonial New England Culture* (Chapel Hill: University of North Carolina Press, 1998), 108–10; John Michael Vlach, *Barns* (New York: W. W. Norton & Co.; Washington, D.C.: Library of Congress, 2003), 16–17; Thomas Durant Visser, *Field Guide to New England Barns and Farm Buildings* (Hanover, N.H.: University Press of New England, 1997), 61; Noble and Cleek, *Old Barn Book,* 77. Noble and Cleek's statement that the form of English and New English barns is identical seems to overlook the use of the structures.

24. Glassie, "The Variation of Concepts within Tradition," 185.

25. Noble and Cleek, *The Old Barn Book,* 78.

26. "A Pennsylvania Barn," *Moore's Rural New-Yorker* 9, no. 42 (October 16, 1858): 333. The article notes that the plans were originally published in Allen's "Rural Architecture" and were reprinted in response to perceived interest "at the present time."

27. Austin M. Fox, ed., *Erie County's Architectural Legacy* ([Buffalo]: Erie County Preservation Board, 1983), 71.

28. Washington Frothingham, *History of Fulton County* (Syracuse: D. Mason & Co., 1892), 54–55; Philip Otterness, *Becoming German: The 1709 Palatine Migration to New York* (Ithaca: Cornell University Press, 2004), vii, 138–45.

29. Fitchen, *New World Dutch Barn,* xli; Rufus A. Grider, "A Collection of Illustrations of Historic Matter Consisting of Tracings of Documents, of Pictures, of Restorations, Curios, Portraits, & &. Relating to the Mohawk Valley, Gathered Mostly during the Years 1889 to 1897," vol. 3, fol. 33, New York State Library, Albany, microfilm (2010).

30. Sally McMurry and J. Ritchie Garrison, "Barns and Agricultural Outbuildings," in *Architecture and Landscape of the Pennsylvania Germans, 1720–1920,* ed. Sally McMurry and Nancy Van Dolsen (Philadelphia: University of Pennsylvania Press, 2011), 99–100.

31. Robert F. Ensminger, *The Pennsylvania Barn: Its Origin, Evolution, and Distribution in North America* (Baltimore: Johns Hopkins University Press, 1992), 10, 15–16, 50.

32. Ibid., 219–20; Noble and Cleek, *The Old Barn Book,* 85–90.

33. Noble and Cleek, *The Old Barn Book,* 84–100.

34. Fox, *Erie County's Architectural Legacy,* 71–72; McMurry and Garrison, "Barns and Agricultural Buildings," 101–6; Noble and Cleek, *The Old Barn Book,* 89–90.

35. Pennsylvania Historical and Museum Commission, "Basement Barns," in *Architecture and Landscapes of Agriculture: A Field Guide,* http://www.phmc.state.pa.us/bhp/Agricultural/Context/FieldGuide/Basement%20Barn.asp (accessed February 18, 2008); Glassie, "The Variation of Concepts within Tradition," 185; Noble and Cleek, *The Old Barn Book,* 81–83.

36. Thomas Summerhill, "The Farmers' Republic: Agrarian Protest and the Capitalist Transformation of Upstate New York, 1840–1900" (Ph.D. diss., University of California, San Diego, 1993), 246–49, 265–84, quote 274; Glassie, "The Variation of Concepts within Tradition," 185; Gilbert T. Vincent, *An Agricultural Legacy: Farm Outbuildings of Central New York* (Cooperstown: Gallery 53 Artworks, 1991), 7; Charles Klamkin, *Barns: Their History, Preservation, and Restoration* (New York: Hawthorn Books, 1973), 56–57.

37. Josiah K. Brown, *Sixth Annual Report of the New York State Dairy Commissioner for the Year 1889* (Albany: James B. Lyon, 1890), 10, 532; Deane G. Carter and W. A. Foster, *Farm Buildings* (New York: Published for the United States Armed Forces Institute by John Wiley and Sons, 1944), 223.

38. Glassie, "The Variation of Concepts within Tradition," 217. For one opinion on the debate over whether barn cladding should be "tight" or "open," see T.E.W., "Should Barns Be Tight or Open?" *Moore's Rural New-Yorker* 3, no. 17 (April 22, 1852): 120.

39. "A Massachusetts Barn," *American Agriculturalist* 5, no. 4 (April 1846): 120.

40. Noble and Cleek, *Old Barn Book,* 79, 81; Visser, *Field Guide to New England Barns,* 70–71.

41. Fink, *Barns of the Genesee Country,* 95.

42. Alan Conway, ed., *The Welsh in America: Letters from Immigrants* (Minneapolis: University of Minnesota Press, 1961), 51–55, 70–71; Paul Demund Evans, "The Welsh in Oneida County, New York" (master's thesis, Cornell University, 1914); reprinted, Electronic Edition 1.0. Siloam Road eBooks, 2001, http://www.roots-web.ancestry.com/˜nyunywh/oneidawelsh/, 6–10, 20–23 (accessed January 7, 2011); Noble and Cleek, *The Old Barn Book,* 84.

43. I. F. Hall, *An Economic Study of Farm Buildings in New York* (Ithaca: Cornell University Agricultural Experiment Station, 1928), 57.

44. Herbert A. Shearer, *Farm Buildings with Plans and Descriptions* (Chicago: Frederick J. Drake & Co., 1917), 10–12.

45. Noble and Cleek, *Old Barn Book,* 37; A. Mecham, "Trussed Roof Arch," U.S. Patent 1,346,229, filed April 1, 1920, issued July 1920.

46. "First Premium Barn," *Moore's Rural New-Yorker* 10, no. 6 (February 5, 1859): 46; W. A. Foster and Deane G. Carter, *Farm Buildings* (New York: John Wiley and Sons, 1922), 102.

47. Little barn building occurred during the Great Depression and World War II, but basement barns predominated in plan books. After the war, while one-story barns were becoming more common, building catalogues suggest that basement barns were still among the options recommended. See National Plan Service, *Practical Farm Buildings* (Chicago: National Plan Service for F. W. Wint Company of Catasauqua, Pa., ca. 1935); Weyerhaeuser 4-Square Farm Buildings Service, *Modern Farm Buildings and Equipment* (St. Paul[?]: Weyerhaeuser Sales Company, ca. 1945). I am grateful to Christopher Sterba for providing me with the latter source.

48. Stanchions are commonly mentioned in farming periodicals by the 1860s; it is likely that they were developed around the same time that basement barns were popularized. U.S. Patent 333,275, filed August 13, 1865, by David J. Barnes of Fort Atkinson, Wisconsin, is for "useful Improvements in Cattle-Stanchions," indicating their use prior to that date.

49. L. D. Snook, "A Farm Barn," *Moore's Rural New-Yorker* 20, no. 50 (December, 11 1869): 791.

50. Hall, *Economic Study of Farm Buildings,* 41. In 1928 a survey of 770 barns showed that in 579 cases, cows faced the exterior walls.

51. Alfred Hopkins, *Modern Farm Buildings* (New York: McBridge, Nast & Co., 1913), 46; R. M. Washburn, *Productive Dairying,* Lippincott's Farm Manuals series,

ed. Kary C. Davis (Philadelphia: J. B. Lippincott, 1925), 179; Heber Bouland, *Barns across America* (St. Josephs, Mich.: American Society of Agricultural Engineers, 1998), 76; Mesick-Cohen-Wilson-Baker Architects, *Shaker Church Family Barn: Historic Structure Report* (Albany: August 2002), 19; Stephen Lewandowski and Elizabeth Mankin, "The Putnam Farm, 1825–1974: Middlefield, Otsego County, New York" (master's project, Cooperstown Graduate Program, SUNY Oneonta, 1974), 22.

52. "Manure," *American Agriculturalist* 1, no. 2 (May 1842): 36; "Making and Saving Manure," *Moore's Rural New-Yorker* 18, no. 4 (January 26, 1867): 29; "Storing Manure," *Moore's Rural New-Yorker* 18, no. 49 (December 7, 1867): 389; "Applying Manures," *Moore's Rural New-Yorker* 20, no. 19 (May 8, 1869): 294.

53. "Model Western New York Barn," *Moore's Rural New-Yorker* 5, no. 1 (January 7, 1854): 5; Richard Rawson, *The Old Hand Book of Barn Plans* (New York: Sterling Publishing, 1990), 81; L. B. Arnold, *American Dairying: A Manual for Butter and Cheese Makers* (Rochester: Rural Home Publishing Company, 1876), 99.

54. "A Complete Stock Barn," *Moore's Rural New-Yorker* 18, no. 76 (November 16, 1867): 365; "A Large Stock Barn," *Moore's Rural New-Yorker* 22, no. 15 (April 15, 1871): 233.

55. "Are Manure Cellars under Barns Best?" *American Agriculturalist* 23, no. 12 (December 1864): 336.

56. David S. Barnes, *The Great Stink of Paris and the Nineteenth-Century Struggle against Filth and Germs* (Baltimore: Johns Hopkins University Press, 2006), 2–3; Nancy Tomes, *The Gospel of Germs: Men, Women, and the Microbe in American Life* (Cambridge: Harvard University Press, 1998), 152–53.

57. *Documents of the Senate of the State of New York, One Hundred and Thirty-ninth Session, 1916,* vol. 13, no. 21, pt. 6 (Albany: J. B. Lyon Company, 1916), 127–33.

58. Washburn, *Productive Dairying,* 179; Mesick-Cohen-Wilson-Baker Architects, *Shaker Church Family Barn,* 19; Hopkins, *Modern Farm Buildings,* 46; Lewandowski and Mankin, "The Putnam Farm, 1825–1974," 22.

59. L. B. Arnold, *American Dairying;* Washburn, *Productive Dairying,* 281; William A. Radford, *Radford's Practical Barn Plans: Outbuildings and Stock Sheds* (Chicago: Radford Agricultural Company, 1909), 117.

60. "Have You Built Your Manure Shed?" *American Agriculturalist* 16, no. 2 (February 1857): 26.

61. William Lawrence Lassiter, *Shaker Architecture* (New York: Vantage Press, 1966), 21. On the care of animals, Lassiter cites Section 7, no. 4, of the sect's millennial laws, which reads as follows: "No beast belonging to the people of God may be left to suffer with hunger, thirst, or cold, in consequence of neglect, on the part of those who have the care of them, but all should be kept in proper places and properly attended to according to their needs."

62. Mesick-Cohen-Wilson-Baker Architects, *Shaker Church Family Barn,* 7–14, 65, 75–79; Elmore Design Collaborative, "Building Structure/Data," *Watervliet*

Shaker Site Master Plan Phase 1, Prepared for the Shaker Heritage Society (Suffield, Conn., 2007).

63. George Mueller, "Planning the Most Perfect Dairy Farm," in Natural Resource, Agriculture, and Engineering Service, *Building Freestall Barns and Milking Centers: Methods and Materials* (Ithaca: NRAES Cooperative Extension, 2003), 5; Andrew W. Wedel, "Manure Removal and Conveyance Options," ibid., 177–79.

64. Lynn R. Miller, *Haying with Horses* (Sisters, Ore.: Small Farmers' Journal, 2000), 229.

65. John Walsh, *The Barn,* DVD (Syracuse: Public Broadcasting Council of Central New York, 2005).

66. Alan Mirken, ed., *1927 Edition of the Sears, Roebuck Catalogue* (New York: Bounty Books, 1970), 1089.

67. Thomas C. Hubka, "The Americanization of the Barn," *Blueprints: The Journal of the National Building Museum* 12, no. 2 (Spring 1994), http://www.nbm.org/blueprints/90s/spring94/page2/page2.htm (accessed February 24, 2008).

68. From this point on, the term "round barn" will be used to refer in general to round, octagonal, and other polygonal barns. Barns discussed here are limited to multistory structures designed, built, and used primarily for dairying unless otherwise noted.

69. Richard Triumpho, *Round Barns of New York* (Syracuse: Syracuse University Press, 2004), 88, 96–101.

70. Randy Leffingwell, *The American Barn* (Osceola, Wis.: Motorbooks International, 1997), 99–100; Triumpho, *Round Barns,* 13, 18, 20–21; National Register Nomination for Central Plan Dairy Barns of New York State Thematic Resources, New York State Historic Preservation Office (1984), "Significance," 1.

71. Orson Fowler, *A Home for All, or, The Gravel Wall and Octagon Method of Building* (New York: Fowler and Wells, 1854), 174–78.

72. Triumpho, *Round Barns,* 26–29; National Register Nomination for Central Plan Dairy Barns of New York State Thematic Resources, "Significance," 3; "An Octagonal Barn," *American Agriculturist* 15, no. 37 (July 1876): 258; J. J. Thomas, *Illustrated Annual Register of Rural Affairs, 1876–7–8* (Albany: Luther Tucker & Son, 1878), 249–50; "A Small Octagon Barn," *Cultivator & Country Gentleman,* May 10, 1888, 373.

73. Triumpho, *Round Barns,* 30–47, 97–101; National Register Nomination for Central Plan Dairy Barns of New York State Thematic Resources, "Significance," 4–5.

74. Triumpho, *Round Barns,* 30–34, 48–50, 53; National Register Nomination for Central Plan Dairy Barns of New York State Thematic Resources, "Significance," 4–5.

75. Triumpho, *Round Barns,* 56; F. H. King, "Plan of a Barn for a Dairy Farm," in *Annual Report of the Agricultural Experiment Station of the University of Wisconsin for the Year 1890* (Madison: University of Wisconsin, 1890), 184, 186–87, 189–90.

76. Triumpho, *Round Barns,* 64–65, 70–71, 73–74, 77; National Register Nomination for Central Plan Dairy Barns of New York State Thematic Resources, "Significance," 6.

77. F. Kennon Moody, John F. Sears, and John Auwaerter, "Historic Resource Study for the Roosevelt Estate, Home of Franklin D. Roosevelt National Historic Site" (Boston: Olmsted Center for Landscape Preservation, National Park Service, draft July 2004), pt. 3, 9 (typescript, Franklin D. Roosevelt Presidential Library and Museum, Hyde Park).

78. Ibid., 42.

79. Robert B. MacKay et al., eds., *Long Island Country Houses and Their Architects, 1860–1940* (New York: Society for the Preservation of Long Island Antiquities, 1997), 11.

80. Norman T. Newton, *Design on the Land: The Development of Landscape Architecture* (Cambridge: Belknap Press, 1971), 444.

81. Bruce E Naramore, *Master Plan for Clermont State Historic Park,* New York State Office of Parks, Recreation, and Historic Preservation, Taconic Region, Originally printed 1982, reprint 1984, 16.

82. Hopkins, *Modern Farm Buildings,* 16.

83. Debby Gordon, "Olana State Historic Site Farm Building Inventory" (working paper, Olana State Historic Site, May 2005).

84. Rodric Coslet, John Crippen, and Eric Paige, "From Cooper to Cow Palace: The Tradition of Gentleman Farmers and Fenimore Farm," *Heritage: The Magazine of the New York State Historical Association* 9, no. 1 (Spring 1993): 32–36.

85. McKinney, also known as the Block Barn, is located in Cuba, New York. It is under private ownership and is still used to keep horses, but it is open to the public on a limited basis. Fink, *Barns of the Genesee Country,* 468–69.

86. Ibid., 468, 474.

87. The site is now part of the Roosevelt National Historic Site, Hyde Park. Historic Resource Study for the Roosevelt Estate, pt. 3, 44.

88. Historic Resource Study for the Roosevelt Estate, pt. 3, 50–51.

89. Frank Futral, "Hyde Park Farm Group: Historic Resource Assessment" (working paper, Roosevelt-Vanderbilt National Historic Sites, National Parks Service, 2006).

90. Futral, "Hyde Park Farm Group," 3–4.

91. Robertson designed the main house at Santanoni, and it has been suggested that he designed the farm complex there as well. See Robert W. Engel, "A History of Camp Santanoni, the Adirondack Retreat of Robert C. Pruyn" (master's thesis, Cooperstown Graduate Program, SUNY Oneonta, 1996), 60–62. Other authors have suggested that the complex was designed by Alfred Hopkins, perhaps in part because of the documented work of Edward Burnett there. See Futral, "Hyde Park Farm Group," 4.

92. United States Department of Agriculture, Economic Research Service, "State Fact Sheets: New York," http://www.ers.usda.gov/Statefacts/NY.HTM (accessed January 20, 2011). Statistics are from 2007–2009.

93. Douglas Harper, *Changing Works: Visions of a Lost Agriculture* (Chicago: University of Chicago Press, 2001), 269–71; Wedel, "Manure Removal and Conveyance Options," 180–86.

94. Noble and Cleek, *The Old Barn Book,* 120; Weyerhaeuser, *Modern Farm Buildings.*

95. Hall, *An Economic Study of Farm Buildings in New York*, 40.

96. Douglas J. Reinemann, "Milking Parlor Types," University of Wisconsin–Madison Milking Research and Instruction Lab, December 2003, http://www.uwex.edu/uwmril/pdf/MilkingParlors/03_UWMRIL_Reinemann_MilkingParlorTypes.pdf (accessed July 8, 2008); Robert Engle, "Milk Center Planning," in Natural Resource, Agriculture, and Engineering Service, *Building Freestall Barns and Milking Centers,* 34–37; Stanley A. Weeks, "Milk Center Building Material Considerations," in Natural Resource, Agriculture, and Engineering Service, *Building Freestall Barns and Milking Centers,* 347–90.

97. Timothy R. Royer, "Options for Construction Contracting," in Natural Resource, Agriculture, and Engineering Service, *Building Freestall Barns and Milking Centers,* 65–71.

2. Sheltering the Flock, Processing the Product

1. Diary of a Tarrytown, N.Y., farmer, 1900, New York State Historical Association Research Library, Cooperstown, Diary A17, entries for October 20–21, November 4, and December 19, 1900.

2. Robert W. Bitz, *Four Hundred Years of Agricultural Change in the Empire State* (Baldwinsville, N.Y.: Ward Bitz Publishing, 2009), 78–79, 192.

3. "Dairy Notes and Queries: Marketing Milk," *Moore's Rural New-Yorker* 23, no. 22 (June 10, 1871): 366.

4. Bitz, *Four Hundred Years,* 78–79; "New York Celebrates Dairy Month," *Inside Pride: The Newsletter of the Pride of New York Program* 4, no. 1 (2004), http://www.prideofny.com/summernews.pdf (accessed January 20, 2011).

5. Byron David Halsted, *Barn Plans and Outbuildings,* rev. ed. (New York: Orange Judd, 1906), 280–86.

6. John J. Craig, "Milk-Houses and Butter-Making," *The Cultivator* 8, no. 8 (March 1851): 115.

7. Halsted, *Barn Plans and Outbuildings*, 261–65; R. M. Washburn, *Productive Dairying*, Lippincott's Farm Manuals series, ed. Kary C. Davis (Philadelphia: J. B. Lippincott, 1925), 294–96.

8. On typhoid cases in downstate New York, see for example: "Bad Milk Caused Typhoid: Source of East Side's Epidemic as Traced by Health Officers,"

New York Times, September 19, 1913; "New Typhoid Cases on Staten Island: Three Reported to Health Board Head and Five Others Suspected," *New York Times,* September 6, 1917.

9. New York State Legislature, *Documents of the Senate of the State of New York, One Hundred and Fortieth Session, 1917,* vol. 14, nos. 29–35 (Albany: J. B. Lyon Company, 1917), 697–706.

10. Eunice R. Stamm, *The History of Cheese Making in New York State* (Endicott, N.Y.: Lewis Group, 1991), 43–44.

11. Ibid., 17, 47, 59.

12. Ibid., 50.

13. L. D. Snook, "Rural Architecture: A Farm Barn," *Moore's Rural New-Yorker* 20, no. 50 (December 11, 1869): 791; "Rural Architecture: Farm Buildings," *Moore's Rural New-Yorker* 31, no. 9 (February 27, 1875): 142.

14. Peter Kalm, *Peter Kalm's Travels in North America: The English Version of 1770,* ed. Adolph B. Benson (New York: Dover Publications, 1987), 118–19.

15. *Documents of the Assembly of the State of New York, One-Hundred and Thirty-seventh Session* 15, no. 21, pt. 6 (Albany: J. B. Lyon Company, 1914), 41.

16. Herbert A. Shearer, *Farm Buildings with Plans and Descriptions* (Chicago: Frederick J. Drake & Co., 1917), 16.

17. Halsted, *Barn Plans and Outbuildings,* 216.

18. William A. Radford, *Radford's Practical Barn Plans: Outbuildings and Stock Sheds* (Chicago: Radford Agricultural Company, 1909), 199.

19. "The Clydesdales," Anheuser-Busch Companies, http://www.anheuser-busch.com/historyClydesdales.html (accessed January 20, 2011).

20. "The Magnificent New Private Stables of Adolphus Busch, Esq.," reprinted in Stanley Schuler, *American Barns: In a Class by Themselves* (Exton, Pa.: Schiffer Publishing, 1984), 191.

21. George Ripley and Charles A. Dana, *American Cyclopedia: A Popular Dictionary of General Knowledge,* vol. 13 (New York: D. Appleton and Company, 1883), 663.

22. E[lam] Tilden, "Sheep Barn—Ruta Baga," *The Cultivator* 9, no. 5 (July 1837): 84; 1830 United States Census, Columbia County, New York State Historical Association Research Library, Cooperstown, microfilm, Town of New Lebanon, page 10, entry for Elam Tilden.

23. U.S. Department of Agriculture, Bureau of Animal Industry, *Special Report on the History and Present Condition of the Sheep Industry of the United States* (Washington, D.C.: Government Printing Office, 1892), 25.

24. A. B. Allen, ed. "Wintering Sheep," *American Agriculturist* 2, no. 12 (December 15, 1843): 355–56.

25. New York State Department of Agriculture, Bureau of Farmers' Institutes, "The Sheep Industry in New York State," *Department of Agriculture Bulletin,* no. 96 (June 1917): 21.

26. Tilden, "Sheep Barn—Ruta Baga," 84; "Sheep Barn," *The Cultivator* 3, no. 11 (November 1846): 334–35.

27. New York State Department of Agriculture, "The Sheep Industry in New York State," 20–21.

28. William James Clarke, *Modern Sheep: Breeds and Management* (Chicago: American Sheep Breeder Company, 1907), 197; Alfred Hopkins, *Modern Farm Buildings* (New York: McBridge, Nast & Co., 1913), 190–94.

29. Len McDougall, *The Encyclopedia of Tracks and Scats* (Guilford, Conn.: Lyons Press, 2004), 72.

30. Daniel Fink, *Barns of the Genesee Country, 1790–1915* (New York: James Brunner, 1987), 344.

31. August Van Cortlandt, "City of New-York, Common Council Chamber, Nov. 22, 1770," *New York Gazette,* November 26, 1770, 3.

32. Matt Cox, "Building a Better Pig: Popular Breeds of Hogs, 1840 to the Present" (research paper, Cooperstown Graduate Program, SUNY Oneonta, Spring 2009).

33. Samuel Deane, *The New-England Farmer or Georgical Dictionary,* 2nd ed. (Worcester, Mass.: Isaiah Thomas, 1797), 157, reprinted in Thomas Durant Visser, *Field Guide to New England Barns and Farm Buildings* (Hanover, N.H.: University Press of New England, 1997), 155–56.

34. New York State, Secretary of State, *Census of the State of New-York for 1845* (Albany: Carroll & Cook, 1846), Recapitulation—No. 3; New York State, Secretary of State, *Census of the State of New-York for 1855* (Albany: Charles Van Benthuysen, 1857), 322; New York State, Secretary of State, *Census of the State of New York for 1865* (Albany: Charles Van Benthuysen, 1867), 402–3; New York State, Secretary of State, *Census of the State of New York for 1875* (Albany: Weed, Parsons & Co., 1877), 411.

35. Radford, *Radford's Practical Barn Plans,* 182.

36. Amos Long Jr., *The Pennsylvania German Family Farm: A Regional Architectural and Folk Cultural Study of an American Agricultural Community* (Breinigsville, Pa.: Pennsylvania German Society, 1972), 393.

37. William Youatt, *The Pig: A Treatise on the Breeds, Management, Feeding, and Medical Treatment, of Swine* (London: Cradock and Co., 1847), 133–34, 141; Stephen W. Jacobs, *Wayne County: The Aesthetic Heritage of a Rural Area* (New York: Publishing Center for Cultural Resources for the Wayne County Historical Society, 1979), 92.

38. Eric Sloane, *An Age of Barns* (New York: Funk & Wagnalls, 1966), 85; Visser, *Field Guide to New England Barns,* 159.

39. Albert Haring and William Hislop, *The Products of the Farm Slaughter House, Sausage Kitchen and Smoke House* (Pullman, Wash.: State College of Washington, Dept. of Extension, 1916), 6, 22; Adrian Room, *Dictionary of Trade Name Origins,* rev. ed. (Boston: Routledge and Kegan Paul, 1983), 99.

40. John Henry McCoy, *Livestock and Meat Marketing* (Westport, Conn.: AVI Publishing Company, 1972), 14–17.

41. Rudolf Alexander Clemen, *The American Livestock and Meat Industry* (New York: Ronald Press Company, 1923), 211, 216–24; William Cronon, *Nature's Metropolis: Chicago and the Great West* (New York: W. W. Norton, 1991), 224, 234.

42. Diary of A. E. Parker, New York State Historical Association Research Library, Diary P223, vol. 1, entries for December 6–26, 1907.

43. H. H. Lyman, *Memories of the Old Homestead* (Oswego: R. J. Oliphant, 1900), 92–93.

44. Richard Rathburn, interview by Anneke Nordmark, Cooperstown, March 28, 2006; Visser, *Field Guide to New England Barns,* 159; Donald D. Stull, Michael J. Broadway, and David Griffith, eds., *Any Way You Cut It: Meat Processing and Small-Town America* (Lawrence: University Press of Kansas, 1995), 53, 115; Halsted, *Barn Plans and Outbuildings,* 371; Gwen Miner, interview by Anneke Nordmark, Otsego County, March 28, 2006.

45. Lyman, *Memories,* 94.

46. McCoy, *Livestock and Meat Marketing,* 19–20; Gilbert T. Vincent, *An Agricultural Legacy: Farm Outbuildings of Central New York* (Cooperstown: Gallery 53 Artworks, 1991), 11.

47. H. H. Lyman recalled "Our smoke-house was the old big fire-place in the cooper-shop, the front part of which was closed up, and sticks put across about four feet from the ground, upon which to hang the hams." Lyman, *Memories,* 93.

48. A *Cultivator* article also suggests that wooden smokehouses helped keep the ashes drier than stone or brick buildings. N. Reed, "Smoke-house," *The Cultivator* 13, no. 5 (May 1865): 151; Radford, *Radford's Practical Barn Plans,* 278–80; Haring and Hislop, *The Products of the Farm Slaughter House,* 13.

49. Vincent, *An Agricultural Legacy,* 11.

50. Miner, interview; Visser, *Field Guide to New England Barns,* 159.

51. Janet Vorwald Dohner, *The Encyclopedia of Historic and Endangered Livestock and Poultry Breeds* (New Haven: Yale University Press, 2001), 412–13; Page Smith and Charles Daniel, *The Chicken Book* (Boston: Little, Brown, 1975), 205–7.

52. United States Census Office, *Compendium of the Enumeration of the Inhabitants and Statistics of the United States as Obtained at the Department of State, from the Returns of the Sixth Census, 1840* (Washington, D.C.: Blair and Rives, 1841), 354.

53. See, for example, Frances Trollope, *Domestic Manners of the Americans,* ed. John Lauritz Larson (St. James, N.Y.: Brandywine Press, 1993), 72–73.

54. James E. Rice, "Poultry-House Construction," in *Cyclopedia of American Agriculture,* ed. L. H. Bailey, vol. 3 (New York: Macmillan, 1907), 557.

55. Homer W. Jackson, ed., *Poultry Houses and Fixtures,* 9th ed. (Dayton: Reliable Poultry Journal Publishing Company, 1926), 70, 79.

56. "Poultry," in Bailey, *Cyclopedia of American Agriculture,* 3:525.

57. Clarence E. Lee, *Profitable Poultry Management,* 8th ed. (Cayuga, N.Y.: Beacon Milling Company, 1935), 12–13.

58. Charles A. Cyphers, "Incubation and Brooding," in Bailey, *Cyclopedia of American Agriculture,* 3:543.

59. Ibid., 544; James E. Rice and Rolla C. Lawry, *A Gasoline Heater Colony Brooder-House,* Cornell University Agricultural Experiment Station of the College of Agriculture Department of Animal Husbandry (Poultry Husbandry) Bulletin 247 (Ithaca: Cornell University, 1907).

60. Cyphers, "Incubation and Brooding," 542; Mount Hope Farm, *The Rise of the Poultry Industry: Mount Hope Cockerels, 1934–1935; Single Comb White Leghorns and Rhode Island Reds* (Williamstown, Mass.: McClelland, 1935), 18.

61. Cyphers, "Incubation and Brooding," 543.

62. Pam Percy, *The Complete Chicken: An Entertaining History of Chickens* (Stillwater, Minn.: Voyageur Press, 2002), 31–33.

63. Lee, *Profitable Poultry Management,* 6–7, 39–41.

64. Vincent, *An Agricultural Legacy,* 21.

65. Page Smith and Charles Daniel, *The Chicken Book* (Boston: Little, Brown, 1975), 276–77; Willard C. Thompson, *Egg Farming* (New York: Orange Judd, 1936, 1950), 253–56.

66. Lee, *Profitable Poultry Management,* 19–20, 41.

67. Ibid., 20, 42–46; Thompson, *Egg Farming,* 158, 240–242.

68. Lee, *Profitable Poultry Management,* 36–38, 67; Thompson, *Egg Farming,* 251–53.

69. John H. Robinson, *The Growing of Ducks and Geese for Profit and Pleasure* (Dayton: Reliable Poultry Journal Publishing Company, 1924), 157–59, 164; 2007 Census of Agriculture, "Table 27. Poultry—Inventory and Number Sold: 2007 and 2002" http://www.agcensus.usda.gov/Publications/2007/Full_Report/Volume_1,_Chapter_1_State_Level/New_York/st36_1_027_028.pdf (accessed June 20, 2011); Richard Jay Scholem, "Long Island's Ducks Are Still Table Favorites," *New York Times,* December 21, 2003, section 14 (Long Island).

70. Robinson, *The Growing of Ducks and Geese,* 188–96.

71. Dohner, *Encyclopedia of Historic and Endangered Livestock and Poultry Breeds,* 458–59.

72. Harry M. Lamon and Rob R. Slocum, *Ducks and Geese* (New York: Orange Judd, 1922), 124–25.

73. Dohner, *Encyclopedia of Historic and Endangered Livestock and Poultry Breeds,* 446.

74. Herbert Myrick, *Turkeys and How to Grow Them* (New York: Orange Judd, 1908), vi–vii, 45, 61, 70, 72, 81, 82, 85–87.

75. Dohner, *Encyclopedia of Historic and Endangered Livestock and Poultry Breeds,* 448–50.

76. Ibid., 467, 470–71.

3. From Haystacks to Silos

1. Diary of E. L. McFetridge, 1869, New York State Historical Association Research Library, Cooperstown, Diary M168 entries for July 14, 23, and 24, and December 14, 1869; 1870 United States Census, Livingston County, New York State Historical Association Research Library, Cooperstown, microfilm, Town of Sparta, entry 120 for Archibald McFetridge household.

2. New York State Census, Livingston County, 1865, New York State Historical Association Research Library, Cooperstown, microfilm, Town of Sparta, Agricultural Statistics, especially the entry for Archid McFetridge.

3. Thomas Summerhill, "The Farmers' Republic: Agrarian Protest and the Capitalist Transformation of Upstate New York, 1840–1900" (Ph.D. diss., University of California, San Diego, 1993), 247–48.

4. Cathy Matson, "'Damned Scoundrels' and 'Libertisme of Trade': Freedom and Regulation in Colonial New York's Fur and Grain Trades," *William and Mary Quarterly,* 3rd ser., 51, no. 3 (July 1994): 399–400; Michael Kammen, *Colonial New York: A History* (New York: Charles Scribner's Sons, 1975), 169–71. The quotation is taken from a report by Cadwallader Colden dated 1723, excerpted in Kammen.

5. *Census of the State of New York for 1845* (Albany: Carroll & Cook, 1846), Recapitulation nos. 2 and 3.

6. R. S. Beck, *Types of Farming in New York* (1938; reprint, Ithaca: Cornell University Agricultural Experiment Station, 1946), 24–31; Richard Beach and Malcolm Fairweather, *Agricultural Atlas of New York State* (Plattsburgh: Department of Geography, State University of New York at Plattsburgh, 1979), 30–35.

7. Peter Kalm, *Peter Kalm's Travels in North America: The English Version of 1770,* ed. Adolph B. Benson (New York: Dover Publications, 1987), 118.

8. Allen G. Noble and Richard K. Cleek, *The Old Barn Book: A Field Guide to North American Barns and Other Farm Structures* (New Brunswick: Rutgers University Press, 1995), 78.

9. "Plan of a Side-Hill Barn," *Moore's Rural New-Yorker* 4, no. 12 (March 19, 1853): 93.

10. "Improvements and Conveniences," *Moore's Rural New-Yorker* 15, no. 3 (January 16, 1864): 22.

11. "Inquiries and Answers: Granary," *The Cultivator,* 3rd ser., 12, no. 2 (February 1864): 67.

12. See, for example, Edward O. Fallis, "Metallic Grain-Storage Building," U.S. Patent 521,951, filed November 3, 1893, and issued June 26, 1894; Edward O. Fallis, "Metallic Grain-Storage Building," U.S. Patent 532,774, filed July 31, 1894, and issued January 22, 1895.

13. U.S. Department of Agriculture, *Farm Bulk Storage for Small Grains,* Farmers' Bulletin no. 1636 (Washington, D.C.: Government Printing Office, 1930), 39–41.

14. Henry H. Baxter, *Grain Elevators, Adventures in Western New York History,* vol. 26 (Buffalo: Buffalo and Erie County Historical Society, 1980), 2, 6.

15. Ibid., 11–14. For an example of an elevator apparatus, see William O. Strong, "Improved Device for Distributing Grain in Elevator-Bins," U.S. Patent 34,379, issued February 11, 1862.

16. Arthur C. Parker, "Iroquois Uses of Maize and Other Food Plants," *New York State Museum Bulletin* 144 (November 1910): 15–17, 34–36; Marcia Eames-Sheavly, *The Three Sisters: Exploring an Iroquois Garden* ([Ithaca]: Cornell Cooperative Extension, 1993), 8; Jason Grant Wilson, ed., "Arent Van Curler and His Journal of 1634–35," in *Annual Report of the American Historical Association for the Year 1895* (Washington, D.C.: Government Printing Office, 1896), 87.

17. *Census of the State of New York for 1845,* Recapitulation no. 2; Franklin B. Hough, *Census of the State of New York for 1865* (Albany: Charles Van Benthuysen and Son, 1867), 396–97.

18. H. Paul Draheim, "The Press Scrapbook—224th in a Series," *Utica Daily Press,* September 19, 1953.

19. L. D. Snook, "About Corn-houses," *Moore's Rural New-Yorker* 20, no. 41 (October 9, 1869): 650.

20. L. D. Snook, "Corn Cribs Again," *Moore's Rural New-Yorker* 20, no. 43 (October 23, 1869): 677.

21. "A Convenient Corn Crib," *Moore's Rural New-Yorker* 17, no. 40 (October 6, 1866): 317.

22. Snook, "About Corn-houses," 650.

23. H.B.H, "A Corn House Wanted," *Moore's Rural New-Yorker* 10, no. 3 (January 15, 1859): 22; "Design for a Corn House," *Moore's Rural New-Yorker* 10, no. 12 (March 19, 1859): 93–94.

24. Charles M. Rowland, "Corn-Crib," U.S. Patent 957,381, filed March 17, 1910, and issued May 10, 1910.

25. Beck, *Types of Farming in New York,* 20–23.

26. "Barracks for Hay or Grain," *Moore's Rural New-Yorker* 17, no. 21 (May 25, 1867): 165; Roderic H. Blackburn and Shirley Dunn, "The Hay Barrack: A Dutch Favorite," *Dutch Barn Preservation Society Newsletter* 2, no. 2 (Fall 1989): 1–6; Rod Blackburn, "An Interview," *Dutch Barn Preservation Society Newsletter* 2, no. 2 (Fall 1989): 6–7.

27. Beck, *Types of Farming in New York,* 20–21.

28. 2007 Census of Agriculture, Table 27, "Field Seeds, Grass Seeds, Hay, Forage, and Silage: 2007 and 2002," http://www.agcensus.usda.gov/Publications/2007/Full_Report/Volume_1,_Chapter_2_County_Level/New_York/st36_2_027_027.pdf (accessed January 12, 2011). These trends were already well under way in the 1970s. See Beach and Fairweather, *Agricultural Atlas of New York State,* 42–47.

29. T.E.W., "Hay Caps," *Moore's Rural New-Yorker* 6, no. 26 (June 30, 1855): 205.

30. C. H. Wendel, *Encyclopedia of American Farm Implements and Antiques* (Iola, Wis.: Krause Publications, 1997), 195–201, 251–62; Lynn R. Miller, *Haying with Horses* (Sisters, Ore.: Small Farmer's Journal, 2000), 91, 93, 147–48.

31. Norm Swineford, *Allis-Chalmers Farm Equipment, 1914–1985* (St. Joseph, Mich.: American Society of Agricultural Engineers, 1994), 274, 278.

32. Miller, *Haying with Horses,* 67, 72.

33. C. E. Gladding and J. N. Gladding, "Improvement in Forks for Elevating Hay," U.S. Patent 20,241, issued May 11, 1858; "Gladding's Hay Elevator," *Moore's Rural New-Yorker* 10, no. 16 (April 16, 1859): 125. Prior to the invention of the type of hay fork described here, the term "hay fork" was used to refer to implements similar to modern pitch forks. Many early references to the new machine call it an elevator rather than a fork.

34. Wendel, *Encyclopedia of American Farm Implements and Antiques,* 207; Miller, *Haying with Horses,* 226.

35. "Beardsley's Hay Elevator, or Horse Power Fork," *Moore's Rural New-Yorker* 12, no. 12 (March 23, 1861): 93.

36. See, for example, "Dederick's Portable Hay Press," *Moore's Rural New-Yorker* 6, no. 20 (May 19, 1855): 157.

37. Wendel, *Encyclopedia of American Farm Implements and Antiques,* 185–86.

38. "A Dairy Barn," *American Agriculturalist* 34, no. 4 (April 1875): 139–40.

39. "An American Silo," *American Agriculturalist* 36, no. 8 (September 1877): 335–36.

40. "Question Box," *Fifty-ninth Annual Report of the New York State Agricultural Society and the Annual Report of New York Bureau of Farmers' Institutes for the Year 1899* (Albany: James B. Lyon, 1900), 491.

41. Noble and Cleek, *The Old Barn Book,* 157–58.

42. W. A. Foster and Deane G. Carter, *Farm Buildings* (New York: John Wiley and Sons, 1922), 156–57.

43. William A. Radford, *Radford's Practical Barn Plans: Outbuildings and Stock Sheds* (Chicago: Radford Agricultural Company, 1909), 120; Noble and Cleek, *Old Barn Book,* 159; Foster and Carter, *Farm Buildings* (1922), 166; Farm Implement News Company, *Farm Implement News Buyer's Guide,* vol. 24 (Chicago: Farm Implement News Company, 1914), 304.

44. Farm Implement News Company, *Farm Implement News Buyer's Guide,* 305–6.

45. Foster and Carter, *Farm Buildings* (1922), 166–70; George Thurber, *Silos and Ensilage: The Preservation of Fodder Corn and Other Green Fodder Crops* (New York: Orange Judd, 1883), 18.

46. Allen G. Noble, *Wood, Brick, and Stone: The North American Settlement Landscape,* vol. 2 (Amherst: University of Massachusetts Press, 1984), 77–79.

47. Noble and Cleek, *The Old Barn Book,* 161.

4. A Farm Building for Every Purpose

1. Diary of R. L. Lamb, 1881–1886, New York State Historical Association Research Library, Cooperstown, Diary L1682. Newspaper clippings pasted in the diary of R. L. Lamb.

2. C. W. Seaton, *Census of the State of New York for 1875* (Albany: Weed, Parsons and Company, 1877), 344.

3. Diary of R. L. Lamb, entries for October 11, 1881, October 30–31, 1885, and November 4–7, 1885.

4. James Fenimore Cooper, *Reminiscences of Mid-Victorian Cooperstown and a Sketch of William Cooper* (Cooperstown: Otsego County Historical Society, 1936), 36.

5. Michael A. Tomlan, *Tinged with Gold: Hop Culture in the United States* (Athens: University of Georgia Press, 1992), 19.

6. Ibid., 12.

7. Michael A. Tomlan, "Hop Houses in Central New York with Guidelines for Their Identification and Evaluation" report for the Madison County Historical Society, Oneida, N.Y. (November 1, 1983), 4–5, 8, 13.

8. Herbert Myrick, *The Hop: Its Culture and Cure, Marketing and Manufacture* (New York: Orange Judd, 1914), 175.

9. "Picking and Drying Hops," *Moore's Rural New-Yorker* 3, no. 25 (June 17, 1852): 193.

10. Albert Bullard, "The Hop Culture in Milford Township," in *Time Once Past Never Returns: A History of the Town of Milford, New York, 1796–1996,* ed. Linda Norris (Milford, N.Y.: Milford Historical Association, 1996), 97.

11. My identification and naming of hop house types in New York is based on Michael A. Tomlan's pioneering work reported in "Hop Houses in Central New York." On the commonality of the common hop house, see Tomlan, *Tinged with Gold*, 174.

12. Sandra M. Bullard, *Hop Time!* (Cooperstown: Barton-Butler Graphics, 1998), unnumbered page.

13. Ibid.

14. W. A. Lawrence, "Hop Culture in the State of New York: Being a Practical Treatise on Hop Growing in Washington Territory" (Puyallup, Washington Territory: E. Meeker & Co., 1883), 105.

15. "Plan for a Hop-House," in Horace R. Allen, *The American Home and Farm Cyclopedia* (Philadelphia: Thompson Publishing Company, 1890), 171–72.

16. "Another Hop Year Begun," *American Agriculturalist* 54, no. 14 (December 1, 1894): 406.

17. "Hop Culture," *Moore's Rural New-Yorker* 19, no. 13 (March 28, 1868): 101.

18. Census data in Tomlan, "Hop Houses in Central New York," 13–14.

19. Bullard, "The Hop Culture in Milford Township," 91.

20. Tomlan, *Tinged with Gold,* 170–74.

21. Tomlan, "Hop Houses in Central New York," 55.

22. "Hops and the Tariff," *New York Times,* December 24, 1889.

23. Cooper, "Reminiscences," 37; Tomlan, *Tinged with Gold,* 108–9.

24. Tomlan, *Tinged with Gold,* 209-210.

25. USDA NASS New York Field Office, "Fruit Report, October 13, 2006, No. 975–5-06," http://www.nass.usda.gov/Statistics_by_State/New_York/Publications/Statistical_Reports/10oct/frt1006.htm (accessed October 23, 2006); Uncork New York, "Wine Country/Lake Erie & Chautauqua," http://www.newyorkwines.org/WineCountry/LakeErieChautauqua.ashx (accessed January 17, 2011); New York Wine and Grape Foundation, "The New York Wine Course and Reference," 9, http://www.newyorkwines.org/resources/a26060b551d6482ebe51c386bed66a90.pdf (accessed January 17, 2011).

26. William D. Barns, "Grape Growing in the Hudson River Valley," in *American Grape Growing and Wine Making,* 4th ed., ed. George Husmann (New York: Orange Judd, 1919), 101–2.

27. G. Denniston, *Grape Culture in Steuben County* (Albany: Van Benthusysen's Steam Printing House, 1865), 7; Daniel Fink, *Barns of the Genesee Country, 1790–1915* (New York: James Brunner, 1987), 431; Ulysses Prentiss Hedrick, *Grapes and Wines from Home Vineyards* (New York: Oxford University Press, 1945), 183, 186, 188.

28. Barns, "Grape Growing in the Hudson River Valley," 108; Richard Sherer, *Crooked Lake and the Grape* (New York: Donning, 1998), 5–6; Lee J. Vance, "Grape-Culture in New York," *Harper's Weekly* 39 (September 28, 1895): 924.

29. Denniston, *Grape Culture in Steuben County,* 7, 13; Hedrick, *Grapes and Wines,* 183–84; D. Bauder, "The Grape-Growing District of Central New York," in Husmann, *American Grape Growing and Wine Making,* 99.

30. New York Wine and Grape Foundation, "The New York Wine Course and Reference," 7.

31. Ibid., 6–7.

32. Bauder, "The Grape-Growing District," 99; Barns, "Grape Growing in the Hudson River Valley," 103; New York Wine and Grape Foundation, "The New York Wine Course and Reference," 9.

33. P. Barry, *The Fruit Garden* (New York: A. O. Moore, 1859), 253; Samuel W. Cole, *The American Fruit Book* (Boston: John P. Jewett, 1849), 244.

34. J. Fisk Allen, *A Practical Treatise on the Culture and Treatment of the Grape Vine,* 3rd ed. (New York: A. O. Moore, 1859), 27; Andrew Fuller, *The Grape Culturist: A Treatise on the Cultivation of the Native Grape,* 2nd ed. (New York: Orange Judd, 1867), 30; George E. Woodward and F. W. Woodward, *Woodward's Graperies and Horticultural Buildings* (New York: G. E. & F. W. Woodward, 1865), 38.

35. Woodward and Woodward, *Woodwards' Graperies,* 7, 66–67, 94.

36. John Fisk Allen, *The Culture of the Grape* (Boston: Dutton and Wentworth, 1847), 6; Allen, *A Practical Treatise,* 20; Barry, *The Fruit Garden,* 254; William Chorlton,

The American Grape Grower's Guide (New York: C. M. Saxton & Co., 1856), 18–19, 23, 26, 27; Cole, *The American Fruit Book,* 244–45; William Strong, *Culture of the Grape* (Boston: J. E. Tilton & Co., 1866), 294, 297, 300–2; Woodward and Woodward, *Woodward's Graperies,* 18, 20.

37. Strong, *Culture of the Grape,* 55–56.

38. Woodward and Woodward, *Woodward's Graperies,* 54.

39. "Fruits," *Transactions of the N.Y. State Agricultural Society with an Abstract of the Proceedings of the County Agricultural Societies* 14 (1854): 598.

40. Fuller, *The Grape Culturist,* 24; Peter Mead, *An Elementary Treatise on American Grape Culture and Wine Making* (New York: Harper & Brothers, 1867), 255; Strong, *Culture of the Grape,* 42, 49–51; Woodward and Woodward, *Woodward's Graperies,* 47, 56.

41. Fuller, *The Grape Culturist,* 29–30; Mead, *An Elementary Treatise,* 260.

42. Allen, *The Culture of the Grape,* 5–6, 24–26; Allen, *A Practical Treatise,* 21–22, 30, 39–41; Chorlton, *The American Grape Grower's Guide,* 29–31; Strong, *Culture of the Grape,* 57, 298–99, 308–9.

43. Allen, *The Culture of the Grape,* 31; Allen, *A Practical Treatise,* 25; Chorlton, *The American Grape Grower's Guide,* 371; Strong, *Culture of the Grape,* 300.

44. Fuller, *The Grape Culturist,* 41, 75; Woodward and Woodward, *Woodward's Graperies,* 20.

45. Husmann, *American Grape Growing and Wine Making,* 140–41.

46. Hedrick, *Grapes and Wines,* 198; Husmann, *American Grape Growing and Wine Making,* 140; Mead, *An Elementary Treatise,* 424.

47. Fuller, *The Grape Culturist,* 183; Hedrick, *Grapes and Wines,* 137–138; Mead, *An Elementary Treatise,* 367; Strong, *Culture of the Grape,* 278.

48. L. H. Bailey, *The Principles of Fruit-Growing* (London: Macmillan, 1918), 408–12; Denniston, *Grape Culture in Steuben County,* 8–9, 16–17.

49. J. C. Folger and S. M. Thomson, *The Commercial Apple Industry of North America* (New York: Macmillan, 1923), 21.

50. Fink, *Barns of the Genesee Country,* 264; J. S. de Campolide, "A Descriptive Account of New-York and Its Environs, with Observations on the Inhabitants, &c," *Monthly Magazine* (London), January 1798, 182.

51. Ibid., 263.

52. U.S. Census Office, *A Compendium of the Ninth Census, 1870* (1872; reprint, New York: Arno Press, 1976), 692–93.

53. U.S. Census Office, *Compendium of the Tenth Census,* pt. 1 (1883; reprint, New York: Arno Press, 1976), 798.

54. Diary of R. L. Lamb, entries for October 24 and 30, and November 13, 1885; Susan A. Dolan, *Fruitful Legacy: A Historic Context of Orchards in the United States, with Technical Information for Registering Orchards in the National Register of Historic Places* ([Seattle]: National Park Service, Olmsted Center for Landscape Preservation, Pacific West Regional Office, Cultural Resources, Park Historic Structures and

Cultural Landscapes Program, 2009), 74–77. Special thanks to Tim Layton at the Olmsted Center for bringing this source to my attention and helping me identify apple varieties. Lamb's "Wispy" apples may have been Winesaps.

55. Diary of R. L. Lamb, entries for October 30 and November 5, 1885; Samuel T. Wiley and W. Scott Garner, eds., *Biographical and Portrait Cyclopedia of Niagara County, New York* (Richmond, Ind.: Gresham Publishing Company, 1892), 126–27.

56. U.S. Census Office, *A Compendium of the Ninth Census,* 863, 865.

57. Seaton, *Census of the State of New York for 1875,* 408.

58. "Commodities," New York State Department of Agriculture and Markets, www.agmkt.state.ny.us/NY_COMMODITIES.html (accessed October 24, 2006).

59. Diary of R. L. Lamb, entries from October and November 1885. The diary mentions a Mr. Logan who helped with apple harvesting. According to the 1870 census, a Henry Logan lived in the nearby town of Porter in Niagara County.

60. Folger and Thomson, *The Commercial Apple Industry of North America,* 299.

61. Diary of R. L. Lamb; Elsie Davy, interview with Jennie Davy, January 18, 2010. Elsie Davy of Albion in Orleans County reported that as early as the mid-1930s, farm workers from other areas—people she called Pennsylvania Dutch—traveled to upstate New York for the apple harvest. She remembers that during or immediately after the Second World War, African Americans were among those seeking seasonal employment. Caribbean and then Latin American workers sought jobs in the orchards by the late twentieth century.

62. Folger and Thomson, *The Commercial Apple Industry of North America,* 299–302.

63. Jacob Biggle, *Biggle Orchard Book* (Philadelphia: Wilmer Atkinson Company, 1908), 131; David Stern, interview with Cynthia Falk, Rose Valley Farm, June 27, 2010.

64. M. C. Burritt, *Apple Growing* (New York: Outing Publishing Company, 1912), 139.

65. Deane G. Carter and W. A. Foster, *Farm Buildings* (New York: John Wiley and Sons, 1941), 292.

66. Barbara Krasner-Khait, "The Impact of Refrigeration," *History Magazine* (February–March 2000), 43, http://www.history-magazine.com/refrig.html (accessed November 1, 2006); Burritt, *Apple Growing,* 137.

67. Cole, *The American Fruit Book,* 80.

68. Alan Rowe, "The Invention and Popular Acceptance of Ice-Cooled Cold Storage: The Social Construction of a New Technology" (master's thesis, Cooperstown Graduate Program, SUNY Oneonta, 2008), 21.

69. Cole, *The American Fruit Book,* 80.

70. N. Hellings, "Improved House for Preserving Fruit and Other Articles," U.S. Patent 69,806, issued October 15, 1867.

71. Rowe, "The Invention and Popular Acceptance of Ice-Cooled Cold Storage," 35–37.

72. J. H. Gourley, *Orchard Management* (New York: Harper & Brothers Publishers, 1925), 232–33.

73. Barry, *The Fruit Garden,* 359.

74. J. S. Buell, *The Cider Makers' Manual* (Buffalo: Haas Navert and Co., 1874), 52–54.

75. National Register of Historic Places Nomination Form, New York State Historic Preservation Office, Kimlin Cider Mill, Poughkeepsie, Dutchess, 02NR04974, sec. 8, 2–3.

76. Stephen W. Jacobs, *Wayne County: The Aesthetic Heritage of a Rural Area* (New York: Publishing Center for Cultural Resources for the Wayne County Historical Society, 1979), 94.

77. Fink, *Barns of the Genesee Country,* 265.

78. Jerry Grant, Director of Research and Library Services, Shaker Museum and Library, e-mail message to author, July 19, 2010; Historic American Buildings Survey, William F. Winter Jr., Photographer, August 1931, "EXTERIOR VIEW OF KILN," Gift of New York State Department of Education, HABS NY, 11-NELEB.V, 14–1; Historic American Buildings Survey, N. E. Baldwin, Photographer, December 1939 and February 1940, "FRUIT DRYING KILN," Gift of New York State Department of Education, HABS NY, 11-NELEB.V, 27–6, 7, and 8. Floor plans of the washhouse building produced in 1939 associate the second-floor with seed cleaning.

79. Jacobs, *Wayne County*, 94.

80. David Stern, interview with Cynthia Falk, Rose Valley Farm, June 27, 2010; Byron David Halsted, *Barn Plans and Outbuildings,* rev. ed. (New York: Orange Judd, 1906), 366–67.

81. United States Department of Agriculture New York Field Office, "New York Is an Agricultural State," June 2010, http://www.nass.usda.gov/Statistics_by_State/New_York/Publications/Statistical_Reports/NY%20is%20an%20Ag%20State2010.pdf (accessed January 17, 2011); Agricultural Statistics Board, NASS, USDA, "Cabbage for Fresh Market: Area Planted and Harvested, Yield, and Production by State and United States, 2007–2009," http://usda.mannlib.cornell.edu/usda/current/VegeSumm/VegeSumm-01–27–2010.pdf (accessed January 17, 2011).

82. William Youatt, *The Pig: A Treatise on the Breeds, Management, Feeding, and Medical Treatment of Swine* (Philadelphia: Lea & Blanchard, 1847), 138.

83. "How to Build Root Houses," *American Agriculturalist* 32, no. 10 (October 1873): 376.

84. Diary of Frank B. Ingraham (b. 1860), 1900, New York State Historical Association Research Library, Cooperstown, Diary In4, entry for November 1, 1900.

85. "Commodities," *New York State Department of Agriculture and Markets* (statistics from 1998), http://www.agmkt.state.ny.us/NY_Commodities.html (accessed October 19, 2006).

86. Diary of Orville M. Slosson (b. 1829), 1860–1862, New York State Historical Association Research Library, Cooperstown, Diary Sl55, entry for November 5, 1860.

87. Ralph L. Watts, *Vegetable Gardening* (New York: Orange Judd, 1912), 276–81.

88. Ibid.

89. Harold Annible, Jim Masters, and Randy Nash, conversations with Lesley Polling, October 20–24, 2006.

90. Franklin B. Hough, *Census of the State of New-York for 1855* (Albany: Charles Van Benthuysen, 1857), recapitulation of agricultural statistics following 316; Seaton, *Census of the State of New York for 1875,* 408; Elmer Otterbein Flippin, *Rural New York* (New York: Macmillan, 1921), 142.

91. John Michael Vlach, *Barns* (New York: W. W. Norton & Company, 2003), 19–20.

92. Nancy Vars, "Tobacco Farming: Lost Onondaga County Calling," *Syracuse Post-Standard*, December 1, 1957.

93. "Culture of Tobacco," *American Agriculturalist* 33, no. 4 (April 1874): 139.

94. Meyer Jacobstein, *The Tobacco Industry in the United States* (New York: Columbia University Press, 1907), 40.

95. "Culture of Tobacco," 139; Richard J. Knoblock, "Raising Tobacco in Onondaga County," *Syracuse Post-Standard*, March 30, 1952.

96. "Tobacco and Its Culture," *Moore's Rural New-Yorker* 8, no. 16 (April 18, 1857): 125–26; E. H. Babcock, *A Treatise on Growing Tobacco in the United States* (Syracuse: E. H. Babcock & Co., 1854), 7.

97. "Tobacco and Its Culture," 125–26

98. Ibid.

99. J. B. Killebrew and Herbert Myrick, *Tobacco Leaf: Its Culture and Cure, Marketing, and Manufacture* (New York: Orange Judd, 1910), 201–205.

100. Babcock, *A Treatise on Growing Tobacco,* 22.

101. "Tobacco Culture in Connecticut," *Moore's Rural New-Yorker* 25, no. 5 (February 10, 1872): 98; Killebrew and Myrick, *Tobacco Leaf*, 202; "Culture of Tobacco—Curing," *Moore's Rural New-Yorker* 12, no. 10 (March 9, 1861): 77; "Cutting and Curing Tobacco," *Moore's Rural New-Yorker* 22, no. 12 (September 17, 1870): 186; John Walsh, *The Barn,* DVD (Syracuse: Public Broadcasting Council of Central New York, 2005).

102. Killebrew and Myrick, *Tobacco Leaf,* 179.

103. New York State Maple Producers Association, press release, July 18, 2005.

104. J. P. Brissot de Warville, *New Travels in the United States of America* (London, 1792), 301, quoted in H. A. Schuette and A. J. Ihde, "Maple Sugar: A Bibliography of Early Records. II," *Transactions of the Wisconsin Academy of Sciences, Arts, and Letters* 38 (1946): 112–14.

105. Susan Fenimore Copper, *Rural Hours* (New York, 1850), 23, quoted in Schuette and Ihde, "Maple Sugar," 161.

106. U.S. Census Office, *Abstract of the Eleventh Census: 1890* (1894; reprint, New York: Arno Press, 1976), 94; Bureau of the Census, *Thirteenth Census of the United States: Abstract of the Census* (1913; reprint, New York: Arno Press, 1976), 407. The exception to this trend is the census year 1870, when both sugar and syrup production decreased significantly in New York.

107. Benjamin Rush, *Transactions of the American Philosophical Society* 3 (1793): 69, quoted in Schuette and Ihde, "Maple Sugar," 223.

108. Robert Rogers, *A Concise History of North America* (London, 1765), 251, and *A New Collection of Voyages, Discoveries and Travels,* vol. 2 (London, 1767), 179, quoted in Schuette and Ihde, "Maple Sugar," 107, 108.

109. Leader Evaporator Company, *Maple Sugar Makers' Guide* (Burlington, Vt.: Leader Evaporator Company, 1953), 14.

110. G. H. Collingwood, *The Production of Maple Sirup and Sugar in New York State* (Ithaca: Cornell Cooperative Extension Bulletin, 1940), 34.

111. J. A. Cope, *Maple Sirup and Sugar* (Ithaca: Cornell Extension Bulletin, 1949), 23.

112. Gene Kritsky, *The Quest for the Perfect Hive: A History of Innovation in Bee Culture* (New York: Oxford University Press, 2010), 79–85.

113. Lorenzo Langstroth, "Beehive," U.S. Patent 9,300, issued October 5, 1852.

114. M. Quinby, *Mysteries of Beekeeping Explained: Being a Complete Analysis of the Whole Subject* (New York: C. M. Saxton, 1864), 7, 14–15, 24–25, 42.

115. *History of Montgomery and Fulton Counties, N.Y., with Illustrations Descriptive of Scenery, Private Residences, Public Buildings, Fine Blocks, and Important Manufactories* (New York: F. W. Beers & Co., 1878), 153, 245, plate following 96.

116. National Agricultural Statistics Service, *United States Honey Report* (Washington, D.C.: USDA, 2006), 3.

5. Powering the Farm

1. Jane Lawliss Murphy, *Sugar on Snow: Memoir of a Northern New York State Farm Kid* (Sea Cliff, N.Y.: DSI Design Group, 2003), 118.

2. Ibid., 178.

3. Ibid., 183–84.

4. New York State Agricultural Society, *Transactions of the New York State Agricultural Society for 1846* (Albany: C. Van Benthuysen and Co., 1847), 648–49.

5. Allen G. Noble and Richard K. Cleek, *The Old Barn Book: A Field Guide to North American Barns and Other Farm Structures* (New Brunswick: Rutgers University Press, 1995), 56–57; New York State Agricultural Society, *Transactions of the New York State Agricultural Society for 1846,* 649.

6. "Sketches of Farming in Western New-York," *The Cultivator* 4, no. 8 (August 1847): 254.

7. David Anthony, Horse-Power, U.S. Patent 5,215, issued August 7, 1847; "'Genius' Former Resident," *Tri-Valley News* (Worcester, N.Y.), September 6, 1984.

8. Samuel M. Shaw, *A Centennial Offering: Being a Brief History of Cooperstown* (Cooperstown: Freeman's Journal, 1886), 213; Orestes Badger, Endless-Floor Horse-Power for Driving Machinery, U.S. Patent 1,898, issued December 14, 1840; Fritz Wilhelm Woll, *A Book on Silage* (Chicago: Rand, McNally & Co., 1900), 152.

9. T. Lindsay Baker, *A Field Guide to American Windmills* (Norman: University of Oklahoma Press, 1985), 5–7.

10. Paul C. Johnson, *Farm Power in the Making of America* (Des Moines: Wallace-Homestead Book Company, 1978), 30.

11. "Self-Regulating Windmill," *American Agriculturalist* 13, no. 2 (September 20, 1854): 37.

12. Baker, *A Field Guide to American Windmills,* 341, 352, 376. Baker provides a complete listing of known American windmill manufacturers in appendix A.

13. Anne Frances Pulling and Gerald A. Leeds, *Windmills and Watermills of Long Island* (Charleston, S.C.: Arcadia, 1999), 7.

14. The Gladden wind turbine is documented in the Historic American Engineering Record, call number NY, 5-NAP, 1-, which can be accessed through the Library of Congress at the American Memory Web site, http://memory.loc.gov.

15. "Steam Power for Threshing and Other Farm Work," *The Cultivator,* 3rd ser., 3, no. 9 (September 1855): 283.

16. J. J. Thomas, "Steaming Food and Farm Management by William Crozier," in *Rural Affairs: A Practical and Copiously Illustrated Register of Rural Economy and Rural Taste* (Albany: Luther Tucker, 1875), 132–33.

17. L. W. Ellis and Edward A. Rumley, *Power and the Plow* (New York: Doubleday, Page & Co., 1911), 42; E. M. Dieffenbach and R. B. Gray, "The Development of the Tractor," in *Power to Produce: Yearbook of Agriculture, 1960* (Washington, D.C.: Government Printing Office, 1960), 29.

18. Albert H. Sanford, *The Story of Agriculture in the United States* (Boston: D. C. Heath and Co., 1916), 259; Victor W. Pagé, *Gas, Gasoline and Oil-Engines* (New York: Norman W. Henley Publishing Company, 1915), 185.

19. U.S. Bureau of the Census, *Fifteenth Census of the United States: 1930—Abstract of the Fifteenth Census of the United States* (Washington, D.C.: Government Printing Office, 1933), 598, http://www2.census.gov/prod2/decennial/documents/00476589ch07.pdf (accessed January 19, 2010).

20. W. A. Foster and Deane G. Carter, *Farm Buildings* (New York: John Wiley and Sons, 1922), 52, 172–78; Fred D. Crawshaw and E. W. Lehman, *Farm Mechanics* (Peoria: Manual Arts Press, 1922), 270; Karl John Theodore Ekblaw, *Farm Structures* (New York: Macmillan, 1920), 123–24.

21. Frank Koester, *Electricity for the Farm and Home* (New York: Sturgis & Walton, 1913), 51–58, 102–3.

22. U.S. Bureau of the Census, *Fifteenth Census of the United States: 1930,* 598–99.

23. Andrey A. Potter, *Farm Motors* (New York: McGraw-Hill, 1913), 3; Clark C. Spence, "Early Uses of Electricity in American Agriculture," *Technology and Culture* 3 (Spring 1962): 153–54.

GLOSSARY

Adze a hand tool with a metal blade oriented perpendicular to the handle that is used to form a squared log from a tree truck (see Figure I.5).

Anchor beam a horizontal framing member that connects two posts and secures them in place; in the H-bent framing typical of Dutch barn construction, the anchor beam forms the cross member of the H-like shape (see Figure 1.6).

Arched roof also known as a rainbow roof or a Gothic roof, this type of barn roof has a distinct curved shape (see Figure 1.21).

Balloon frame a wood framing system that makes use of sawn lumber, such as two-by-sixes, nailed together rather than larger timbers connected with mortise and tenon joints.

Bargeboard decorative trim applied under the roof eaves often used on buildings designed in nineteenth-century revival styles (see Figure I.15).

Barrack a building used to provide shelter; although often used to refer to military housing, in agriculture the term can refer to a long building for keeping a sizable poultry folk or even a structure with an adjustable covering to protect a crop of hay (see Figures 2.37, 3.16).

Battery series of cages used to confine birds, usually laying hens, to increase production in poultry farming (see Figure 2.39).

Bay the open area between two framing bents in a barn; barns are often described by the number of bays they contain, with a typical English barn consisting of three bays and therefore four bents.

Bent although the name suggests something that is curved or crooked, in barn construction a bent is a straight plane defined by the posts and beams that support the building; bents typically run perpendicular to the ridge of a gable roofed barn and are separated by open bays where storage or work can occur.

Board and batten siding exterior cladding using vertical lumber butted side to side with a thin vertical strip of wood applied to cover any gap between the boards (see Figure 4.1).

Box stall an enclosed area within a barn or stable for housing an animal, such as a horse.

Bridge an entryway to the upper story of a multistory barn that spans an open space beneath (see Figure 1.19).

Circular saw a cutting device with a disk-shaped blade that rotates as a result of a power source such as water, steam, or electricity; a circular saw leaves arched marks on the wood it cuts (see Figure I.8).

Cladding material applied to the exterior of a building to make it weather tight.

Clapboard horizontal boards, generally tapering from bottom to top, applied as cladding to the exterior of a building with the bottom edge overlapping the board below (see Figure 2.4).

Cobblestone stone washed round by water or retreating glaciers (see Figures I.1, 4.7).

Combine a machine for harvesting grain that combines the functions of reaping (cutting the plant), threshing (loosening the grain), and winnowing (separating the grain).

Cowl a sheet-metal device applied to the roof of a hop house to assist in creating an upward draft; cowls loosely resemble the monk's hoods of the same name and rotate based on wind direction (see Figure 4.6).

Cupola a stationary feature on the roof of a structure that provides a means for ventilation, often through openings fitted with slats; unlike ventilators made of sheet metal, cupolas are usually square in cross-section and built of wood (see Figure I.13).

Cure the process of preserving a crop such as hay, tobacco, or hops, usually by drying.

Cut nail a type of nail, widely used by the early nineteenth century, cut from metal stock; the shaft of a cut nail is tapered on only two sides, and the head can be produced by machine or by hand (see Figure I.11).

Draft kiln a structure for drying a product, which operates by creating a current of hot air; in the context of New York State agriculture the term draft kiln usually refers to a building for drying hops.

Dropping board a shelflike area within a chicken coop, usually under the roosts, for catching chicken manure so it can be easily removed.

Eave the portion of a roof that overhangs the side walls of the building.

Ensilage the process of creating silage; see also "silage."

Fieldstone loose stone that occurs naturally in a given area; fieldstone is not "dressed," or cut into rectangular blocks, and it does not have to be cut or blasted from a rock formation (see Figure I.4).

Flail a hand tool used to thresh cereal crops by beating the harvested plants with a swinging club in order to loosen the grain from the seed covering and stalk.

Forebay an extension of the upper story of a barn beyond the wall of the lower story; this feature is characteristic of the so-called Pennsylvania barn (see Figure 1.14).

Gable end on a building with a gable or gambrel roof, the shorter side where the wall surface extends upward to the peak of the roof.

Gable roof a roof composed of two planes that meet at the roof peak; looking at the gable end of a building, the gable roof forms a triangle (see Figure I.17).

Gambrel roof a roof with a "broken" pitch, which when viewed from the gable end takes the shape of a pentagon; gambrel roofs are typically found on late-nineteenth-century and early-twentieth-century barns and on Dutch Colonial Revival houses (see Figure 1.20).

Gothic roof see "arched roof."

H-bent a framing technique characteristic of Dutch barns in which the arrangement of posts and beams resembles the letter H (see Figure 1.5).

Harpoon fork a type of hay fork with one or two tines used to lift a gather of hay from a hay wagon and transport it to storage space within a barn (see Figure 3.20).

Hay cap a portable covering, usually of cloth or canvas, placed over a haystack to protect it from the weather.

Hay cock small piles of hay left to dry in the field; the term "cock" can be used as a verb to refer to the process of putting hay in small piles.

Hay fork a device used to move hay from a wagon into a haymow or hayloft of a barn; although the term was once used to refer to a hand tool similar to a pitchfork, after the mid-nineteenth century it more typically referred to a piece of equipment for lifting hay, which was powered by the motion of a horse or horses led forward and backward to raise or lower the device (see Figure 1.29).

Hay hood an extension of the barn roof on one or both gable ends, which covers the end of the hay track and shelters doors to the hayloft in the upper story (see Figure 1.32).

Haylage silage made from alfalfa; see also "silage."

Haymow see "mow."

Horse wheel a device, either fixed in place or portable, that uses the motion produced by horses walking in a circular pattern to power other equipment (see Figure 5.2).

Hot bed a "mini" greenhouse for starting plants; hot beds usually use glazed panels resembling window sash that help hold in the heat from the sun and decomposing plant matter or manure (see Figure 4.15).

Hover as a verb used in an agricultural context, to brood or incubate; as a noun, an enclosure for young chicks that simulates the warmth and closeness of a mother hen.

Laminated truss in barn construction, a roof-framing system composed of multiple pieces of wood, often glued together, to form the roof framing; while the term "truss" refers to a framework made of multiple pieces, the adjective "laminated" indicates that the wooden members are oriented with their grain running parallel to one another to create multiple layers, usually forming an arch.

Laying cage see "battery."

Line shaft a mechanical component, usually in the shape of a rod rotated by an external power source such as water or steam, that provides power, often through belts, to nearby machines (see Figure 5.12).

Martin hole a small opening in the wall of a barn that provides for ventilation and allows birds access to help control pests such as rodents and insects (see Figure 1.4).

Mortise one component of a mortise and tenon joint, the mortise is the rectangular hole into which the tenon is inserted (see Figure I.6).

Mow an area within a barn where a crop, usually hay, is stored; in an English barn or a basement barn, mows are typically found to one or both sides of the central threshing floor.

Nesting box a dry, relatively dark area, enclosed on three sides, with soft material such as straw at the base where hens can lay their eggs; nesting boxes are used for both domestic and wild birds (see Figure 2.29).

Nogging a material, such as brick, stone, or earth, used to fill the spaces between the members of a wood frame.

Oatlage silage made from oats; see also "silage."

Offal waste material, which in butchering usually includes the entrails and internal organs of an animal.

Pasteurization the process of heating a food to a temperature below boiling and then cooling it to inhibit the growth of microorganisms; pasteurization is named for Louis Pasteur, who experimented with the process in the 1860s for wine, but it is now typically associated with milk.

Pentice a small section of roof constructed to help shelter an entrance; usually narrower than a porch, a pentice is not supported by columns or posts (see Figures 1.2, 1.4).

Pole barn a twentieth-century building type, often low in comparison with its length and width, constructed with posts of wood or metal that support a roof; a pole barn does not need to have solid side walls nor does it require a floor or foundation other than the ground on which it sits (see Figures 1.44, 4.19).

Post a vertical framing member, square or circular in cross-section and typically large in diameter.

Rainbow roof see "arched roof."

Ridge and furrow house a type of greenhouse composed of a series of buildings with gable roofs, which are arranged side to side so that the roof arrangement resembles a series of V's; the location of the greenhouses next to one another creates less exposure to the cold air outside (see Figure 4.13).

Rosehead nail a wrought nail with a hand-hammered, faceted head that loosely resembles a flower with petals (see Figure I.10).

Sash saw see "up-and-down saw."

Scratching place a location where chickens can scratch and peck the earth in search of bugs, worms, and other edible items; chickens are typically also fed grain in their scratching place.

Silage animal feed made from crops, such as corn, that includes the whole plant, stored moist and preserved through anaerobic fermentation.

Skep a container for housing a bee colony; skeps can be made of several different materials but are often woven from straw (see Figure 4.42).

Stanchion an upright bar or post; in agriculture "stanchion" refers to the apparatus, constructed of wood or metal, that secures a cow's head in place so that it cannot move about the barn (see Figure 1.23).

Super a box that is part of a beehive, which contains the honeycomb and houses the bees; sometimes termed a "superhive" (see Figure 4.45)

Tenon one component of a mortise and tenon joint; the tenon is the "male" extension at the end of a piece of wood, which is typically narrower and thinner than the remainder of the board.

Thatch a roofing material made from plant matter; in the United States thatch is typically composed of bundles of straw or coarse grass (see Figures 1.3, 3.16).

Up-and-down saw a device for cutting wood that moves vertically, powered by an external source such as a waterwheel; up-and-down, or sash, saws leave straight, parallel saw marks on the wood they cut (see Figure I.7).

Windrow a row of cut hay in a field; windrows are used temporarily after hay is harvested to allow it to dry before storage.

Wire nail a type of nail with a round head and a shaft that is circular in cross-section; commonly used after the late nineteenth century (see Figure I.12).

Wrought nail a type of nail, common before the nineteenth century, that is individually made by a blacksmith who hammers heated iron into the desired shape; the shaft of a wrought nail typically tapers on all four sides.

FURTHER READING

This is not the first book to be written about barns in New York State nor will it be the last. Several other published studies of specific types of buildings or specific regions within the state stand out and are highly recommended for those who want to learn more. John Fitchen's landmark volume on New York Dutch barns is one example. First published in 1968, the book was reissued in a second revised edition with additional text by Greg Huber. The new version of *The New World Dutch Barn: The Evolution, Forms, and Structure of a Disappearing Icon* (Syracuse: Syracuse University Press, 2001) is based on significant fieldwork in eastern New York and New Jersey and expands the scope of inquiry into the nineteenth century.

Like New World Dutch barns, other unusual or distinctive barns types, such as round and polygonal barns or hop houses, have also attracted the attention of other students of vernacular architecture. Non-orthogonal barns are the subject of a monograph titled *Round Barns of New York* (Syracuse: Syracuse University Press, 2004) by Richard Triumpho. Michael Tomlan's *Tinged with Gold: Hop Culture in the United States* (Athens: University of Georgia Press, 1992) chronicles the rise and fall of hops production in central New York with special attention to the built environment.

Many individuals or local groups have been responsible for important publications on the agricultural buildings in a given community or county. On Otsego County, my own local area, Henry Glassie's 1974 article "The Variation of Concepts within Tradition: Barn Building in Otsego County, New York" (*Geoscience and Man* 5) and Gilbert Vincent's study *An Agricultural Legacy: Farm Outbuildings of Central New York* (Cooperstown: Gallery 53 Artworks, 1991) are both noted examples. On the regional level, Daniel Fink's *Barns of the Genesee Country, 1790–1915* (New York: James Brunner, 1987) provides a thorough, well-illustrated examination of barns and rural life in western New York.

Books on barns in neighboring states contain information that allows for important comparisons with New York buildings. Two of note are Thomas Visser's *Field Guide to New England Barns and Farm Buildings* (Hanover, N.H.: University

Press of New England, 1997) and *The Pennsylvania Barn: Its Origin, Evolution, and Distribution in North America* (Baltimore: Johns Hopkins University Press, 1992) by Robert Ensminger. Other volumes, such as Allen Noble and Richard Cleek's *Old Barn Book: A Field Guide to North American Barns and Other Farm Structures* (New Brunswick: Rutgers University Press, 1995), offer a more comprehensive view of agricultural buildings throughout the United States. Of special note in this regard is John Michael Vlach's book simply titled *Barns* (New York: W. W. Norton & Company; Washington, D.C.: Library of Congress, 2003), which features numerous images of farm buildings from the Historic American Buildings Survey.

Finally, for those interested in learning about the relationship between farming and barn building, there is nothing like looking at primary source material. The periodicals *American Agriculturalist, The Cultivator,* and *Moore's Rural New-Yorker* all offer a plethora of material for those willing to sit down and read through the often yellowed pages.

Books published by professionals engaged in the design of model farm buildings also provide an important avenue for learning about ideal barn plans. Some of my favorites include Alfred Hopkins's *Modern Farm Buildings* (New York: McBridge, Nast & Co., 1913), W. A. Foster and Deane G. Carter's *Farm Buildings* (New York: John Wiley and Sons, 1922), Byron David Halsted's *Barn Plans and Outbuildings* (New York: Orange Judd, 1881), and Herbert A. Shearer's *Farm Buildings with Plans and Descriptions* (Chicago: Frederick J. Drake & Co., 1917). Both Foster and Carter's volume and Halsted's were published in multiple editions, allowing for comparison of recommendations in different years.

Today, professionals continue to issue volumes dedicated to designing farm buildings to suit modern needs. One example is *Building Freestall Barns and Milking Centers: Methods and Materials* (Ithaca: NRAES Cooperative Extension, 2003), which is based on papers presented at a conference held on the subject in 2003. The Internet also plays an important role in disseminating information. The full text of older agricultural volumes can often be found there, and new information, provided by organizations such as the Cornell Cooperative Extension, is easily accessible on-line.

Index

Note: Page numbers in italics refer to the information in photographs, illustrations, and figure captions.